MARTIAL AESTHETICS

MARTIAL AESTHETICS

How War Became an Art Form

Anders Engberg-Pedersen

STANFORD UNIVERSITY PRESS
Stanford, California

STANFORD UNIVERSITY PRESS
Stanford, California

CARLSBERG FOUNDATION

ELITE FORSK

THE VELUX FOUNDATIONS
VILLUM FONDEN ✂ VELUX FONDEN

Printed and bound by CPI Group (UK) Ltd, Croydon, CR0 4YY

Cataloging-in-Publication Data available upon request.
Library of Congress Control Number: 2022019748
ISBN: 9780804799942 (paper), 9781503634862 (ebook)

Cover art: Playing board of Hellwig's wargame.
Source: Johann Christian Ludwig Hellwig,
Das Kriegsspiel (Braunschweig, 1803).
Cover design: Jason Anscomb

In memory of Mette Teilmann Nielsen

April 12, 1979, Roskilde—January 17, 2014, Kabul

It is futile, even wrong, to try to turn a blind eye to the brutality of war because of unwillingness to accept its true nature.

—Carl von Clausewitz

CONTENTS

PREFACE

The twenty-first century has witnessed a pervasive militarization of aesthetics. Western military institutions have co-opted the creative worldmaking of art and aesthetics and merged it with the destructive forces of warfare. This unusual merger has taken place both in the material domain of media and technologies and in the theoretical domain of military ideas and doctrines. Artificial aesthetic worlds such as 3D terrain simulations and synthetic training environments pervade contemporary war efforts, and thinkers in several leading Western militaries have adopted key aesthetic concepts from the discourse on design. Today, military institutions form an unexpected avant-garde in both senses of the term: as the military front-runner for a new operational aesthetics.

What are we to make of this curious imbrication of two phenomena that seemingly belong to entirely different realms and orders of human experience? How is the brutal business of war and the disastrous effects it has on people's lives tied up with artistry, artifacts, and creative worldmaking? And when did military thinkers begin to speak the language of art and aesthetics? *Martial Aesthetics: How War Became an Art Form* examines the origins of this at once strange and sinister phenomenon. It shows that the creative warfare of the twenty-first century is merely the most recent moment in a historical development that began much longer ago. Indeed, the emergence of martial aesthetics harkens back to a series of inventions, ideas, and debates in the eighteenth and early nineteenth centuries. Already then, military thinkers and inventors adopted ideas from the field of aesthetics about the nature, purpose, and force of art and retooled them into innovative military technologies and a new theory that conceptualized war not merely as a practical art but as an aesthetic art form. Adopting an approach that is simultaneously historical and theoretical, the book shows how early war media (from star charts and horoscopes to the Prussian *Kriegsspiel*, or wargame) and military discourses (from Kepler to Clausewitz) were entangled with classical ideas in philosophy and aesthetic theory (by thinkers such as Leibniz, Baumgarten, Kant, and Schiller), in order to trace the emergence of martial aesthetics. Against this historical background, the book also presents a new theoretical frame for war in the twenty-first century. The book argues that, as counterintuitive as it may seem, we need to acknowledge the constitutive role of aesthetics in war. Inventing and shaping desired futures like works of art, the military has long sought to frame war as a creative and artistic activity. But the book also points to the perils of this endeavor. Martial aesthetics not only designates a set of inventions and ideas that military institutions have produced over the past 250 years. It also signifies the systematic erasure of brutality, suffering, and death, and the troubling transfiguration of collective violence into the free and noble endeavor of art—the enchantment of war as an art form.

INTRODUCTION

Creative Warfare

The first time Watson died, he was on a gently sloping hill surrounded by hazy mountains. It was back in October 2009, and his fellow soldiers from the US Marine Corps' First Tank Battalion Scout Platoon were driving their tank across the desert landscape. A few minutes earlier, a helicopter had taken out a tank far ahead in the distance, and the squad was expecting a violent encounter with enemy forces. Veering off the paved road that carved through the valley, the driver pushed up the hillside. As they reached the top, the vista that opened below them under the gray skies revealed numerous insurgents, who soon began to shoot. Perched on top of the tank, Watson, the gunner, returned fire. As the smoke from his crackling quick-fire rounds began to lift, the scene became clear. They were all dead. In the distance, on the other side of the road, two new insurgents unexpectedly appeared. Another tank to Watson's left immediately eliminated them. But as Watson would soon realize, the danger wasn't over. The turret of the armored vehicle offered some protection, but out in the open he remained highly exposed. Two dry, barely audible sounds suddenly clicked in quick succession. The second shot hit Watson and sent him tumbling to the ground. He was killed on the spot. But it wasn't necessarily the last time he would die that day.

Using the training platform *Virtual Battle Space 2* (VBS2), Watson had been engaged in a simulation designed to provide soldiers with an immersive virtual experience of war before going into actual combat. Safely ensconced inside the Marine Corps base in Twentynine Palms, California, Watson was located inside the Battle Simulation Center, where he drove along a virtual terrain based on actual cartographic data from a potential combat zone. Playing a "serious game," Watson and his comrades were immersed in a half-imagined, half-real world where a series of exchanges and transfers took place between the ludic events in VBS2 and the minds of the scout platoon of the First Tank Battalion.

This highly dramatic and entirely uneventful scene itself unfolds inside an art installation by the German documentarist Harun Farocki. *Serious Games I–IV* is the title of a series of video artworks first featured at the biennale in Sao Paolo in 2010 and since shown in art galleries across the world. Displayed on four separate screens, they examine the complex apparatus that subtends and organizes such simulations. As Watson and the other platoon members play the game, an instructor concurrently builds the simulated world they move around in and creates the dangers they are exposed to. Also visible to the audience, the instructor selects different types of explosive devices and templates of enemies from a drop-down menu and places them at strategic locations with a few mouse clicks. *Watson Is Down*, the first of Farocki's four art installations, shows how this martial worldmaking—with its imagined objects and potential events—eventually leads to the fatal shots that bring a temporary end to Watson's gaming. Observing his own imagined death on the screen in front of him, Watson pushes himself away from the console with an annoyed sigh.

Watson's death leads us directly into a complex of institutions, technologies, and representations that has decisively come to shape warfare in the twenty-first century. In recent decades, war has become thoroughly pervaded by imaginary worlds in the form of simulations, virtual scenarios, serious games, and synthetic training environments that have created odd passageways, overlaps, and frictions among different realms of war. Actual operations, imagined worlds, and aesthetic representations have been bundled into curious hybrid entities that merge and blend different modalities. Just in this short scene, Watson dies in multiple ways at the same time: he suffers a purely imaginary death in the game, a potential future death in the "serious game," and an aesthetic death in Farocki's art installation—an artwork that highlights the paradoxical nature of the entire setup by showing Watson at once dead and alive.

The strange imbrication of warfare with the imaginary, the virtual, and art becomes no less odd if we turn from media and technology to ideas. In recent years, military thinkers have increasingly adopted the language of art and aesthetics when theorizing the nature of contemporary warfare. *Creativity, the imagination, artistry,* and even *genius* have become buzzwords in military circles as new tools to handle the complexities of twenty-first-century global warfare; and soldiers are told they must learn to unleash their creative potential to wage war successfully. In 2008 and 2009, during the wars in Afghanistan and Iraq, the highest echelon of the US military lent these ideas its stamp of approval, when General James Norman Mattis issued two memoranda that mandated a shift in how the US understands war.[1] Mattis argued that in an environment of extreme volatility, uncertainty, complexity, and ambiguity—high VUCA in military jargon—older doctrinal concepts such as Effects-Based Operations (EBO) or Operational Net Assessment (ONA) no longer work. Developed for a military world picture largely governed by relatively clear cause-and-effect relationships and a high degree of predictability, these traditional ideas did not seem to be useful guides for the complexities of modern nonlinear warfare. Instead, focusing on the "creative imagination," Mattis promoted a range of concepts taken from the realm of art. And ever since, aesthetic terms such as *artworks, artists, artistry, intuition, creativity,* and *the creative imagination* have migrated into field manuals, doctrinal documents, military theory, and teaching materials in military academies. In other words, the military discourse of war has adopted and actively promoted the figure of the artist as an ideal for the contemporary soldier.

MARTIAL AESTHETICS

Farocki's installation *Serious Games* and Mattis's memoranda on the creative imagination reveal how contemporary warfare blends two fields and areas of experience that are conventionally considered to be quite distinct from each other: warfare and aesthetics. Traditionally, the discipline of philosophical aesthetics has concerned itself with the nature of artworks, with their construction, their rules, their nature and meaning, as well as with the subjective experience of artworks by readers, spectators, or listeners. What is the function of a work of art? What are the parameters of realistic representation? How do we experience a play? When is a painting beautiful or sublime? And by which aesthetic categories do we judge a work of art to begin with? Such questions form the crux of aesthetic debates from Plato and Aristotle via Kant and Schiller to John Dewey and Sianne Ngai.

The term *aesthetics* itself, however, is elusive. Today, the term is used in a variety of ways both within and across the fields of literary and cultural studies, musicology, philosophy, architecture, and many others, and there is little consensus about basic definitions. The folk theory of "aesthetics" is often vaguely associated with beauty and, perhaps, art, and the term still has sufficient cachet to market everything from clothing to cars. In recent years, however, a particular understanding of aesthetics, at once new and old, has come to dominate several academic disciplines. This is an understanding that expands aesthetics beyond the borders of art as traditionally delimited. With reference to its Greek etymology (*aesthesis* denoting sensibility and perception), "aesthetics," in this sense, designates forms of sensibility that constitute both the shared experience of our common world and the representations of artworks. Although the basis for this understanding of aesthetics can be traced back to Alexander Baumgarten, who founded the philosophical discipline of aesthetics as the science of sensibility, it is Jacques Rancière who has developed it most forcefully in recent years. By reorienting, in both senses of the word, aesthetics toward distributions and relations of the sensible, Rancière has also brought aesthetics into close contact with the political and the social. If we are indeed witnessing an "aesthetic turn," or if aesthetics is being established as "a new intellectual foundation" for numerous disciplines, as Mark Foster Gage has argued, then it involves a turn away from its traditional association with beauty.[2] Against a nonutilitarian pure aestheticism that proclaims with Oscar Wilde that "all art is quite useless," aesthetics in the twenty-first century has left the comfort of the armchair behind to face the pressures and conflicts of our collective and political existence.

These shifts have opened up new possibilities. By reorganizing our perception of social relations, creating space for more voices on the public stage, and rendering visible what has been pushed to the margins of our shared field of vision, art has come to be seen as an argument, an aesthetic intervention in the political debate. But this alleged power of aesthetics may also be turned on its head—that is, the potential that Rancière, the philosopher of emancipation and dissent, finds in aesthetics can also be co-opted and redirected to other purposes or subsumed by other logics. Indeed, both as a trove of concepts at the level of theory and as the production and organization of forms of sensibility, aesthetics has in recent years come to occupy a central place in Western militaries. By retooling established aesthetic categories and propagating creative violence at the level of theory, and by inventing lifelike digital war imaginaries that format soldiers' perceptual apparatus and increasingly blend into actual operations, Western militaries have transformed aesthetics into a powerful tool of warfare. Subjecting it to a logic of optimization, military institutions have drafted aesthetics in the quest to imagine the best of all possible wars and to inculcate it as an experiential fact before it is implemented in the real. The military has thereby become an agent of some of the most radical experiments in contemporary aesthetics. It has emerged as an unexpected avant-garde in which the aesthetic and the military sense of the term have merged to form the cutting edge in the production, management, and thinking of war. It is the process of this merger, the products it generates, and the ideas that govern it that I gather under the term *martial aesthetics*.

As weird and uncanny as all this may sound, it is not new. Watson's multiple deaths and Mattis's "creative imagination" may bring us into the heart of contemporary martial aesthetics, but they also form a prismatic vantage point onto a much deeper history. For even as twenty-first-century military institutions have merged war and aesthetics, we are merely witnessing the contemporary development and elaboration of a process with origins dating back several hundred years. The emergence of a martial aesthetics—considered both as a technological artifact and as an idea within military theory—harkens back to the late eighteenth and early nineteenth centuries with the invention of the modern wargame and the first sustained theoretical conceptualization of warfare as an art form. This period marks a decisive shift from an even older set of premodern war media and ideas that had governed warfare from antiquity until the early modern period. To grasp the emergence, development, and ethical pitfalls of martial aesthetics, a deep historical perspective is therefore essential.

To this end, the book begins in the first chapter by taking us far back in time to examine one of the most important premodern war media—the celestial orbs. For more than two millennia, astrological war media decisively shaped the conduct of warfare. Military commanders relied on the imagined futures that astrologers elaborated from astrolabes, horoscopes, and star charts. Devised as tools to handle uncertain futures and as guides for decision-making within the military realm, these contingency media were also at the center of heated debates. A famous exchange between Johannes Kepler and Albrecht von Wallenstein, then supreme commander of the armies of the Holy Roman Empire, spells out the disagreements about the reach and force of such projective imaginaries and the media that subtend them. Taking Schiller's war play *Wallenstein* as its point of departure, chapter 1 charts the rise and demise of astrological war media along with the emergence in the eighteenth century of a set of ideas within philosophical aesthetics that effectively disconnected art from any practical engagement with warfare. In Kant's famous and somewhat inelegant formulation, art is art because it displays a "purposiveness without purpose" and has no practical utility outside the realm of art itself.

Yet as theorists and philosophers of high art sought to cordon off aesthetics as a self-contained, autonomous realm, a group of military thinkers invented a self-contained artifact whose imaginary scenarios and projections of potential futures served the practical purpose of waging and optimizing war—the wargame. Transplanting foundational ideas from aesthetics to the realm of war, these inventors sought to unite creativity, play, sensuous perception, and cognitive as well as emotional interpellation into an autonomous artifact, a self-contained imaginary world that would allow them to invent, test, and realize the *optimum bellum*—the best of all possible wars. Chapter 2 traces their endeavors as they begin to incorporate aesthetic concepts and objects into the field of war. It is through their efforts and seemingly quaint inventions that the military first developed a martial aesthetics, one that has since morphed into new shapes through the affordances of contemporary digital technologies.

In chapter 3, I show how military inventors and designers moved to the forefront of a new *operational aesthetics*. Breaking down the wall that philosophers of aesthetics had sought to erect between art and craft, between autonomy and functionality, and between the imaginary and the real, operational aesthetics effects a collapse of these distinctions. Situated at the exact threshold, the new artifactual military worlds straddle war and aesthetics and unite them as a liminal phenomenon. They form the site for a demiurgic production of war, for the invention and implementation of factitious futures in a process of martial worldmaking.

Where the first chapters of the book lead us into the virtual military worlds generated by media technologies old and new, the later chapters take us directly into the military brain. The second part of the book examines the provocative idea within military theory that war is an art form. Chapter 4 delves into the origins of this claim by engaging the work of Carl von Clausewitz and Otto August Rühle von Lilienstern. Clausewitz and Rühle von Lilienstern do not simply advance the old idea that war is a practical art rather than a precise science governed by laws (as suggested, for example, by the inaccurate but well-known English translation of the famous ancient Chinese military treatise commonly ascribed to Sun Tzu—*The Art of War*).[3] Rather, they consider warfare as an aesthetic art form in its own right. Clausewitz's and Rühle von Lilienstern's writings on aesthetics and war effect a transfer of concepts from the realm of art to the military realm. They begin to associate genius, artistry, virtuosity, intuition, and creativity with soldiers as much as with artists. Indeed, they cast officers and commanders as "war artists" and war itself as "a work of art." Tracing the development of this aesthetic theory of war in the nineteenth and twentieth centuries, the chapter discusses the epistemological and ethical dilemmas that pertain to the transfiguration of collective violence into an art form.

These dilemmas are even more relevant because of the return of the aesthetic frame of war in the twenty-first century. Following General Mattis's adoption of the vocabulary of creativity, genius, and virtuosity, a movement of military thinkers, educators, and scholars has formed that promotes these ideas around the globe under the guise of a new discourse on "military design." Design thinking now pervades militaries from Great Britain to Denmark, from Australia to Canada. Chapter 5 examines contemporary military thought and the aesthetic frame that organizes it. Ostensibly a method for problem solving and managing the complexity of contemporary warfare, military design inscribes itself in the deeper historical trajectory as the current manifestation of the aesthetic theory of war. Modeled on the figure of the free artistic genius, military design projects a vision of liberating self-realization and creative martial worldmaking that lends war the aura of a noble, even desirable activity.

In short, from a contemporary vantage point, *Martial Aesthetics* traces how military inventors and thinkers have co-opted aesthetic artifacts and concepts. Charting this eerie and dark phenomenon through several historical manifestations, the book seeks to extract a theoretical frame from these historical examples that may lead to a better understanding of the truly strange character of contemporary warfare. In other words, I have written this book in the belief that there is indeed something to be learned from our violent past that is of immediate relevance for our violent present and for the violence to come.

Martial Aesthetics continues a larger investigation into war and its role in the history of knowledge. My previous book, *Empire of Chance: The Napoleonic Wars and the Disorder of Things* (Harvard University Press, 2015) analyzed the shift in the epistemology of war against the background of mass warfare. Adopting a synoptic perspective, I charted the emergence of chance as a pervasive problem across the literature, historiography, military theory, games, and mapping efforts of this momentous historical period. I showed how in their attempts to manage the chaos and contingencies—which they diagnosed as the essence of modern warfare—military thinkers, literary authors, game designers, and mapmakers invented new representational forms and new knowledge models to handle uncertainty. *Martial Aesthetics* similarly examines war as a field of knowledge, but it proceeds to trace the constitutive role of aesthetics within military science and technology. Then as now, the field of military knowledge is permeated by aesthetic artifacts and concepts that frame war as an art form, and a historical account of the birth of martial aesthetics may cast a new light on the powerful digital tools and ideas that shape war in our present moment.

A book of this kind has many limitations. First, it does not pretend to offer an exhaustive account of the multiple overlaps and intersections of war and aesthetics. For example, one of the more striking and already well-documented encounters took place in the early twentieth century when the artistic avant-garde made war into the engine of a radically new aesthetic. Even after the senseless mass slaughter of World War I, the futurist Filippo Tommaso Marinetti continued to rebel against the idea that war is "anti-aesthetic." In his 1935 manifesto, *The Futurist Aesthetic of War*, Marinetti insisted on the beauty of flame-throwers, gas masks, tanks, and even the fragrance of putrefaction, and he repeats, almost as an incantation, that "la guerra ha una sua bellezza" (war has its own beauty). By reframing and expanding the concept of beauty, Marinetti sought to claim war as a valid and desirable object of representation in works of art.[4] Walter Benjamin reflected on Marinetti's credo the following year in "The Work of Art in the Age of Its Technological Reproducibility." In an equally famous statement, Benjamin argued that fascism turns politics into an aesthetic spectacle—a process of aestheticization that can only lead to war. In Benjamin's view, the aestheticization of politics by fascism realizes the futurist vision as it transforms war into the ultimate artwork. Indeed, for Benjamin, fascist warfare becomes "the consummation of *l'art pour l'art*."[5]

Marinetti's conception of aesthetics as a matter of beauty and Benjamin's analysis of the aestheticization of politics are emblematic for a whole field of inquiry that I will occasionally remark on. In *Martial Aesthetics*, however, I seek to redirect aesthetics away from its traditional association with "beauty" and even away from art itself, in order to examine the militarization of aesthetics. This involves an inversion of perspectives. The question is not that of the futurists—how war may be claimed for aesthetics—but when and how aesthetics has been claimed by the military. In other words, the line of inquiry pursued here focuses on the media and the concepts of creative worldmaking developed by the military as tools for planning, training, and waging war. War is an aesthetic phenomenon not only because it can be placed in the category of the beautiful, as Marinetti did, but because military institutions import aesthetic products and aesthetic concepts to train soldiers for war and because the very act of waging war is framed as an artistic discipline in its own right.[6]

This aesthetic approach to the military itself is a departure from some dominant ways of thinking. Since the turn of the century, scholars of literature, film, and art history have developed a rich trove of analyses of the multiple ways in which war has shaped individual works of art. How, for example, modernist painting and sculpture developed a particular aesthetic language in response to World War I. Or how the wars in Iraq, Afghanistan, and Syria have left their stamp on the representational patterns that pervade the literature of these recent wars.[7] Such treatments of cultural products generally regard war as the originary agent or force whose often devastating consequences are subsequently recorded and refracted in works of art. Implicit in many of these accounts is a conception of war as a historical force that precedes and impacts on its aesthetic depiction in art.

At the same time, other scholars have examined the history of military representational media and technologies, charting the mutations of wargames, mapping, and various optical media. Paul Virilio, for example, famously charted the history of the "logistics of perception" and the overlap of imaging techniques, or "watching machines," as he once called them, with military targeting. In his account, the parallel emergence of cinema and aviation marks a turning point when mediated representations produced by the camera transformed the character of warfare as the immediate perception of the martial world was supplanted by a world of images.[8] Following Virilio's lead, Antoine Bousquet has more recently unearthed the deeper technoscientific foundations underlying the gradual convergence of perception and military targeting.[9] Meanwhile, the media theorist Friedrich Kittler has argued throughout most of his career that war has been the driver of technology—that the media and technologies that today sustain our civilian lives are spin-offs of military inventions and thus owe their existence to the exigencies of armed conflict.[10] For Kittler, too, war is a primary force, if not *the* primary force, that shapes the media and the life forms of civil society.

Together, these efforts have greatly enriched our understanding of both the aesthetics and the technologies of war. But the general separation of warfare and aesthetics into distinct realms and the primacy given to military technologies over civilian technologies neglect the ways in which war, aesthetics, and technology have frequently intersected and entwined to form closely knit structures in which creative techno-aesthetic imaginaries are integrated directly into the war effort.[11] Artists have long been positioned as the belated observers of the horrors and the devastation of war, but this construction has overshadowed how creative imaginary worlds have themselves served as engines of violence and destruction. *Martial Aesthetics* unearths this creative dimension of war in its double manifestation in a set of media and technologies as well as in the military's aesthetic self-fashioning as it reframes its own violent activities as a creative art form. In other words, the book seeks to bring to light the martial force of aesthetics—that is, the transformative, operational power that aesthetic artifacts and concepts acquire the moment they are plugged into the military apparatus. And it puts pressure on the dilemmas that arise once war becomes a form of violent creation.

This latter point is important. Within German media studies it has long been an acknowledged but uncomfortable truth that Friedrich Kittler's writings display an obsession with war and its media that at times seems to spill over into a fetishistic reverence for war as the driver of history and an active promotion of military media and technologies.[12] Even though military media and ideas are often presented as closed systems boasting admirable technological or conceptual sophistication, their endpoint and ultimate purpose lie outside these systems—in a world of violence, displacement, and brutality. Even the abstract and often abstruse language of military doctrine is an instrument of force that translates directly into injury and death. Broaching the subject of a martial aesthetics therefore involves a careful balance of perspectives. On the one hand, I argue that there *is* an aesthetic dimension to war that we cannot simply ignore. To grasp it, we must trace its various historical manifestations. But I also argue that the militarization of aesthetics has a number of dire, but unacknowledged, ethical consequences. Lurking in the background, we find an aesthetic martialism that promotes war as an aesthetic phenomenon.

Indeed, a central purpose of *Martial Aesthetics* is to make evident the dark side of framing war as an art form. When the German composer Karl-Heinz Stockhausen made his infamous statement that 9/11 was "the greatest artwork there has ever been," he may well have referred to a satanic figure in a personal artistic myth of creation and destruction. And in the same interview, he assured the interviewer that such a satanic work of art that cost thousands of lives was evidently a crime.[13] Regardless, this offhand statement caused a global moral outcry and led to a public apology. Meanwhile, the much more pervasive and systematic attempts to frame war in terms of artistry and creativity that are currently taking place inside the military have met with barely any form of critique.[14] Thriving silently out of the public eye, this far more influential discourse contains an inherent justification for war, and it shapes the way many military institutions are coming to understand the use of violence. *Martial Aesthetics* attempts to bring this discourse into the open and to complement a sober assessment of historical developments with a critical outside perspective. By historicizing and theorizing martial aesthetics, we may begin to counter the fetishization of war media and the ennoblement of war into an art form.

My approach takes its methodological cue from several thinkers who have brought the analytical apparatus from the humanities to bear on matters of concern within contemporary society. Eyal Weizman, for example, has examined architecture as a strategy of occupation, and he has teased out the historical background and philosophical underpinnings of the humanitarianism that has dominated perceptions of military intervention since the Cold War. In particular, I owe a debt to his appraisal of the performative role of philosophical concepts within military organizations.[15] *Martial Aesthetics* also builds on Elaine Scarry's classic study of torture, *The Body in Pain*, and her reflections on "making and unmaking" as they enable us to put the particular nature of contemporary martial worldmaking into relief. To gauge the effects and tease out the underlying ideologies inherent to media and technologies, I follow the lead of scholars such as Hans Belting, Pasi Vähliaho, and Jonathan Crary who situate concrete objects and inventions within larger assemblages of events, institutions, and power. As Crary writes about optical media, they are "points of intersection where philosophical, scientific, and aesthetic discourses overlap with mechanical techniques, institutional requirements, and socioeconomic forces."[16] Situating war media in a broader context of institutions, knowledges, and aesthetics, I analyze not only the forms of martial worldmaking implicit in their particular configurations but also the explicit debates that surround them. I therefore discuss a diverse array of texts and materials: classical works of philosophy and aesthetic theory—Leibniz, Baumgarten, Kant, and Schiller, among others—are juxtaposed with a series of war media from premodern horoscopes via early wargames to recent digital scenarios and synthetic training environments, which are in turn related to military texts from Clausewitz and Rühle von Lilienstern to twenty-first-century military doctrines and army manuals. The method, in other words, is to align and entangle a story of aesthetics, a story of media, and a story of military theory.

This approach brings the book within the orbit of Ryan Bishop and John Phillips's work. In their examination of the "technicities of perception," they relate modernist avant-garde aesthetics to twenty-first-century military technology.[17] The unusual rapprochement between worlds seemingly apart also structures *Martial Aesthetics*. But whereas Bishop and Phillips show the resistance of aesthetic thought to the logic of military technological development and the gap between them, my study traces their increasing infiltration.[18] While the beginning of the twentieth century witnessed a plethora of radical aesthetic experiments performed by several artistic avant-gardes, in the first decades of the twenty-first century such aesthetic experimentation is conducted under the aegis of the military.

By tracing this entanglement, *Martial Aesthetics* follows the impulses of Joseph Vogl's genealogical critique of the forms of contemporary capitalism, but redirects it to a different field. Across several books, Vogl has shown how economic theories since Adam Smith's "invisible hand" have been structured by philosophical and moral imaginaries and how the current regime of finance that governs the world economy is deeply entwined with, and to a large extent constituted by, a spectral host of fictions, imagined scenarios, and projected futures.[19] As I argue in this book, the field of war is in a similar fashion informed by powerful creative imaginaries that profoundly shape military practice and military theory. In the field of war, too, such imaginaries are pervasive and performative. Anything but airy nothings, they make and they shape the wars that militaries seek to realize. They are the creative demons that now inhabit the war machine, that lend aesthetics a diabolical force far beyond its previous reach, and that transform contemporary war into an alluring aesthetic phenomenon.

1

ASTROLOGICAL WAR MEDIA

In the winter of 1634 in the Bohemian town of Pilsen, Albrecht von Wallenstein—then generalissimo of the Holy Roman Empire and supreme commander of the armies of the Habsburg monarchy—found himself pacing his chamber while pondering his military options. It was a defining moment of the Thirty Years' War. The Swedish adversary was edging closer; Wallenstein was losing the trust of his employer, the Habsburg emperor Ferdinand II; and even within the ranks of his own army, voices were beginning to question his leadership. All of these threats were coming to a head, and Wallenstein was keenly aware that he had to act. Inside his chamber, he imagined one military strategy after the other until he was juggling a whole array of potential strategic scenarios. He only needed to choose among them. But which?

To help him decide, Wallenstein turned to the stars. Since ancient times, beginning in Mesopotamia, the science of astrology had formed an integral part of military planning, and Wallenstein is the last commander known to consult astrology in matters of war. His chamber was plastered with star charts, quadrants, globes, and other astrological equipment. At one point Wallenstein stopped in front of a so-called *speculum astrologicum*, a blackboard that displayed the positions of the planets or "wandering stars," as they were known since antiquity. In accordance with the science of astrology, Wallenstein believed that the celestial constellations—the particular position of the planets at a given time—reveal events of the immediate future on earth. Inspecting the *speculum astrologicum*, he suddenly noticed that the stars had aligned in a promising constellation, and he exclaimed: "fortunate aspect!" The time for action had come.

This scene is entirely made up. It appears in Friedrich Schiller's three-part drama *Wallenstein*, completed in 1799. Schiller zooms in on the final days of Wallenstein's life before he was murdered in late February 1634. But as Schiller knew well, the scene has a famous historical background. Not only was the historical Wallenstein indeed beholden to the science of astrology; he had initiated a famous correspondence about the nature and power of astrology with one of the leading scientists of the day—Johannes Kepler. In 1608, Kepler had made a horoscope for Wallenstein.

Wallenstein's horoscope is divided into twelve contiguous triangles representing the houses of the zodiac. The horoscope's spatial order shows the exact position of the sun, moon, and planets at the time of Wallenstein's birth. Observing the various positions and alignments of the planets, Kepler proceeded to predict a number of events in Wallenstein's life. He concluded that the horoscope "was not a bad nativity, but contained exceptionally important signs."[1] Yet Wallenstein was not satisfied. As the years went by, he felt that the horoscope and the events in his life fell increasingly out of sync. Some of the predicted life events had occurred too early, some too late. He therefore asked Kepler to update the original horoscope. And now Wallenstein demanded new and very concrete astrological predictions based on a careful recalculation and correction of the original horoscope.[2]

Kepler refused. Or, he refused to offer the degree of detail Wallenstein demanded. In a wry response, Kepler lectured Wallenstein on the limits of astrological knowledge. Astrology, he writes, can predict only general tendencies, not particular events. As he puts it, "It is an erroneous illusion to think that such *Accidentia*, which mostly follow from the workings of the human will, occur in accordance with concrete, calculated celestial events, and can therefore be predicted."[3] In spite of his reservations, however, Kepler did actually update Wallenstein's horoscope. He proceeded to predict a number of events until—remarkably—the winter of 1634, in which, as he wrote, "horrible disorder" threatened.[4]

It is this discussion about the force and reach of astrological war

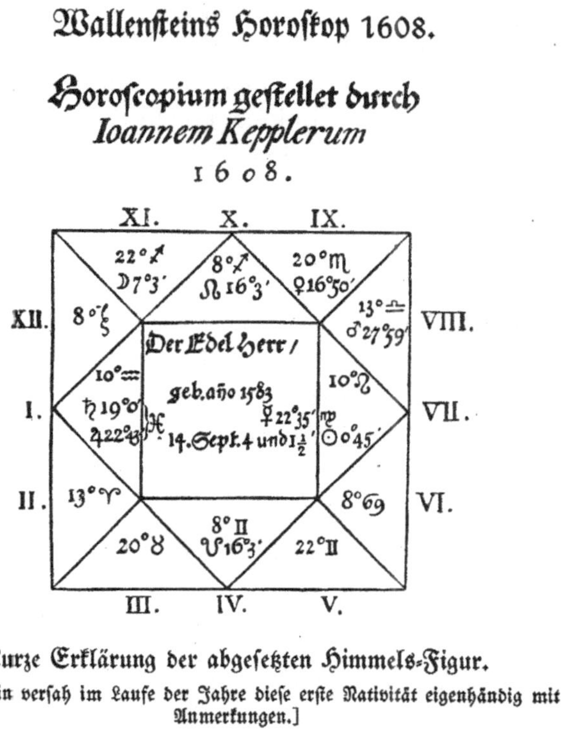

FIGURE 1.1. The horoscope Kepler made for Wallenstein in 1608. Source: Johannes Kepler, *Die Astrologie des Johannes Kepler: Eine Auswahl aus seinen Schriften*, ed. Heinz Artur Strauss and Sigrid Strauss-Kloebe (Munich: Oldenburg, 1926).

media that Schiller evokes in 1799 when he places Wallenstein in front of the blackboard with the planetary aspects. In Schiller's play, though, Wallenstein does not heed Kepler's warnings about the limitations of the science of astrology. When he notices the favorable alignment of the stars on the blackboard in front of him, he is convinced of the scientific and metaphysical backing for his plan of action. The time to transform his numerous potential scenarios into an actual decision has finally arrived.

But Wallenstein does nothing. He ponders, he reflects, he evaluates his array of imaginary futures. But he refuses to act. As time begins to run out, his military advisers urge him to make a decision, but to no avail.

Wallenstein keeps thinking. Then his wife insists that he get on with it, but Wallenstein keeps thinking. With increasing desperation, first his son and then his in-house astrologer both implore him to act, but Wallenstein simply keeps on thinking. Finally, Wallenstein's sister-in-law, Countess Terzky, has had enough and exclaims:

> The moment has arrived, when you should draw
> The sum conclusion of your life's account;
> The signs of victory stand above your head,
> The planets nod good fortune from above,
> And cry: the time is come! Is it in vain
> That all your days you have so closely told
> The courses of the stars? Wielded the compass
> And quadrant? painted on these walls the vault
> Of heaven and the zodiac, and gathered
> About you with their silent, bodeful signs
> The seven lords of destiny?
> Was it an idle game that you were playing?[5]

This curious scene in which the mastermind of military strategy is beseeched by his family members to transform imagined futures into concrete action raises some fundamental questions about the media of war. Set in the first half of the seventeenth century, Schiller's play marks the end of a belief system that had informed the conduct of war for almost two millennia. The origin of the era that Wallenstein's demise brings to a conclusion can be traced back to the Assyrian emperor Sargon II in the eighth century BCE. According to the historical record, Sargon II (721–705 BCE) is the first Assyrian monarch reported to consult the heavens in matters of war. Before one of his several campaigns, he turned to his astrologer, who informed him that Nabû (Mercury), Marduk (Jupiter), and Magur (the moon) had entered into a favorable constellation and appeared to herald the destruction of the enemy. Sargon was quick to take action. As he wrote: "Upon the precious approval of the warrior Shamash [the sun], who wrote encouraging omens on the exta that he would walk at my side . . . I mustered my army."[6] With the invention of the horoscope in the fifth century BCE, the integration of media, science, and war established a powerful astrological war imaginary that would deeply influence military decision-making.[7]

Central to this imaginary was a particular modality of events. Espying among the celestial orbs the future of his king and kingdom, Sargon's astrologer was engaged with events that were neither impossible nor necessary. Aristotle, in *On Interpretation*, would later call such an event *endechomenon*—that is, an event that "may either take place or not take place."[8] In Boethius's early sixth-century translation, the Latin term for an event that is neither impossible nor necessary, that may take place or not take place, became *contingens*, and today such events are known in the plural form as *future contingents*. For more than two millennia, astrology was regarded as the science best equipped to handle this critical but elusive and unwieldy type of event. Politically savvy astrologers developed a highly elaborate war imaginary comprising a kaleidoscopic array of contingent futures and contingent worlds. They thereby set the parameters for a military futurology whose overall structure and basic validity were widely accepted until the seventeenth century.

What was the nature of the astrological war imaginary, and what was the status of the imagined events produced by its media? As the debate between Kepler and Wallenstein indicates, there were various cracks and fissures in the assemblage. Even as the basic framework of astrology long went unquestioned, key elements in its war imaginary were frequently contested. In particular, the force and level of predictions formed the subject of continuing debates. Within which time frame and with what specificity of detail might military events emerge? Could the stars mark the exact day of an attack? Did they predict events at an individual level or merely general tendencies? With which tools should astrologers translate between celestial and terrestrial movements, and which among the various systems of divination formed the superior celestial hermeneutics? In other words, even if it went without saying that war, astrology, and media were locked in an intimate relationship, the exact nature of this relationship remained contentious.

Schiller taps directly into these debates, but he also raises some fundamental questions about the role of aesthetics in war. Wallenstein creates a war imaginary of potential scenarios and imagined futures developed from the media available at the time—horoscopes, astrolabes, and star charts. But are these imagined futures mere potentialities, self-contained artificial worlds designed for detached appreciation? Are they purely aesthetic, only an "idle game," in Countess Terzky's words, without any purchase on the actual world? Or do these imaginaries have practical consequences? Do they contain what Aristotle calls *dunamis*—that is, the power to become real? What, this play asks, is the *force* of aesthetics? While Harun Farocki's *Serious Games* bring out the intricacies of the contemporary war assemblage, Friedrich Schiller's *Wallenstein* can reveal the paradoxes that attend its longer history. Written at the height of philosophical aesthetics, Schiller's war play pries open the fissures that beset the astrological war assemblage and address head-on the tensions between use and autonomy, purpose and play, and war and aesthetics.

CONTINGENCY MEDIA

The Thirty Years' War (1618–1648) was one of the bloodiest wars in Europe. The fervor of the religious disagreements that pitted Protestants against Catholics and the ferocity with which the war was fought caused massive devastation and deaths in the millions. For Schiller, the period marked a traumatic caesura in German history. His play *Wallenstein* relates a central episode at the midpoint of the wars. Ostensibly tracing the fall and murder of the renowned general, however, Schiller's focus is not the historical chronicle. He had already published a historical account of the wars in 1792. With his famous play, Schiller instead examines the nature of future contingents. Everyone plays a game of war in *Wallenstein.* The opening scene itself already announces the main theme of the play. A lowly peasant who wants to try his luck approaches a tent crowded with soldiers and a group of boys playing dice on a drum. Soon engaged in a game of chance, both the peasant and the soldiers give themselves over to the uncertainty of events that may come to be and may not—the allure of the game being contingency itself paired with the material rewards of a fortunate outcome. Unsatisfied with the equal distribution of chance, however, the peasant brings along a pair of "lucky dice" manipulated to shift the odds in his favor.[9] His deception is soon discovered, and the soldiers seize him along with his "false dice," ready to execute him for "cheating in the game."[10]

Playing and playing falsely are part of a larger material and metaphorical complex that frames the activities of all agents, from children and the lowest ranks of peasants and private soldiers to the highest military and political echelons.[11] Civilians, whose livelihood has been destroyed by the war now in its sixteenth year, play for money to alleviate their hardships; soldiers play to pass the time, but they also take active part in the "bloody wargame" of the Thirty Years' War;[12] officers such as Butler and Octavio Piccolomini play a game of self-interest and personal advancement; with his proxies and spies, the Austrian emperor plays a strategic-political game against and behind the back of Wallenstein, who in turn subsumes everyone to his military calculation as if it were a "board game."[13]

Common to these variations of the game are the type of event they produce and the material objects with which they are connected. As the opening scene demonstrates, dice are not only the agents of contingent events. The peasant also manipulates them to control and limit the number of potential events they produce. False dice are tools to navigate contingency, to transform the nimbus of possible futures into a strategic advantage.

In Schiller's *Wallenstein*, a range of objects is tasked with this purpose. The false dice clearly fall within the category of the game, as does the "board game" that forms the metaphor for Wallenstein's military calculations, but other nonludic phenomena are similarly used to offer knowledge of the future.[14] Through the art of chiromancy, or palm reading, the palm of Wallenstein's own hand as well as that of his daughter Thekla are transformed from simple body parts into a collection of signs that allows divination of future events.[15] And indeed, the central objects in the play pertain to the science from which chiromancy was eventually derived—the science of astrology. Horoscopes, astrological tables, and celestial drawings are the astrological tools that offer Schiller's Wallenstein a window into the future.

We may subsume this otherwise heterogeneous array of games, inscriptions, and tools under the larger category of *contingency media*. I understand this term as referring to media that serve as tools to facilitate strategic thought and action under conditions of uncertainty. Media are notoriously difficult to define, but the variety of the objects analyzed in the field of media studies suggests that the starting point for thinking about media should not necessarily be ontological.[16] Eva Horn and Joseph Vogl have suggested that we think of media as *dispositifs*—that is, as "assemblages or constellations of certain technologies, fields of knowledge, and social institutions."[17] From this point of view, the differences among objects, technologies, and material inscriptions of various kinds matter less than the practical ways they are put to use, the particular historical juncture at which they emerge, and the epistemic or metaphysical framework within which they are made to operate. A medium, as Vogl argues, does not belong to an ahistorical category of stable objects. An object first "*becomes a medium*, precisely by becoming epistemologically productive" in a constellation of an institutional development, a technological invention, and a theoretical framework. A medium does not simply produce events; it constitutes an event in itself.[18] In the history of warfare, a range of objects have in this way all become media at specific historical junctures, when they have been invented, reappropriated, and put to use to display and manage contingent events. Within the framework of astrology, as Schiller's *Wallenstein* highlights, horoscopes, astrological tables, the spatial patterns of the palm, and the stars themselves have all been transformed from simple, asignifying objects into epistemologically productive media to handle the contingencies of warfare.

But just as media emerge at particular historical junctures when a larger constellation makes them productive, their malfunction has also spurred debates over their efficiency. In the early seventeenth century, a key part of the larger assemblage—namely, the metaphysical framework of astrological science—was being seriously questioned, and with it the very status of contingency media as media. In other words, were horoscopes, palms, and revolving celestial spheres media at all? Were they signifying objects that could predict the contingent futures of war, make it legible, and, perhaps, manipulable? Or were they channeling nothing at all other than the misguided hermeneutic practices of self-authorized astrologers?

Since its emergence in ancient Mesopotamia, astrology relied on the fundamental assumption that celestial dynamics translate into terrestrial dynamics. In *Tetrabiblos*, the standard reference for all things astrological for over a millennium, Ptolemy writes:

> The cause of both universal and of particular events is the motion of the planets, sun, and moon; and the prognostic art is the scientific observation of precisely the change in the subject natures which corresponds to parallel movements of the heavenly bodies through the surrounding heavens.[19]

The science of astrology was therefore infused with a spatial metaphysics:

the celestial configuration in itself carries what Ptolemy called an "effective power."[20] In other words, star events are made possible because astrologers project a spatial field infused with metaphysical assumptions onto the planets and their movements. For the astrologer looking up at the skies, the heavens constitute not only a mobile spatial arrangement but a field of possible events.[21]

Even if this assumption for centuries had the status of a natural law much like gravity has for us today, critiques appeared at regular intervals and with heightened frequency in the late Middle Ages and the early modern period.[22] In 1373, one of the most productive scholars of the fourteenth century, Heinrich von Langenstein, wrote his *Tractatus contra astrologos coniunctionistas de eventibus futurorum* (Treatise against astrologers conjunctionists of future events). In this work, he criticized the assumptions of astrologers who deemed themselves capable of predicting terrestrial events based on the observation of celestial conjunctions. With a wide arsenal of arguments, Giovanni Pico della Mirandola in his twelve-volume *Disputationum adversus astrologos* (Arguments against astrologers) would later renew the attack on astrology, questioning the coherence of its cosmological foundations as well as its numerous practical failures.[23] A particularly caustic critique was articulated by Martin Luther, for whom astrology conflicted with his theological notions and the faith in the goodwill of God. As he put it in one of his sermons, "There comes fashionable astrology or mathematics, which greatly desires to be a science, but it cannot cast off its inborn foolishness" (Sequitur lauta illa Astrologia seu Mathematica, quae valde cupit esse scientia, sed non potest stulticiam ingenitam exuere).[24] Luther's sarcasm extended also to the media of astrology. The individual horoscope was drawn based on the constellation of the stars at the moment of birth. But what justified that celestial influence on the life of a human being set in at just that moment and not earlier? "Are the stars not just as effective *in utero* as *extra uterum*? Do you think that the stars inquire about a small piece of skin over a woman's stomach?"[25]

THE POWER OF PREDICTION: KEPLER CONTRA WALLENSTEIN

An important element in the critique of astrology and its media concerned the type of contingency that astrologers could predict. Was it possible to predict concrete events for named individuals, or could the starry skies only indicate larger trends, such as conflicts, disasters, or peace at a general level? That was precisely the bone of contention in the celebrated debate between Kepler and Wallenstein. Along with his request of an update and recalculation of the horoscope, Wallenstein demanded to know how long he would continue in military service and whether he would be blessed with luck in all his military endeavors.[26] Moreover, he believed that the horoscope would even be able to reveal the nationality and profession of his "hidden and public enemies," for, as he writes, "that can easily be deduced."[27] Kepler's reply deserves to be quoted at some length:

> I state this solely for the purpose of removing the illusion entertained by the subject of the nativity that all the *Particularia* can be predicted from the heavens. This much is true, that from the heavens follow heavenly *Particularia*, but not terrestrial ones, neither *specialia* nor *individua*, rather, all terrestrial *Eventus* take their form and shape from terrestrial causes, since every particular has its particular cause. . . . For even though certain time periods are a celestial particularity, and can be taken from heaven, understand, then, what heaven does all for itself: thus it has been stated above that heaven very rarely, almost never is alone, but that the subject of the nativity and others with whom he has commerce, do much and undertake endeavors of their own free will that they could also have refrained from, and had not been forced to do by heaven, but whereby they promote or hinder the natural chance events, something that their celestial time, measure, and particularity cannot do.[28]

Distinguishing between what is today commonly referred to as natural and judicial astrology, Kepler seeks to secure the scientific basis of astrology by limiting its reach.[29] Only the general predictions of natural astrology have validity. The belief of judicial astrology that celestial patterns can be translated into particular terrestrial events, however, is pure superstition. Concrete events on earth are the product of a complex of causes, most of them terrestrial. The influence of human will, chance, and political circumstances in the sublunary realm have the greatest sway and hinder a direct correlation of the stars and human affairs. So although the metaphysics of the astrological system remains intact, Kepler goes out of his way to emphasize that his medium and his science cannot provide the information Wallenstein demands of it. Thus his conclusion that it is an erroneous illusion to think "that such *Accidentia* . . . can be predicted."[30]

The debate between Kepler and Wallenstein brings out the many interwoven components of the astrological war imaginary. A blend of discursive, metaphysical, scientific, military, aesthetic, and media elements, it forms the stuff that military dreams are made on. The disagreement in this debate concerns the *force* of such dreams—not whether this assemblage carries powers of prediction but how and to what extent. The starry skies and the horoscope are unquestionably media of a celestial force governing the sublunary realm, but according to which system should they be interpreted, and what is the reach of their force? From Wallenstein's perspective, the horoscope is an epistemically highly robust representation that accurately maps spatial constellations onto future contingents at all levels, if only for the scientifically trained beholder. From Kepler's perspective, the horoscope generates both knowledge and pure fantasy. It accurately maps the positions of the stars onto supraindividual future events, but at the level of the individual and particular it has no power to produce reliable knowledge—only empty fictions and illusions.

That Kepler, the last renowned astrological adviser to a major military commander, nevertheless agrees to update Wallenstein's horoscope and offers a series of often fairly specific predictions is a good example of what Dan Edelstein has called the "Super-Enlightenment"—the curious blend of the hermetic and the occult with what we today recognize as well-reasoned science. With its amalgamation of astronomical observation and astrological metaphysics, the horoscope precisely maps the "epistemological no-man's land" in which many scientists operated at the time.[31]

When Schiller writes his play about war and astrology some 175 years later, he enters directly into this debate about the force of the astrological war imaginary. By then astrology had long been abandoned as a serious guide to the affairs of the world, but with his historical play Schiller presents the astrological war imaginary at the very moment of its unraveling. Wallenstein's initial belief in its force is indisputable. Standing in front of the *speculum astrologicum*, he has no doubt that he is looking at the diagram of his imminent victory. When one of Wallenstein's allies is captured and his military plans are revealed, this unforeseen event therefore challenges the entire metaphysical order of his belief system.

The favorable constellation on his star chart did not translate into favorable military events on the ground.

In an attempt to save the science of astrology, however, Wallenstein reconceptualizes the nature of the stars' predictive force. No longer a representation of the immediate future as it is about to unfold, the stars now represent what *ought* to unfold according to the natural course of things:

> The stars don't lie, *that* however
> took place against the course of the stars and against destiny.
> The art is honest, but this false heart
> brings lie and deceit into the truthful heavens.
> Divination is based only on truth,
> Where nature exceeds its bounds, all science errs.[32]

The predictive force of the astrological war imaginary is now revealed to be predicated on a set of rules and procedures that fall within the "natural" course of terrestrial events. Beyond that, the stars lose all their influence. Wallenstein thereby transforms the heavens from an *ontic* force to a *normative* force—from events that *will be* to events that *should have been*. No longer a strategic military tool for concrete action in the field, astrological prediction marks instead the degree to which warfare exceeds the natural order of things, producing events and actions that lie beyond the usual epistemological and moral sphere.

As the play progresses, the force of the stars wanes even further until Wallenstein's celestial map of events loses all its metaphysical underpinnings. Paying no heed to the warnings of his astrologer Seni, Wallenstein eventually abandons astrology as a guide in military affairs. Deprived of their power to influence, the heavens have ceased to represent a celestial force and now constitute only an infinite, meaningless territory. Where Kepler lectured the historical Wallenstein on the limits of astrological predictions, Schiller's fictional Wallenstein comes to dismiss their power entirely.

In the move from fervent believer to disillusioned agnostic, Schiller's protagonist condenses a two-thousand-year-long history of the astrological war imaginary. The larger interest of the play, however, lies in Wallenstein's curious misinterpretation and misuse of its war media. Once again, horoscopes play a central role. When Wallenstein's officers warn him against his own general, Octavio Piccolomini, they are rejected out of hand because Wallenstein has himself "cast his horoscope / We are born under the same stars," as he puts it.[33] Assuming a celestial bond between them, Wallenstein never suspects Octavio's deceit, but he also interprets all astrological signs in his own favor when, according to the horoscope he himself cast for Octavio, they would apply equally well to him. Likewise with the figure of luck that Wallenstein notices on the *speculum astrologicum*. Immediately after his jubilant exclamation, he is advised that the constellation of events on the ground have instead favored those plotting against him.[34]

Misidentifying the subject of the horoscopes, Wallenstein's graver error is his misuse of the war medium. Schiller's Wallenstein not only makes use of the tools of astrology. Like the historical Wallenstein, he has transformed his castle into a gigantic celestial representation, painting the zodiac signs on the walls and surrounding himself with pictures of the planets.[35] While his astrologer Seni observes the actual sky and derives lessons for concrete action, Wallenstein is living inside a representation and becomes increasingly oblivious to its alleged referent, to what Kepler called the "terrestrial causes." Immersed in the medium, Wallenstein is oddly uninterested in using it for practical military purposes. Famously governed by a pervasive inaction,[36] the play sees Wallenstein hesitate, ponder, imagine, project, and reflect, but he is unwilling to transform the potentiality he derives from his astrological representations into terrestrial reality. Thus Countess Terzky's question: Are his astrological operations *serious games* with practical consequences? Are the star charts, horoscopes, and celestial representations on the castle vaults media at all? In other words, are they part of a larger complex of institutions and epistemology that endows them with a practical efficacy and a measurable impact, as had been the case for astrological contingency media for millennia? And if not, what purpose do they serve?

THE GREAT DIVIDE: WAR AND PHILOSOPHICAL AESTHETICS

Wallenstein's misuse of astrological war media is inscribed within a larger discussion in eighteenth-century philosophical aesthetics about the nature and purpose of art. The eighteenth century is traditionally regarded as the period in which a conception of art as an autonomous realm was first developed. Building on a thesis first propounded by Paul Oskar Kristeller in 1951, Larry Shiner argues that an important conceptual separation took place during the eighteenth century, with wide implications for the understanding of art in the past 250 years.[37] In ancient Greek and Roman theories of art, *techne* and *ars* designated a much wider array of phenomena than the modern concept of art does today. Poetry and sculpture belonged to this category, but so did carpentry, medicine, and horse breaking. In this older system of art, the separation between what would later be called "fine art" and "craft" did not yet exist. The poet and the doctor, the embroiderer and the shoemaker, the sculptor and the military commander were as much artisans as artists, defined by their common ability make and perform. As skills, *techne* and *ars* contained a distinctly utilitarian element, lending these concepts an applied dimension absent from the modern concept of art. Often the products of *techne* and *ars* served a particular purpose, whether in the form of clothing or entertainment. Horace's dictum in his *Ars Poetica*, "He who has mixed utility and pleasure has won everyone's approval," encapsulates this understanding of art.

Only in the eighteenth century does this broad notion of art begin to fracture. In three main phases, Shiner argues, a modern understanding of art emerges, first tentatively from 1680 to 1750, then more forcefully between 1750 and 1800, only to consolidate itself between 1800 and 1830. In the modern conception of art, different aspects of the older system are separated into distinct spheres. Art is separated into the fine arts, on the one hand, and crafts and popular arts, on the other; the artist is distinguished from the artisan; and the artwork is separated from the product. From here on, the poet and the potter no longer participate in an activity that carries the same name or has a similar function. For along with these distinctions, a new set of criteria emerged to characterize the fine arts. Whereas potters follow the habits and rules of their craft to make a product that serves a particular purpose, the fine arts are now characterized by the autonomy of the work of art, the originality of the artist, and the refined, disinterested pleasure of the spectator or listener.

The emphasis on genius, the imagination, creativity, and nonutility and the separation and safeguarding of these characteristics within the realm of fine art as opposed to the realm of craft and popular arts mark a decisive break with a conception of art that had dominated for about two millennia. By the 1750s, the notion that artists were not only distinct from artisans but were indeed defined by their opposition to each other was widespread.[38] A clear indication of this shift is found in Didérot and d'Alembert's *Encyclopédie* (1751–72), which divides the field of knowledge into three main categories and places the fine arts (here organized into poetry, painting, sculpture, engraving, and music) under the faculty of the imagination while all other arts and sciences are subsumed within the faculties of memory and reason.[39]

By the end of the century, the idea that fine art belonged to a separate realm and was characterized by a unique set of attributes dominated aesthetic theory. Shiner sums up the shift in the following manner:

> Whereas the ideal qualities desired in an artisan/artist in the old system combined genius and rule, inspiration and facility, innovation and imitation, freedom and service, these qualities were finally pulled apart in the course of the eighteenth century. As this happened, all the "poetic" attributes—such as inspiration, imagination, freedom, and genius—were ascribed to the artist and all the "mechanical" attributes—such as skill, rules, imitation, and service—went to the artisan. . . . Among the many attributes of the artist, genius and freedom seemed to sum up all the superlative qualities that now separated the free, creative artist from the supposedly dependent and routine craftsperson.[40]

One may dispute the extent and degree of Shiner's thesis about the grand divide in the theory of art in the eighteenth century. The notion that aesthetic experience was predicated on a state of disinterest was, for example, a topic of serious debate. Yet even if there was no uniform critical consensus about all the different concepts involved in the larger shift, and many of them remained, in the words of one influential scholar, "essentially contested concepts," eighteenth-century thinkers did establish a whole new frame for thinking about art.[41]

What do these debates have to do with war? For us to grasp the place of warfare in aesthetic thought at this time, one idea in the emerging conception of art is central. The separation of art from practical purposes involved a rethinking of the status of the work of art itself. No longer tied to a specific purpose, nor regarded primarily as an imitation of nature, the work of art gradually came to be seen as a second creation, the invention of a self-contained world in its own right. In 1728, Johann Jakob Bodmer and Johann Jakob Breitinger conceived of the writer as the creator of "new worlds, which he populates with new inhabitants who are of a different nature and follow their own laws."[42] The creative imagination invented new ideas and new representations, the origins for which were to be found "not in the actual world of real things, but rather in the world of possible things."[43] The philosophical basis for this idea was Leibniz's theory of possible worlds. In his *Theodicy*, Leibniz had argued that the present world was just one among an "infinity of possible worlds" in the mind of God.[44] While the actual world was, in his famous phrase, the "best of all possible worlds," it was surrounded by a nebula of compossible worlds that were just as real, but that had not been actualized. In the aesthetic application of Leibniz's theory of possible worlds, Bodmer and Breitinger envisaged the author as a secular demiurge in the position parallel to that of God in Genesis and similarly engaged in the creation of an internally coherent, self-contained world unto itself.[45]

A key moment in the development of this conception of the work of art was the publication in 1785 of Karl Philipp Moritz's essay "Versuch einer Vereinigung aller schönen Künste und Wissenschaften unter dem Begriff des in sich selbst Vollendeten" (Toward a unification of all the fine arts and letters under the concept of self-sufficiency).[46] As the title indicates, Moritz argues that the purpose of a work of art should not be conceived instrumentally; that is, its purpose does not reside in any external effects it may have on human beings, such as pleasure.[47] Rather, the work of art constitutes a "totality" that is "self-sufficient" and whose purpose is purely intrinsic to the work of art itself.[48] As he puts it:

> In contemplating the beautiful object . . . I roll the purpose away from me and back into the object itself: I regard it as something which is completed, not in me, but *in itself*, which therefore constitutes a whole in itself.[49]

The purposes of crafts, objects, and popular arts lie outside themselves (he offers the example of a watch, a knife, and plays that seek to evoke the emotions of the masses); but in the proper artwork, Moritz relocates the purpose to the artwork itself, to an "inner purposiveness," thereby sealing the artwork off from any external dependencies and establishing its raison d'être solely in its inner coherence and unity.[50]

By transposing the purpose of art from the external world to the inner realm of art itself, Moritz's brief and unassuming essay made a decisive break with a set of beliefs that had governed the theory of art for two millennia. But it would take the more substantial efforts of Immanuel Kant to cement the notion of art as an autotelic self-sufficient totality. In his *Critique of the Power of Judgment* published five years later in 1790, Kant pulled together and organized the new conception of art in a more systematic manner. Drawing even more sharply a line between the fine arts and craft, Kant distinguished fine art, or "die schöne Kunst," both from *Geschicklichkeit*, or skill—that is, the human practical ability to perform some task—and from *Handwerk*, or craft, which characterizes work performed not for its own sake but for some other purpose, such as wages.[51] Fine art is instead, in Kant's famous phrase, governed by a "purposiveness without purpose."[52] Transposing purpose from the external realm into an autotelic formal inner purposiveness, Kant ultimately considers art a subjective, cognitive phenomenon. Introducing the notion of "play," Kant claims that when viewing a beautiful work of art, two of the art consumer's cognitive faculties, the imagination and the understanding, are brought into a state of harmonious free play. Where the power of judgment is wont to subsume the percepts presented by the imagination to the concepts of the understanding and thereby categorize them, this categorizing judgment is suspended in aesthetic experience. Seeing beautiful art gives rise to the pleasurable sensation of the two different parts of the mental machinery being themselves purposefully attuned to one another.[53] From the mundane, pragmatic, and actual purposes of craft or the merely entertaining function of popular "pleasant arts,"[54] Kant not only transforms the notion of purpose into an internal affair within the work of art; when he does consider effects beyond the work of art, his aesthetic theory regards art as a phenomenon that sets into motion a subjective, cognitive phenomenon in which the mind relishes its own internal coherence as the faculties spin freely in a state of play.

Uniting these ideas with a range of other concepts of the eighteenth-century discourse on aesthetics, such as genius, originality, beauty, taste, and the aesthetic, Kant's *Critique of the Power of Judgment* provided a philosophical grounding of the new conception of art that had developed in the eighteenth century. He cemented the separation of art and craft, the artist from the artisan, and the work of art from the artisanal object, in the process elevating the artwork to a realm of a higher, more refined appreciation that was not just in practice but in principle incompatible with practical functionality. Withdrawing art from the mundane world of everyday human affairs, Kant cemented the idea of the work of art as a self-sufficient creation, adding further the idea that its primary function was to effect a state of cognitive free play whose premise was the suspension of conventional purposiveness.

SCHILLER'S AESTHETIC THEORY

Such is the intellectual background that informs Schiller's own thinking about the purpose and power of art. While doing preliminary work on *Wallenstein*, he was concurrently developing a theory of aesthetics, which was published in 1795 with the title *Letters on the Aesthetic Education of Man*.[55] Gripped by the revolutionary fervor that swept across Europe in the 1780s, Schiller had initially been favorably disposed toward the ideals of the French Revolution, but as it soon devolved into the Reign of Terror, he sought a different path for effecting the deep societal changes he desired that might lead to the experience of freedom. The letters on aesthetics are his response. In a grandiose argument, Schiller claims that the ideal of freedom may be obtained not by way of a bloody revolution but by the cultivation of aesthetic experience through exposure to the refined realm of fine art.

A central part of this argument involves a new conception of "play." This concept harkens back to Kant, but in Schiller's work it takes on a different form. Like Kant, Schiller is keen to distinguish his novel concept of play from concrete games such as board games or games of chance. Instead, what he labels the "the play drive" (*Spieltrieb*) is an anthropological category that may well be activated by concrete games but cannot be reduced to them.[56] Rethinking Kant's transcendental faculties of the imagination that processes percepts and the understanding that supplies concepts, Schiller posits two analogous drives, the sense drive (*Stofftrieb*) and the form drive (*Formtrieb*), which constitute the main forces determining human lives and comportment. In this equation, the play drive is a subjective drive that mediates between the two former drives and thereby between a series of subsidiary dichotomies: contingency and necessity, passivity and action, seriousness and play. The main function of the play drive is to cancel out extremes, to reconcile the drives and obtain a harmonious balance between them:

> To the extent that it deprives feelings and passions of their dynamic power, it will bring them into harmony with the ideas of reason; and to

> the extent that it deprives the laws of reason of their moral compulsion, it will reconcile them with the interests of the senses.[57]

Activated by the contemplation of beauty, the play drive places the subject into an "aesthetic state," which Schiller describes as at once "nothing" and "the highest reality." Nothing "if you turn your attention to individual and concrete effects," but also a state of the highest reality "if you consider the absence of all limitations and the sum of the powers that are active together in it."[58] Because of this dual nature of play, it figures both as "*mere* play" and as the very essence of human nature: "it is play and *only* play that makes the human being complete."[59] Not directed toward anything specific, the play drive, in Schiller's account, puts the individual in an aesthetic state whose reality is that of an intensified but purely potential freedom. In such a state we may disregard the limits that reality would otherwise impose on us and act according to our own will.

Toward the end of his letters, Schiller boldly outlines the emergence of an "aesthetic state" as a political entity in which the aesthetic reconciliation of humanity's sensual and rational nature will lead to a balanced and harmonious society. As he puts it:

> In the midst of the formidable realm of forces, and of the sacred empire of laws, the aesthetic impulse of form creates by degrees a third and a joyous realm, that of play and of the appearance, where she emancipates man from fetters, in all his relations, and from all that is named constraint, whether physical or moral.[60]

But critical caveats follow. Such an aesthetic state is at odds with actual political reality. It exists only in "a few chosen circles,"[61] and, while cast as a potential societal ideal, it appears more as a withdrawal from the realm of politics than as a viable model of government. Moreover, the sovereignty individuals wield when beauty places them in the aesthetic condition of play has jurisdiction only in the "*world of appearance*, in the unreal realm of the imagination."[62] A virtual freedom, it must remain uncontaminated by the limits of the real. Otherwise it is nothing but "a lowly tool for material purposes, and can establish nothing for the freedom of the spirit."[63] In Schiller's aesthetic theory, the play drive emerges as at once the prerequisite for a society in harmonious balance—make play, not revolution—and at the same time it is entirely withdrawn from practical, worldly affairs. Once the *Stofftrieb* and the

Formtrieb are balanced and left in suspension in the aesthetic state by the play drive, the mind reaches a state of pure potentiality. The purpose of play does not lie outside of subjective experience in the realization of a choice freely made. Rather, it resides within the world of play itself as the thrilling experience of unconstrained freedom.

FROM WAR MEDIA TO PURE AESTHETICS

Schiller's aesthetic theory offers a frame for understanding Wallenstein's curious handling of war media. The general's notorious hesitation, the inaction that forms the central void around which the play revolves, is indissociable from Schiller's newly developed conception of play. For in Wallenstein's hands, war media undergo a transformation from practical instruments of war into works of art. Wielded by Wallenstein, the horoscopes and astrological tables serve to induce an aesthetic state in which he can revel in the infinite possibilities of boundless freedom. In his own words: "I was attracted to the freedom and the power."[64] Any choice that would turn his play with potentiality into actuality would also entail a loss of freedom: "What? Must it then be carried out in earnest, / Because I played too freely with the thought? Curses on playing with the devil!"[65]

The modality of Wallenstein's imaginative worlds can be explained by recourse to an influential distinction. For Aristotle, a future contingent, *endechomenon*, contains a potential power, or *dunamis*.[66] In *Metaphysics*, Aristotle offers two main definitions of the nature of this inherent force. Often translated as "force" or "power," *dunamis* is "a source of change in another thing or in the same thing *qua* other."[67] For example, the arts and crafts (*techne*), such as the medical sciences, are potentialities because as productive forms of knowledge they are "originative sources of change in another thing"—in this case, the health of a patient.[68] A broadly applicable concept in the sense of a force of change, *dunamis* may refer to a concrete object as well as more abstract phenomena, such as political influence or the force of a legislative act.[69]

The effective force to produce a change designated by this definition, however, appears in a different guise in Aristotle's alternative understanding of the term. In this second definition, *dunamis* is often translated as "potentiality" or "potency" because it designates the potential of a thing or phenomenon to be actualized and become real. Aristotle explains this by way of a contrast with "actuality," or *energeia*. A thing that has the potentiality of being but does not exist lacks *energeia*,[70] and its being remains a potentiality: "of non-existent things some exist potentially; but they do not *exist*, because they do not exist in complete reality."[71] The force of change in this second definition refers, then, to a change of modality from potential being to actual being. Only when something is fully at work is its *dunamis* transformed into the more completed state of *energeia*—its "potentiality" into "actuality." For rational beings, however, this change does not happen on its own but rather requires a will or desire. In Aristotle's terms:

> the delimiting mark of that which as a result of *thought* comes to exist in complete reality from having existed potentially is that if the agent has willed it it comes to pass if nothing external hinders.[72]

For Wallenstein, however, *energeia* is to be avoided at all costs. To the last moment he tries to remain ensconced within the realm of *dunamis*, using the contingency media of astrology to produce an array of potentialities but to withhold being from them all by not putting any of them to work. The question that opens his central monologue in the third part of the play—"Can it be possible? I can no longer act as I might choose?"—does not refer to a given plan of action that has now been blocked.[73] The devilish choice he is eventually forced to make is the metachoice of having to choose at all. Pressed by Countess Terzky's husband, Count Terzky, to follow up on yet another imagined scenario with the seriousness of action, Wallenstein refuses to let the real infringe on his possible worlds and restrict his sovereignty in the realm of his imagination:

> Wallenstein: Yes, *if* I wished,
> I could repay him ill for ill most sorely.
> It is my pleasure to know the power I have;
> But whether I shall ever use it, that, I think,
> *You* know no better than another man.
> Terzky: You've always played your game with us like that![74]

The game Wallenstein plays is the idle game of aesthetics, not the practical wargame that his sister and his officers insist he play. More the artist than the military commander, Wallenstein builds a fictional world in which he can live inside his astrological representations and use them to operate only within imaginary futures. Wallenstein's misuse of military contingency media thereby transforms their medial nature. No longer part of a military assemblage, they cease to be war media for the realization of the best of all possible wars and become instead pure aesthetic media for the purpose of inducing a psychological state of virtual freedom.

DYING FOR AESTHETICS

Schiller's *Wallenstein* presents a significant statement on the relationship between war and aesthetics. Over and above the historical subject matter, Schiller weaves two much longer stories into the textual fabric of the play. Evoking long-standing debates about the force of war media and the imagined futures they generate, the play combines the history of the demise of the astrological war assemblage with the more recent eighteenth-century debates about the purpose and force of aesthetics. Yet with this double exposure the play not only cements the divide between craft and aesthetics that had emerged in eighteenth-century theory but also the separation of aesthetics from the realm of war. War media are emptied of their *energeia*, and their dynamic force is withdrawn to an autonomous aesthetic sphere of purely imaginary worlds. In other words, at the pinnacle of the late Enlightenment theory of art, warfare becomes an exemplary test case for the fundamental separation of art and craft. If Wallenstein, entering his numerous counterfactual worlds, is transformed into a nimbus of virtual, alternative Wallensteins, who in each imagined world may choose and act differently, as Joseph Vogl has suggested,[75] this virtual freedom is predicated on the severance of the link between these imaginary realms and the singular reality that surrounds him, on the refusal to acknowledge an aesthetic function with a purchase on the real. *Wallenstein*, the play, transforms Wallenstein the military commander into Wallenstein the artist who draws up alternate drafts of war as so many works of art—autonomous, self-contained, purposive without purpose. When the enemies threaten the Habsburg Empire, Wallenstein builds a number of invisible, parallel "aesthetic states" above its borders, installing himself as their sole architect and sovereign ruler. The sovereignty of his artistic governance, however, is premised on its absolute independence from the actual political and military landscape. Wallenstein the artist partitions himself out from Wallenstein the commander. In Schiller's play, then, the refined, autonomous, free realm of art emerges as the very counterpoint to the practical, functional, immanent realm of warfare.

And so, Wallenstein must die. Throughout the play, Wallenstein's "celestial art" (*Sternenkunst*) is pitted against a different conception of war entertained by both his adversaries and several of his allies.[76] They believe in a pragmatic "statecraft" (*Staatskunst*), and, eschewing all metaphysics, they play the political-military game with spies, intelligence, plots, and double-dealings.[77] This understanding of war is summed up by Wallenstein's field marshal when he claims that war is a "raw, violent craft" (*Handwerk*).[78] As a craft, war is not subject to metaphysical certainties or celestial prevision. In the collision of multiple immanent forces, military operations are pervaded by contingency. As one proponent of this conception puts it: "It is a bloody war, to which we go / Uncertain, hidden is for us the outcome."[79] Wallenstein, who either flat-out denies the existence of contingency or seeks to escape the "dark rule" of blind chance in the controlled aesthetic worlds of his own design, increasingly becomes "the plaything of a blind force," until he eventually succumbs to it.[80] Schiller's earlier historical account of the Thirty Years' War published in 1792 is marked by the confessional and political differences between Wallenstein and the Holy Roman emperor Ferdinand II. But in his play, war serves as a catalyst to forcefully split up art and craft: art is separated out in an alternate self-contained world of intellectual and sensuous pleasure without any effective force to act on the military and political situation, whereas the nonaesthetic, pragmatic craft of war comes to dominate in the actual world. Wallenstein must die, not simply out of faithfulness to the historical record, but also because art must be kept apart and safeguarded from the effective, practical dealings of his adversaries' warcraft. Wallenstein's death is the sacrifice that Schiller performs to ensure that art remains uncontaminated by the reality of war.

Wallenstein, then, may serve as the emblematic figure of a new view developed in late eighteenth-century philosophical aesthetics from Moritz via Kant to Schiller. After imaginary worlds had been part and parcel of war for over two millennia, the astrological war assemblage eventually came apart; and with the rise of philosophical aesthetics, the old debates about the force of imaginary worlds took a different turn. The new belief held that since art is autotelic and fulfills its purposes within its own boundaries, military aesthetics carries no effective force. The price art pays for its conceptual elevation into an autonomous, autotelic world is precisely the loss of its purchase on the real. Dynamic, but never energetic; potential, but never actual; Schiller's late Enlightenment play seeks to end the debate about the practical force of imaginary martial worlds.

If we leave the high theory of philosophical aesthetics, however, and turn to an adjacent field peopled by a much less renowned group of thinkers—officers, gamers, and part-time inventors—the debate reappears with a new energy and sense of urgency. For while many literary theorists and philosophers were busy withdrawing functionality from aesthetics, an emerging military tradition was concurrently just as busy co-opting several of the main aesthetic concepts: autonomy, creativity, emotions, and play. Seeking to develop a tool for the management of war, these officers built a series of imaginary military worlds whose aesthetic components they infused with a powerful operational force: they invented the modern wargame. Their efforts mark the media technological origins of martial aesthetics.

2

THE ARTIFACT OF WAR

In 1824, the Prussian lieutenant Georg Heinrich Rudolf Johann Freiheer von Reisswitz was summoned by Prince Wilhelm, then commanding general of the Third Battalion of the Prussian Army. The prince had heard of a new *Kriegsspiel*—a wargame originally invented by Reisswitz's father. Reisswitz junior had since worked to improve the game, and now the prince wanted a demonstration of the device. Intrigued by the game and convinced of its usefulness, Prince Wilhelm promised to recommend it to the king as well as to the head of the general staff, General Müffling. And, indeed, a few days later, Reisswitz was ordered to military headquarters. This time, however, the immediate reception was somewhat cool. Surrounded by the officers of the general staff, Müffling declared: "Gentleman, Herr Lieutenant Reisswitz wants to show us something new." Ernst Heinrich Dannhauer, Reisswitz's friend who relates the story, writes that the inventor "was undeterred by the somewhat chilly reception" and proceeded to place a topographical map on the table. Somewhat baffled by the presence of a map, Müffling exclaimed, "Your game is played on an actual military map and not on a chessboard?" Reisswitz proceeded to set up the game, and with everything in place, two officers were chosen to play against each other, and the game began. Less interested in the events of the game, however, Dannhauer instead turned his attention to the General Müffling. As the game developed, Müffling underwent a noticeable transformation. Dannhauer writes: "It's fair to say that the old man, who had been so cold at the beginning, grew warmer and warmer with each move as the maneuver developed, and in the end exclaimed enthusiastically: 'That is no ordinary game, that is a war school. I must and will give it my warmest recommendation to the army.'"[1]

This scene is well known as a key moment in the history of warfare and media.[2] The genealogy of wargames is usually traced back to a fifty-year period from 1780 to 1830, and for media studies, Dannhauer's account stands out prominently because it offers an evocative description of a novel technology and its adoption by the military. The topographical map that Reisswitz, Dannhauer, Müffling, and the other officers of the general staff were poring over during the demonstration and the pieces they could manipulate and move across its surface combined to form a powerful tool to train officers in the art of war. Playing Reisswitz's *Kriegsspiel*, along with those of inventors such as Hellwig, Venturini, Opiz, and Chamblanc, they could practice the complex skill of moving their corps across an actual terrain at both a tactical and a strategic scale.

The games of the period therefore form a natural starting point for a history of the increasingly complex simulations of the world at war—simulations of the reach of weapons, of the affordances and limitations of the terrain, of the entire operative logic of warfare. The primary concern of such histories has been to chart the development of the relation between the simulation and actual warfare. Which changes were introduced to minimize the difference between the board and the terrain? When did the figures lose their likeness to those of chess? How might the pervasive uncertainties of war be modeled by the introduction of dice, and what are the effects of contingency for the calculations and decisions that are part and parcel of the management of large-scale war? Examining all these parts of the device, media historians have traced the stages and developments of a technology designed to help individuals control and manage the complexities of warfare.

If we zoom out from a narrow history of technology and media, however, and broaden the perspective to include the discourses on aesthetics, the inventions of the period appear in a different light. During the decades around 1800, the disparate group of retired officers, amateur inventors, and civilian gamers established a new war assemblage that yoked war, media, and the imaginary together in a novel constellation. Just when the philosophers of art were at work to separate art from its practical engagement with the world at large, the thinkers and practitioners of war were moving in the opposite direction, seeking to co-opt and harness the power of the imaginary for the purpose of warfare. These creative imagineers of war developed not only a war medium that was designed to handle the contingent futures of military engagements but a medium that itself constituted a self-contained, imaginary martial world. Moreover, the colored pins, the topographical maps, and the dice gave body and shape to the imaginary contingent futures and transformed purely abstract ideas into a sensuous material. War, in other words, came to involve aesthetic artifacts: sensuous, autonomous artificial worlds created by military inventors and played by military officers.

At the same time, the games themselves seemed to manipulate the players and even the spectators. Again, Dannhauer's account is instructive. Turning away from the procedures on the map, he begins to describe the transformation in General Müffling's reaction to the game and correlates the two directly. From his initial chilly reception of Reisswitz, Müffling is heated up with every new move the officers make on the map in front of him, and in the end, seemingly as a consequence of the heat it has generated, he offers his warmest recommendation of the game. As the two officers playing the game were operating on the map, the game itself performed some kind of operation on Müffling's emotions.

Already at the beginning of the development that laid the foundations for the far more advanced contemporary military simulations, the wargame emerged as a self-contained artifact that united autonomy, emotions, the imaginary, creativity, and play. It had become an aesthetic artifact of such power that the military institution was eager to adopt it in order to harness these key aesthetic elements for the immediate, practical purpose of waging war. The period from 1780 to 1830 thereby exhibits a decisive shift from the astrological assemblage of media, war, and the imaginary, and marks the origins of a martial aesthetics. Once we leave the high theory of philosophical aesthetics and turn to the games and manuals devised by this group of inventors and to the implicit conceptions of war folded into the boards, pieces, and manuals, we may be able to trace how aesthetics was integrated with warfare and to outline the main parameters of the new war assemblage.

MARTIAL GENESIS

When Johann Christian Ludwig Hellwig published his wargame, *Versuch eines aufs Schachspiel gebaueten taktischen Spiels von zwey und mehreren Personen zu Spielen* (Attempt at a tactical game based on chess to be played by two or more persons), in 1780, it contained a manual of some two hundred pages. The second edition and his updated version of the wargame from 1803 also included a playing board of 1,617 squares.

The wargame was based on chess, as the title indicates, but Hellwig's tactical game expands the board dramatically, supplants the abstract squares with a varied terrain, and boosts the complexity of the rules far beyond those of its predecessor. And that is just the easy version. Toward the end of the manual, Hellwig outlines a second game with a board of 2,640 squares and additional terrain markers. Hellwig's expansive ideas made the game exceedingly slow, and the inventor Chamblanc later criticized it for being essentially unplayable,[3] but his endeavors reveal the quest to build an imaginary world from scratch—a rich, self-contained martial world complete with the basic elements of soldiers, munitions, terrain, and a set of complex rules to structure the logic of their interaction. Visually marked by the squares and terrain indications, this invented world has its grounding in the spatial expanse of the playing board and is clearly demarcated by its borders. On this self-contained territory, then, the manual develops in painstaking detail the rules and the operative logic that organize this imagined world.

The world-building character of Hellwig's invention has since become a widespread notion in the theoretical discussion of games. In Johan Huizinga's classic study, *Homo Ludens*, games are regarded as "temporary worlds within the ordinary world."[4] This view is echoed in contemporary game studies. Discussing the relationship between the fictional and the real in modern games, Jesper Juul writes that "a video game is a set of rules as well as a fictional world."[5] By way of graphics, text, game title, and the rules or the manual, games project fictional worlds and cue the players to suspend their disbelief and buy into the illusion.[6] Even if the graphics of modern video games have significantly boosted the sense that gamers are immersed in a fully formed world of its own, already Hellwig and his contemporaries conceived of their games as self-contained worlds. Whether the board measured 1,617 squares, 2,640 squares, or 3,600 squares as in Georg Venturini's *Beschreibung*

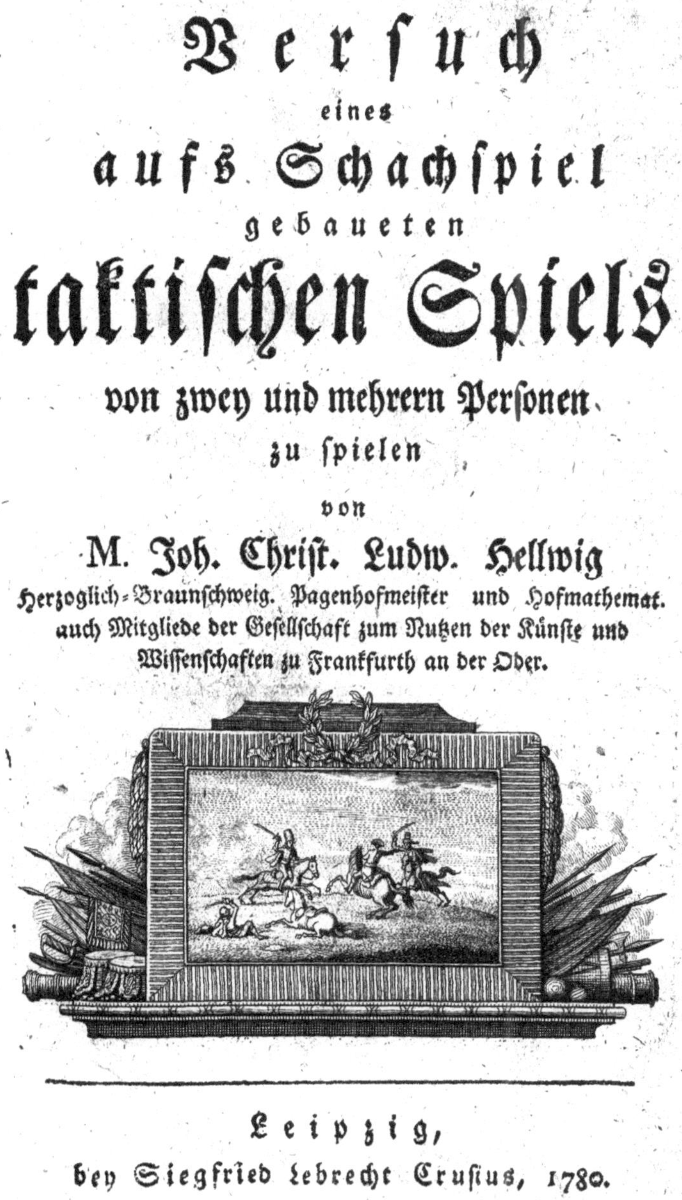

Versuch

eines

aufs Schachspiel

gebaueten

taktischen Spiels

von zwey und mehrern Personen

zu spielen

von

M. Joh. Christ. Ludw. Hellwig

Herzoglich-Braunschweig. Pagenhofmeister und Hofmathemat. auch Mitgliede der Gesellschaft zum Nutzen der Künste und Wissenschaften zu Frankfurth an der Oder.

Leipzig,

bey Siegfried Lebrecht Crusius, 1780.

FIGURE 2.1. Frontispiece for Hellwig's wargame. Source: Johann Christian Ludwig Hellwig, *Versuch eines aufs Schachspiel gebaueten taktischen Spiels von zwey und mehreren Personen zu Spielen* (Leipzig: Crusius, 1780). Bayerische Staatsbibliothek München, Gymn. 30-1/2.

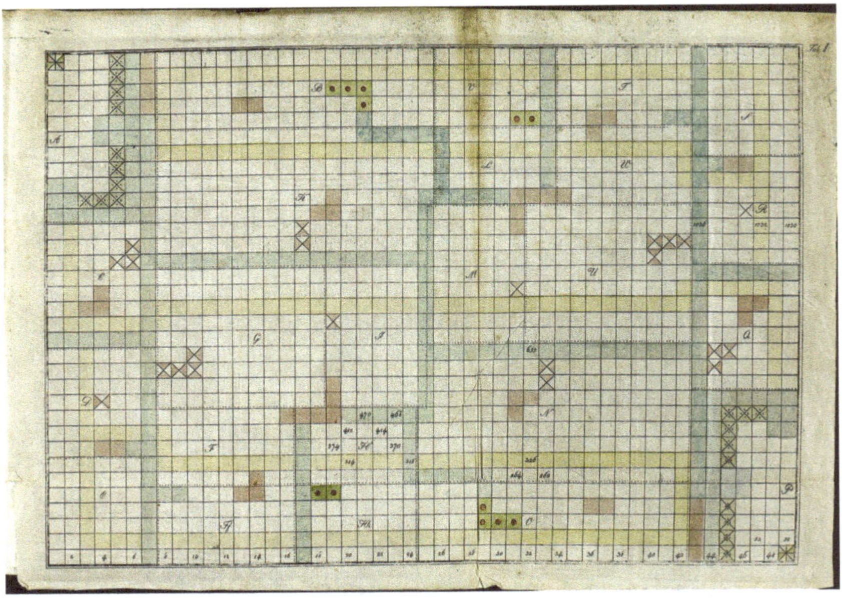

FIGURE 2.2. The playing board that accompanied the later version of Hellwig's wargame. Source: Johann Christian Ludwig Hellwig, *Das Kriegsspiel—ein Versuch die Wahrheit verschiederner Regeln der Kriegskunst in einem unterhaltenden Spiele anschaulich zu machen* (Braunschweig: bei Karl Reichard, 1803). Forsvarets Bibliotek.

und Regeln eines neuen Krieges-Spiels, zum Nutzen und Vergnügen, besonders aber zum Gebrauch in Militair-Schulen (Description and rules of a new wargame, for usefulness and enjoyment, but particularly for use in military schools), issued in 1797, the demarcated space and the emerging realism of the terrain and of the rules that organized action and movement combined to produce a separate, self-sufficient, internally coherent world at war. Indeed, in the introduction to his game, Venturini described his invention as a world in miniature:

> You will realize that because of the dependency of all operations on the player's will, it will become much easier to see the connection, the causes and effects of the main events of war in a *single* view and through the experience on the small scale to deduce the possible consequences from the first causes also on the large stage of the world.[7]

The construction of a martial world unto itself at the end of the eighteenth century can be seen as the material correlate of the aesthetic theory propounded by the art critics and philosophers. Just as Bodmer and Breitinger conceived of art as the invention of a new world complete with its own inhabitants and its own set of rules, the military inventors brought into being new martial worlds governed by particular sets of rules as laid out in detail in the accompanying instruction manuals. Next to the martial world in miniature, bodied forth by the boards, maps, colors, and pins, the manual served as a military version of Genesis, establishing the elements, the parameters, and the operative logic that constitute the martial world of the wargame. In the ludic realm, the creation of the world could be comparatively quick. In the manual to Hellwig's game from 1780, Hellwig estimates that setting up the game takes one-and-a-half hours.[8] For some, however, the invention of the wargame itself was a task of seemingly biblical proportions. Only after an "almost infinite labor" did Venturini manage to complete his "whole new creation." In the manual to his new and updated wargame *Darstellung eines neuen Kriegesspiels zum Gebrauch für Officiere und Militärschulen* (Presentation of a new wargame for officers and for use in military schools) published posthumously in 1804, Venturini expresses his quasi-divine creative fatigue: "Would that this work fulfill its purpose; among *all* the tasks I have ever undertaken, this has cost me the greatest effort and the most time."[9]

OPTIMUM BELLUM: THE BEST OF ALL POSSIBLE WARS

The creative energies of the military inventors around 1800 resulted in an artifact that went far beyond the precepts staked out by the theoreticians of aesthetics. Once the fatigue of martial genesis had subsided and the game had been set up, the inventors could present an artifact that constituted not only a martial world in miniature but a machine that could generate a whole range of possible worlds. Manipulating the pieces on the terrain according to the rules that governed the wargame, officers like Reisswitz and Dannhauer, and commanders like General Müffling and King Wilhelm could play through a multiplicity of tactical and strategic scenarios in the hypothetical realm of possibilities. The purpose of games of strategy is, in Claus Pias's words, "to generate and to optimize microcosmoses,"[10] and the new wargames produced these imaginary worlds of war in order to find the optimal variation of a given future conflict.

The wargames thereby constitute a curious military version of Leibniz's theory of possible worlds. Where eighteenth-century aestheticians such as Bodmer and Breitinger based their theories of artworks as self-contained worlds on Leibniz's theory, the wargames developed at the end of the century push his ideas further. In his short text *Monadology* from 1714, Leibniz argues that there is an infinity of possible universes in the mind of God, and he famously concluded that it is impossible to improve the world we inhabit because it constitutes the best of all possible worlds.[11] Framed by the problem of evil, the *Theodicy*, which Leibniz published four years earlier in 1710, develops a similar argument in greater detail. In Leibniz's account, genesis is preceded by a divine choice. The present world is merely one among an infinity of equally possible worlds that all strive toward existence and compete with one another based on their degree of perfection:

> The wisdom of God, not content to behold all the possibles, penetrates them, compares them, weighs one against the other, to judge their degree of perfection or imperfection, the strong and the weak, the good and the evil: it even goes beyond the finite combinations, it makes of them an infinity of infinites, that is an infinity of possible sequences of the Universe each of which contains an infinity of creatures; and thereby the divine wisdom distributes all the possibles it has already contemplated separately into just as many universal systems, which it further compares to one another: and the result of all these comparisons and reflections is the choice of the best among all these possible systems, which the wisdom of God makes in order to satisfy goodness completely; which is precisely the plan of the actual Universe.[12]

The criterion that governs the competition among the possible worlds that all pretend to existence is therefore the maximization of perfection—the *loi du meilleur* (law of the best).[13] Choosing the most perfect—"optimum"—of all possible worlds, God then proceeds to grant it the ultimate perfection of existence with an omnipotent fiat.

What does a possible world look like? Toward the end of the book, Leibniz senses the need to provide a salient image of his theory, to visualize how the purely spiritual possible worlds in the mind of God might appear to mere mortals. The scene is as famous as it is striking. Imagining an encounter between the priest Théodore and Pallas Athena,

Leibniz describes how, in a dream, the goddess reveals to him a "Palace of Destinies"[14]—a pyramid-shaped palace that contains representations of all the possible worlds that Jupiter could choose from before he made his choice of the world Théodore inhabits. As Athena leads Théodore through the palace, every room is transformed into a whole world by a feat of magic as soon as Théodore enters it. In one of them he can see a whole human life unfold "as if with the glance of an eye and as in a theatrical representation."[15] Supplementing the theatrical visualization of every possible world, each room is equipped with a large book that in numbered chapters relates the detailed story of this particular world. As Athena instructs Théodore, he only has to place his finger on a line of text, and immediately he "will see represented effectively in all its detail what this line only broadly indicates."[16]

Uniting visual and textual means, each room in the palace functions as a projector that transforms an alternate abstract possibility into a concrete representation visible to the human eye. The Palace of Destinies thereby becomes the material representation necessary to explain to Théodore and to the reader of the *Theodicy* not merely the existence of possible worlds but also—as he enters the room at the top of the pyramid—that the world he himself inhabits is indeed the best of all the possible worlds. But Athena goes further. Even Jupiter himself made use of the magical palace as a tool to visualize and compare compossible worlds before making his choice about which of them to admit into existence. As Athena explains:

> You see here the Palace of Destinies, where I keep watch and ward. There are representations not merely of what happens, but also of everything that is possible; and Jupiter, having surveyed them before the beginning of the existing world, classified the possibilities into worlds and chose the best of all. He sometimes comes to visit these places to enjoy the pleasure of recapitulating things and of renewing his own choice, which cannot fail to please him.[17]

Leibniz's Palace of Destinies functions as an imaginary tool that visualizes alternate possible worlds and their futures, transforms the limited space of representation into a world in itself, is governed by a logic of optimization, and enables the choice of which possible world to realize. In this, it forms a philosophical analog of the wargame. What in

Leibniz's imagination could appear only in a dream by divine magic, however, is materialized by the wargame as a practical, manipulable, and immanent tool. Supported by the texts of the manuals, the game boards or topographical maps in a sense compress all the palatial suites into a single, limited space on which an infinity of alternate configurations can be played through. The comparison to the *Theodicy* makes the demiurgic qualities of the wargamer evident, but unlike the divine architect in Leibniz's theory, the military commander is not seeking the best of all possible worlds. The martial variation of Leibniz's *Theodicy* finds its objective in the *optimum bellum*, the best of all possible wars. A Leibnizian war machine, the wargame generates a nimbus of hypothetical martial worlds whose varying degrees of perfection are measured by their military efficiency. Not merely a self-contained world in miniature, as in Bodmer and Breitinger's account of the artwork, the wargame is a generator of possible worlds emerging from the small expanse of symbolic terrain as the commander moves his pieces across the board playing through multiple scenarios. In search of the optimal strategy, he then chooses the best of all the possible wars and seeks to grant this possibility the privilege of existence by transforming ludic potentiality into real-world actuality.

Leibniz's theory of possible worlds thereby forms a philosophical basis for both the aesthetic theory of the eighteenth century and for the emerging modern wargame. Indeed, Leibniz suggests the link himself. During his extended reflections on games, he at one point outlines a

> newly invented wargame in which colonels and captains and also other commanders can practice in place of chess and cardgames, and can develop great science, speed, and invention; with individual game pieces one might then represent specific battles and skirmishes on the table, as well as the character of the weapons and the ground, and even, if one desires, historical battles such as the Battle of Lützen, the skirmish with the French at Ensisheim, and others[;] thereby one would often find what others missed and how we might learn from the historical defeats.[18]

In Leibniz's proposal for a new wargame from 1681, officers would be able to play imaginary wars and to replay historical battles. Learning from the mistakes of the past, they might then train their creative capacity to develop the best of all possible strategies for any future conflicts. Key to Leibniz's imagined wargame, however, was its development from the abstract space of chess. Leibniz may have known the wargame invented by Christoph Weickmann, the *New-erfundenes Großes Königs-Spiel* (Newly invented great game of kings) from 1664 with its more elaborate playing board,[19] but if the wargame were to serve as a proper tool to develop possible worlds, Leibniz argues, the isomorphic surface will have to represent both weapons and the terrain on which the battle takes place. In 1681, Leibniz could only outline a blueprint of such a world-producing training device; it was left to the inventors around 1800 to build it.

VISUALIZING WAR

Compared to Leibniz, the inventors around 1800 put an even greater premium on visualization. In the manuals, forewords, and other descriptions of their inventions, these game designers frequently articulate a central function—that the possible worlds they were constructing were not solely cognitive tools of abstract ratiocination. Rather, they were effective as strategic devices because they transformed cognitive problems into sensuous matter. This transformation is expressly stated as the main purpose of Hellwig's original wargame from 1780. His preface opens with this claim: "The ultimate purpose of a tactical game is to visualize the finest and most important events of war."[20] His later game from 1803 includes this desideratum in the title itself: *Das Kriegsspiel—ein Versuch die Wahrheit verschiedener Regeln der Kriegskunst in einem unterhaltenden Spiele anschaulich zu machen* (The wargame: An attempt to visualize the various rules of the art of war in an entertaining game).[21] This later game does not differ significantly from the previous version, but Hellwig downplays the earlier comparisons to chess while emphasizing the wargame's capacity for visualization. Even if "a complete representation" of the elements of war is impossible given its vertiginous complexity, the objective of the game will be met if it "visualizes the most important elements of war."[22]

That the intention of the inventor was matched by the reception of the user is indicated by an account by a young officer in the Austrian Army included in the introduction to the wargame published by Opiz in 1806: *Das Opiz'sche Kriegsspiel—ein Beitrag zur Bildung künftiger und zur Unterhaltung selbst der erfahrensten Taktiker* (The Opiz wargame—a contribution to the *Bildung* of future tacticians and to the entertainment of even the most experienced tacticians). The officer praises the game for including dice, which allows for a more realistic simulation of the contingent operative logic of actual war,[23] and he notes the shift in the representation of space as compared to Hellwig's and earlier games:

> Your game has no likeness to chess at all, just as your playing board has no likeness at all to a chessboard.
>
> *Your game* consists of a *randomly chosen terrain,* painted in different colors and divided into squares filled with forests, rivers, lakes, ponds, mountains of varying height and incline, fortresses, cities, towns, mountain passes, ravines etc.
>
> . . . *What a difference!* What incomparably more important, far superior advantage compared to chess!—which admittedly practices the mind immensely in how to think, but in no way teaches the soldier the various and often mind-boggling impediments in an operation.[24]

Like the abstract topography of its surface, chess may train the mind in abstract thought, but the novelty and advance of Opiz's wargame lies in the concrete representation of an actual terrain. Only by operating with a material representation can the player come to grasp the complexities of war. This, at any rate, was the experience of the Austrian officer himself. Playing the game, he claims, "several ideas that would otherwise have remained obscure in my mind became clear on your board."[25] The conventional metaphor that equates sight and comprehension is here literalized and given a material correlate in the medium of the wargame. Only by way of the externalized, visual perception of the figures across the terrain do the cognitive insights emerge from the obscure recesses of the mind into the clarity of understanding—much as Théodore could only grasp Leibniz's philosophy once presented with a dynamic, visual representation of the abstract discourse. It is an essential feature of this new military artifact that it constitutes and projects elaborate sensuous worlds. In other words, the cognitive function of the new wargame as a tool of strategy is predicated on its organization and dynamization of the sensible. Working with the sensible rather than with pure cognition, the players take visual lessons that solve complex problems of military strategy by externalizing and instantiating them in the visual matter of the game world. To wage war efficiently, already around 1800 officers must learn not simply a way of thinking but a way of seeing—habits of perceiving, navigating, and working with the sensible.

TECHNOLOGIES OF EMOTION

Simulating conflict in an elaborate fictional world that combined cognitive and sensible capacities, the new wargames added a further dimension that enhanced their power as tools of war. A striking feature in Dannhauer's account of Reisswitz's demonstration of his wargame is that it was not merely the officers who operated on the game; the game itself seemed to perform some kind of operation on the officers. If we follow Dannhauer's gaze and redirect our eyes from the map to its users, we notice that over and above their role as tools for the management of military events, the wargames functioned as technologies of emotion that recalibrated the affective apparatus of the players. Inviting players to project themselves into the representation, the small world grounded by the board, the map, or the sand box in the case of Reisswitz's game, constructs a simulation that transforms passive spectators into active agents and allows them to live vicariously a life of passions and emotions across its surface. Evoking a range of emotional states and intensities from boredom and fatigue to tension, frustration, excitement, and fear, the wargame served both as a tool to generate an emotional investment in order to secure an unflagging interest in its pedagogical lessons, and as a means to manage and train the emotions for the actual experience on the battlefield.[26]

This perspective is usually left out of histories of the wargame. For media historians, the period around 1800 marks a significant development in the rationalization of war.[27] In the idiom of Charles Sanders Peirce, wargames are often described as tools for abductive reasoning.[28] Wargames, in other words, seek to temper the violence and chaos of war with their dice, grids, and rulebooks, and they thereby transform warfare into a rational endeavor subject to simulation, planning, testing, and control. As Pat Harrigan and Matthew G. Kirschenbaum recently put it, wargames are "ordered and rationalized spaces, wherein rules and procedure—sculpted out of algorithmic steps and probabilistic curves—reign supreme."[29] As tools of reason, both the tactical and the ludic map seek to impose an order on a notoriously elusive phenomenon in order to obtain some measure of control.

As Dannhauer's account suggests, however, wargames are themselves agents that perform operations on their users, interpellating them and evoking a range of emotions. But to notice these emotions, we need to zoom out from the game itself and pay attention to the context in which it appears. The game does not end at the borders of the playing board or the topographical map that mark the limits of its physical dimensions. The historian of cartography Christian Jacob has offered a tentative but accurate definition of maps that is of some relevance. "A map," he writes, "is defined perhaps less by formal traits than by the particular conditions of its production and reception, and by its status as an artifact and as a mediation in a process of social communication."[30] We may extend this definition to the wargame. Hidden in Dannhauer's foundational scene we find performative effects that appear only when we include the users in the loop and their role in a process of communication. Severed from the human beings and practical engagements that surround them, wargames might easily pass for the objects of reason that their totalizing, disembodied gaze suggests, but this reductive approach obscures what is just as important: what maps do. Speaking of images in general, Hans Belting has bemoaned that "in dealing with technological images, it is still customary to concentrate on the technology, on the methods by which they are produced, rather than on the relationship between the medium and the beholder and his [or her] experience of a new kind of image."[31] Belting argues instead for an "anthropology of images" that supplements the analysis of the technological object itself with "the way it is put to use by a culture."[32] For far from barring emotions, wargames invite projection and immersion, and its users experience a range of emotional states while virtually immersed. Since the map does not contain any emotion but serves as a catalyst for them, we must attend to the contextual documents and representations for clues about how the maps were used, what pedagogical intentions guided the design of the wargames, and how the players responded to them.

The most elemental emotions evoked by the wargame were of a pedagogical nature. To catch the attention and interest of the officers, wargames were deemed a more efficient method than the usual instructional formats of books and lectures. Venturini, for example, worried that the two traditional fields of military science—the study of history and the study of geography—would deter potential students: "As significant and important as these two sciences are, I am nevertheless convinced that already their large, encyclopaedic names will discourage many from the zealous study of the science of war." With his wargame, Venturini therefore sought to lure the novice into the study of war "under the attractive guise of a game" in order to "generate more interest in its more difficult parts."[33]

The Bavarian lieutenant Wilhelm Freiherr von Aretin concurred. He published his own wargame in 1830: *Strategonon: Versuch, die Kriegführung durch ein Spiel anschaulich darzustellen* (Strategonon: Attempt to visualize the conduct of war in a game) in which he recommends that the traditional medium for the teaching of military science—the text—be exchanged for a new one: the game. For Aretin, the most efficient pedagogical praxis does not consist in

> long, tiresome, half-understood lectures you try to have the students memorize and that are soon forgotten; rather, you should show and teach them the rules of warfare in an entertaining and vivid manner. This sharpens their mind incomparably more and gives them pleasure at the same time. Playing, they thereby learn everything and understand the content of the lecture much more easily once it has been elucidated in this manner, compared to if they had to leaf through books for hours on end and really had to make an effort to grasp what their teacher was saying.[34]

The boredom, complexity, and opacity of books give way to the fascination, transparency, and vivid immediacy of the game. Visualizing the dynamics of war, wargames generate emotions that tether the attention of the players to the board and keep them immersed in the learning activity. The emotions function simply as a catalyst, but a catalyst necessary for the pedagogical efficacy of the game.

TRAINING EMOTIONS

It was one thing for the wargame to evoke emotions, but was it possible to train them? Might the dynamic miniature world projected by the topographical map and its pieces and rules operate on the emotions just as they were intended to operate on the rational, calculating mind of the player? For some, the answer was no. In 1825, Ludwig Freiherr von Welden, then a colonel in the Austrian Army and former director of its topographical bureau, published his *Entwurf für die Verfertigung und Benützung der Plane zur praktischen Erläuterung mehrerer Theorien der Kriegskunst* (Essay on the production and use of maps for the practical elucidation of various theories of the art of war). As the title indicates, von Welden advocated the use of topographical maps and drawings to visualize and test basic tenets of contemporary military theory. Overlaying the map with a grid, the readers might themselves construct a simple "game space" for this purpose.[35] For von Welden, however, only some parts of the elements of war are subject to calculation:

> Since we do not consider the moral forces because they are not subject to calculation, then we will first treat the main part of the higher theory of warfare, which consists in the ability to bring together the majority of the physical forces at the decisive point.[36]

Welden's exclusion of all moral (psychological) forces from the military calculus would seem to confirm the traditional view of wargames as a cognitive instrument for the rationalization of war. Yet Welden's exclusion of the emotions goes against the trend. The period around 1800 saw the development of a discourse within military theory on the central role of the emotions. These ideas find their most influential articulation in Clausewitz's *On War*.[37] In his famous trinity, a "blind natural drive" that manifests itself in the form of "hatred and enmity" is said to range alongside chance and politics. For a full anthropological theory of war, Clausewitz states, the *emotions* are just as important as the *imagination* in dealing with the uncertainties of war and the *understanding* in negotiating the relationship between war and politics.[38] Traditionally, military theory has ignored emotions because of their elusive nature, but Clausewitz is quite explicit about their importance:

> Should theory abandon him [the soldier] here and complacently move ahead with absolute arguments and rules? Then it is useless for life. Theory must also take the human element into consideration and grant courage, audacity, even temerity their place. The art of war has to do with living and moral forces.[39]

Clausewitz's theory of war therefore includes extensive discussions of the role of emotions such as courage and fear as well as basic character traits such as melancholia, determination, and perseverance.[40]

The bombardment of the soldier's sensory apparatus on the battlefield can easily cause intense emotions to overpower cognitive abilities. Two kinds of courage are therefore necessary: the courage not to be overwhelmed by personal danger and the courage to act on imperfect knowledge.[41] For Clausewitz, the emotions are at once a potential liability and a potential bulwark against the violent impressions and the pervasive uncertainty of military action. They therefore ought to form the bedrock of any theory that claims to address war as it unfolds in practice and not just as it is imagined by the strategist on the drawing board. Thus, as Clausewitz writes elsewhere, the "courage of despair is just as much an object of the military calculus as is any other variable," and "whoever does not want to calculate with all these things, will never be a good general."[42]

Given the prominent role of the psychological and emotional aspects of war in the military theory of the time, might they be trained with symbolic means far from the battlefield in the safety of one's study? Clausewitz appears to have been wary of wargames because they focused primarily on the material and not the moral forces of war.[43] Like his contemporaries General Scharnhorst and Otto August Rühle von Lilienstern, Clausewitz instead believed in the power of texts. Whether historical or fictional, texts, he claimed, offer the kind of simulated experience and "living representation"[44] that might prepare the soldier's psychological state and inoculate it against the dangers and violent impressions of actual warfare.

Yet at least two contemporary inventors claimed that the wargame had a similar function. Johann Ferdinand Opiz, mentioned earlier, is an important figure in that he is the first to make contingency a central aspect of the wargame. He included dice and thereby allowed the officers to train in an epistemic environment that approximated the state of knowledge in war much more closely than any previous wargame.[45] But thereby the game also trained the second kind of courage that Clausewitz would later describe in *On War*—the courage to act in such a deficient epistemic environment. The Austrian officer who lauded Opiz for using an actual terrain on the board also praises the fact that you cannot always rely on your knowledge, your experience, and your fearlessness (*Unerschrockenheit*). In the game, chance events constantly disrupt the plans and maneuvers attempted on the board.[46] That fear and fearlessness should even play a role in a game was such a novel idea that the officer felt compelled to include an explanatory footnote:

> Don't be surprised by the expression: fearlessness. That is also necessary in our game; for every player has ambition and desires the best result for himself. Yet, since he must really strain his mental powers to their utmost in order to carry out his plans and still, in spite of all his prudence, cannot be certain that he will reach his goal, then he must expose his figures to various dangers, yes even march courageously into them.[47]

The simulation of randomness and danger first generates the fear that the player then learns to handle and transform into fearlessness as the game progresses. For the officer, the game functions as an anesthetic, offering the player an emotional inoculation through repeated virtual exposure to the emotion that would otherwise, as Clausewitz put it, deprive anyone of "the ability to make an immediate decision."[48]

In his *Strategonon*, Aretin claimed that the game would not only visualize the rules and principles of the art of war, train the officer's ability to predict maneuvers in future wars, and help him read military maps. It would also train his emotional response to battle: "It will further teach him that necessary quality in a warrior, cold-bloodedness, because it is difficult to remain cold-blooded in the heat of the game, especially when an unexpected loss occurs."[49] For Aretin, too, the two-dimensional board at once serves as an emotional catalyst and as a tool to keep the emotions flat: it heats them up to cool them down.

Cold-bloodedness, fearlessness, and courage, the desiderata of military training, thereby emerge as the effects of a flat technology whose projected dynamic world operates on the emotional apparatus of the players. In this, the function of the wargame both resembles and deviates from Aristotle's analysis of the relation between fiction and the emotions in the *Poetics*. In his aesthetic theory, Aristotle famously argues that tragedy, by arousing fear and pity, leads to a cathartic purging of these emotions.[50] The wargame has a similar impact on the player, but it forms part of a training regime designed to instill an emotional numbness that will preempt fear from arising in an actual military situation in the future. The wargame is a technology for keeping violent emotions flat and reducing their intensity: fear is tempered, emotional heat reduced to coolness.

While early wargames targeted the cognitive and emotional apparatus of the players as individuals, they could also be used to forge a collective emotional bond. This function was particularly important in the wake of the Napoleonic Wars when the feeling of unity and common purpose that the soldiers had experienced in the preceding years was beginning to fade. In his history of the Twenty-Fourth Infantry Regiment, the Prussian officer Franz von Zychlinski describes the regiment's emotional state after the war.

> The flames of martial enthusiasm had been extinguished. Will it be possible in peacetime to warm up the soldiers for their task such that through the awareness of it they will coalesce into an innerly unified whole? Will we succeed in infusing the officers, in whose hands lie the continued reformation and vitalization of the military profession, with such a high opinion of their vocation that it will produce a feeling of heartfelt kinship?[51]

To improve the emotional situation, the senior officers decided to make use of Reisswitz's wargame—the early prototype invented by Reisswitz senior. They thereby transformed the game into a memory device, a ludic technology repurposed to revivify the collective emotions of the past. Instead of flattening emotions, the wargame should produce them as intensely as possible. In this instance, however, the technology of emotion malfunctioned miserably. Thwarted by the complexities of Reisswitz's rules and by poor instruction from the senior officers, the younger officers quickly tired of the game. Hindering easy immersion into the simulated world, the game produced only disinterest rather than the unity of an emotional community, and the soldiers ultimately abandoned it.[52]

As this alternative account of the modern wargame suggests, the period around 1800 saw the tentative beginnings of the military's endeavor to simulate the human sensorium and the emotions. Maps and games served primarily as tools of reason, but they also conjured the emotions as a vehicle for learning and as objects in their own right. To operate successfully in the field, officers should first go through a virtual but real emotional training: project yourself onto the map and submit to the operations performed on you by the game; this will prepare your entire cognitive, perceptual, and emotional apparatus for the experience of actual warfare. This was the promise folded into the dice, the figures, the boards, and the maps of the wargame.

The emergence of the modern wargame around the turn of the nineteenth century marks the origin of a new military assemblage. While the literati and philosophers of the eighteenth century in their aesthetic theory labored to establish art as a realm that united the imaginary, the emotions, creativity, and play into an autonomous, self-sufficient world, the inventors of the wargame transplanted these very elements to the realm of war. Military commanders and institutions had long lost their belief in the force of the media in the old astrological war assemblage, but they were eager to promote the new martial artifact, which gained its efficacy from the aesthetic elements it imported into the realm of war. For the first time, invented aesthetic worlds served as serious military instruments. These early games were certainly primitive when compared to contemporary digital simulations and synthetic training environments. Still, it had become evident that the field of aesthetics carries a vast potential that the military can appropriate to always have at its disposal an array of possible martial worlds from which it can seek to realize the optimum bellum.

3

OPERATIONAL AESTHETICS

The military inventors of the modern wargame at the turn of the nineteenth century developed a new and radical aesthetics. No longer adhering to the doxa of the philosophical aesthetics of the eighteenth century, game designers operationalized classical aesthetic concepts and objects and tethered them to immediate practical military purposes. They thereby set in motion an ongoing process of operationalizing aesthetics that has only become more elaborate over the years with the development of new and increasingly sophisticated tools—from Hellwig's tactical wargame from 1780 to the 3D synthetic training environments currently developed by the US Army Futures Command.[1] This process of operationalization has profoundly transformed standard assumptions that governed the traditional theory of aesthetics. The game designers, computer programmers, and military institutions themselves, however, have primarily been concerned with developing the most efficacious war machines. Their reflections therefore center on the more mundane practicalities of optimization. The question remains open: How do we theorize these curious artifacts?

As I propose in this chapter, military institutions, along with the artists, designers, psychologists, and academics they employ, have developed a new brand of aesthetics through increasingly advanced artifacts of war. This "operational aesthetics," as we may call it, blends autonomy with functionality, play with seriousness, the imaginary with the actual, and aesthetics with war.[2] No longer limited to the private, leisurely endeavors of a small group of happy amateurs, operational aesthetics is a main driver of military innovation today. It is the promise of the still untapped transformative force inherent to the hybrid unity of war and aesthetics that motivates large sections of technological research and development in contemporary Western militaries. Instead of tracing the long road from the Prussian *Kriegsspiel* to twenty-first-century synthetic training environments—something that has been done well by others[3]—this chapter lays out the parameters of operational aesthetics. Using examples from among the first wargames around 1800 and the most recent ones in the twenty-first century, the chapter shows what operational aesthetics is and how it works, with the aim of outlining a broader theoretical frame of contemporary relevance.

AESTHETIC FORCE

The nature of operational aesthetics is already indicated by the balance that early wargame inventors tried to maintain between entertainment and training. Although the emphasis of wargames gradually shifted from frivolous entertainment to serious practical use, the inventors stressed the importance of both modes of engagement. Venturini's 1797 game, for example, is, as the subtitle proclaims, "for use and entertainment, but in particular for use in military schools." Opiz, whose own subtitle echoes that of Venturini—"a contribution to the *Bildung* of future tacticians and to the entertainment of even the most experienced tacticians"—claims to have successfully reached "the dual purpose, *education* and *entertainment*."[4] Where Hellwig's is too close to chess and thus only a game, Opiz states, the complexity of Venturini's game destroys the entertainment value and makes it only a cumbersome teaching tool. By steering a middle course between the two previous games, however, Opiz believes he has found the optimal balance between entertainment and seriousness.[5] Reisswitz's game that so thrilled the chief of the Prussian general staff, General Müffling, likewise articulates both functions in the same breath: "The purpose of the game is with a mechanical device to visualize a single maneuver that follows the tactical rules for the education and practice of young military personnel or for the purposeful entertainment of older officers."[6]

The merger of pure play and practical purpose makes these artifacts of war into an early form of what has later been dubbed "serious games." Such games have a carefully thought-out educational purpose, but they achieve this aim by way of a ludic mode of engagement. As Clark C. Abt puts it, "Serious games combine the analytic and questioning concentration of the scientific viewpoint with the intuitive freedom and rewards of imaginative, artistic acts."[7] The seemingly oxymoronic combination of "serious" with "games" captures well the composite nature of the wargames. They have one foot in aesthetics and one foot in war. Merging the two realms in a single artifact, however, and insisting on their simultaneity, "operational aesthetics" sets a new frame for the aesthetic elements it reformatted. Locating the telos of the imaginary worlds outside the artifact itself, the wargames have their rationale in the concrete operations that the imaginary could perform in the actual world.

Co-opting aesthetics from the self-contained realm of art, the inventors thereby changed its basic parameters. If Schiller's character Wallenstein may serve as the figure for the withdrawal of aesthetics into a secluded realm of infinite potentiality, the wargame pulls aesthetics in the opposite direction. What inventors such as Hellwig, Venturini, and Opiz realized and what struck General Müffling during the demonstration of Reisswitz's game was that imaginary aesthetic worlds contain a powerful force that can do concrete military work. In other words, the demonstration marks the moment when the central elements in aesthetic theory—invented worlds, sensuous matter, and emotional and perceptual interpellation—are merged and integrated into the institutional setting of the military. This integration pushes the imaginary beyond an ontological threshold. Because wargames merge the "as if" modality of play with the concrete exigencies of war, the turn to wargames does not mean a turning away from the real. Rather, the wargame is the artifact through which the imaginary can reach such density that it may produce a new reality. The wargame is the birthplace of the real. What Jussi Parikka writes of "operational images," and of "operations" more broadly, that they are "ontogenetic forces that bring about realities," applies equally to wargames.[8] From their origin in the pure potentiality of chess, the miniature martial worlds become the tools of an applied operational aesthetics that enables the conversion of hypothetical scenarios into concrete action. In other words, the wargame is an ontological machine that can realize the force of aesthetics by transforming, in Aristotle's terms, potentiality into actuality—*dunamis* into *energeia*.

This, at least, is the new regulatory ideal of operational aesthetics. It marks a significant departure from the ideals of the aestheticians. Instead of the Kantian aesthetic principle that art displays only an inner, formal "purposiveness without purpose," operational aesthetics tethers the internal purposiveness to a practical objective and displays, rather, an external telos, a "purposiveness with purpose." And where for Kant the artwork put the mental faculties of the imagination and the understanding in a state of free play marked by the suspension of their usual categorizing activity, the imaginary worlds of the wargames were designed to help the players categorize potential strategies in a hierarchy that would lead to the best of all possible wars. The regulatory ideal of operational aesthetics shifts the measure of evaluation from an internal to an external one. The aesthetic criterion is no longer the beauty or the inner coherence of the invented world nor the subjective pleasure of a freewheeling cognitive apparatus but utility and practical efficacy—the power to transform.

The potentially transformative power of the imaginary world of wargames taps into a wider debate within aesthetics proper. In literary and cultural studies, scholars have long propounded the transformative power of art (and art criticism) in terms of oppositional politics, of the artistic subversion of institutional oppression, of speaking truth to power. As Rita Felski has argued, however, the actual force that artists and critics wield is often very limited and frequently overstated. Speaking specifically about literature, Felski makes the point succinctly when she writes that "we see frequent attempts to endow literary works with what Amanda Anderson calls aggrandized agency, to portray them as uniquely powerful objects, able to single-handedly impose coercive regimes of power or to unleash insurrectionary surges of resistance."[9] Most often, art is disconnected from well-organized movements and central institutions of power, and the often complex politics they articulate and embody in their subtle formal structures is rarely focused into a transformative force with concrete societal effects. As Felski concludes: "Political function cannot be deduced or derived from literary structure."[10] Indeed, because art's critique is often leveled against powerful institutions, but is itself disconnected from equally powerful institutions, tracing its immediate impact on political discourse is often difficult.

This sobering view of the limits of art's transformative power should not, however, lead us to dismiss the force of aesthetics altogether. Once aesthetics is plugged into the machinery of military institutions, once it becomes a part of a larger military assemblage and is operationalized, its potential worlds can be put to work by these very institutions. Müffling's enthusiastic reception of the wargame forms the all-important link that connects the aesthetic artifact with the muscular organization of the Prussian military. More than simply the official introduction of a new technology into the military arsenal, the scene marks the moment when aesthetics itself is operationalized and the potential of its imaginary is transformed into a powerful military force. Via the game, "as if" could be converted into "is." Thus the early wargame acquired the power to make the strategic dreams of a group of Prussian commanders come true.

LIMINAL WAR

War in the military aesthetic assemblage is characterized by a curious ontological liminality. In 1969, the anthropologist Victor Turner described "play" as a "liminal" or "liminoid" activity in that it is located on the threshold between the real and the imaginary.[11] Turner's understanding of play goes against classic definitions. Gregory Bateson defines play by the clear limit between play and nonplay,[12] and although Huizinga acknowledges the occasional fluidity between play and seriousness, his standard definition sees play as "the direct opposite of seriousness" characterized by its fundamental "disinterestedness."[13] Huizinga does devote a whole chapter of *Homo Ludens* to the linkage of war and play, but for him the common denominator is the adherence to rules, laws, and codes of honor—that is, the formal structure of a scripted ritualized activity, not the liminality of an ontological threshold.[14] Before the codified nature of war unraveled in the modern period, Huizinga claims, war was "bloody play" because it was governed by rules—rules that also structure ludic activities.[15]

The modern tradition of defining play vis-à-vis seriousness, Huizinga points out, has a venerable precedent in Plato. But Plato reverses the terms. In *Laws* he writes:

> "I say that a man must be serious with the serious," he says . . . "God alone is worthy of supreme seriousness, but man is made God's play-

> thing, and that is the best part of him. Therefore every man and woman should live life accordingly, and play the noblest games and be of another mind from what they are at present. . . . For they deem war a serious thing, though in war there is neither play nor culture worthy the name, which are the things *we* deem most serious. Hence all must live in peace as well as they possibly can. What, then, is the right way of living? Life must be lived as play, playing certain games, making sacrifices, singing and dancing, and then a man will be able to propitiate the gods, and defend himself against his enemies, and win in the contest.[16]

Plato not only deems play the most serious and valuable activity as part of religious ritual activities but also identifies it in opposition to warfare. Only indirectly does play have a bearing on military events, in that the play of the religious ritual may appease the gods, but the activity of playing takes place during peacetime—not in war.

Operational aesthetics reshuffles these relations between play, seriousness, and war into a new configuration. As a liminal or liminoid phenomenon, the wargame brings the three elements together in an artifact to produce scenarios that hover between the imaginary and the real. Initially, the strategic worlds the players conjure forth exist purely as potentialities. As part of a larger military assemblage, however, they contain within them the seeds of realities to come. The liminality of operational aesthetics is therefore characterized by an ambiguity that differs from the kind of ambiguity that is often ascribed to play. Even if play is usually defined as a world as opposed to the world of nonplay, Brian Sutton-Smith names "ambiguity" the central feature of play and lists numerous play theorists who in various ways outline its elusive nature. Referring to William Empson's classic *Seven Types of Ambiguity*, Sutton-Smith invokes the uncertainty of reference, of intent, of sense, and so on, that often characterizes games and play. Modern wargames, however, do not display this kind of uncertainty. They do indeed occupy a threshold between the imaginary and the real, but the imaginary process of playing serves the clear purpose of testing scenarios through simulation in order to realize the best of all possible wars. The wargame gains its use as a flexible strategic tool through its ability to produce a nimbus of potential worlds in the imaginary mode of play, but once it is plugged into the military apparatus, there is little uncertainty about the serious purpose of artifactual war. Rather than the either-or ambiguity of conventional games, the wargame displays the both-and liminality of a virtual tool. The wargame is autonomous yet functional, playful yet serious, an instrument of the imagination and a catalyst of the real.

By operationalizing aesthetics, the inventors around 1800 bridged the gap between art and craft that the eighteenth-century philosophers took great pains to establish. Uniting the roles of artist and artisan, these inventors produced complex artifacts for distinctly utilitarian purposes. Not simply "self-sufficient worlds"—nonpurposive representations of war to be enjoyed at times of leisure—the wargames served as creative tools to produce actual strategies for imminent operations. In this, the operational aesthetics developed by the military officers invokes the applied dimension of the old concept of art and glues together the fractured unity of art and utility in a creative act of violent worldmaking. The force of the new war assemblage lies precisely in its ability to span the divide, to make war at once an art and a craft.

MANAGING EMOTIONS

Practical functionality is one of the central criteria of the operational aesthetics that emerges around 1800. Its operational character, however, is not limited to the link it builds between the artifact and the world it seeks to control. The wargame performs a double operation—on the rational part of the mind and on the perceptual and emotional apparatus of the players themselves. As we saw, Hellwig, Venturini, Reisswitz, and others primarily considered their inventions as cerebral tools of tactics and strategy. But they also stressed the importance of concrete perceptions and the calibration of emotional states. Even if the flat board games from around 1800 can seem almost quaint and their perceptual and emotional engagement simplistic when compared to today's hypertechnical war apparatus, they included elements in the new war assemblage that have only gained in importance in more recent times. Tactical and strategic interests drove the second wave of inventions toward the end of the nineteenth century as well as the third wave after World War II. During the Cold War, the nuclear threat led to an increased focus on future scenarios and modeling, and research and development funding was soon funneled into the realm of simulations.[17] Works by the leading US nuclear strategist, Herman Kahn, such as *On Thermonuclear War* from 1960 and *On Escalation: Metaphors and Scenarios* from 1965, encapsulate the logic of simulation and deterrence in Cold War military thought. In *On Escalation*, Kahn famously devised an "escalation ladder"—a set of scenarios that in forty-four steps would lead to "Spasm or Insensate War."[18] As we know, the threat remained entirely within the virtual, and all-out nuclear war was fortunately avoided. When military officers criticized his expertise, Kahn, with some justification, could therefore retort: "How many thermonuclear wars have *you* fought recently?"[19] From this perspective, Jean Baudrillard was right when he stated that "the nuclear" is the "apotheosis of simulation."[20]

The aim of Cold War simulations and political wargames was large-scale strategy and deterrence. But they did engage the emotions. The wargames developed by the RAND corporation in the 1950s and 1960s struck nearly all the commentators with their emotional intensity. In 1965, researchers at MIT published a study that sought to quantify the players' degree of emotional involvement. It showed that 64.9 percent of the wargamers described the experience as "extreme or intense."[21] Still, even though analysts noted the pedagogical importance of emotional investment, the psychological state of the player did not constitute a central object of the game.

The year 1977 marks a turning point. At a conference organized by the Department of Defense (DoD), the game developer Jim Dunnigan argued that the design of wargames should involve its users to a greater extent. Designers needed to engage the players at an emotional level to lure them into the game. Dunnigan, who designed hobby games for entertainment, was subsequently hired as a consultant to the US military. As Sharon Gamari-Tabrizi notes, this coalition between the military and the entertainment industry meant that wargame designers "became ever more sensitive to the requirement for emotionally appealing game scenarios and rules."[22]

Yet very few games sought to include the psychological aspect of war as an independent variable. An exception was *Call of Cthulhu*, which was released in 1981—a year after PTSD was first recognized as a mental illness category and included in the third edition of the *Diagnostic and Statistical Manual of Mental Disorders* published by the American Psychiatric Association. *Call of Cthulhu* was a role-playing game based on H. P. Lovecraft's horror stories and took into consideration the emotional and psychological impact of war experience. Tracking the mental health of the players with a point system, the trauma of combat, torture, and pain could reduce them to a state of insanity.[23] But together with a few others, *Call of Cthulhu* remained the exception to the rule.

Technological developments in the 1990s, however, would pave the way for a new emotional management system. With the evolution of first-person shooter games, the two-dimensional, cartographic representation of the ludic world gave way to situated, perspectival simulations that brought the player directly into the thick of computer-generated things.[24] The computer wargame could thereby simulate directly the images of violence that literary and historical texts had until then prompted only indirectly in the reader's imagination. A key attraction of first-person shooter games was and is the emotional effects generated by these images. Their utility for the recruitment and training of soldiers was therefore obvious to the military and has contributed to the porous borders between the military and the entertainment industry in past decades.[25]

Only in the twenty-first century, however, were there more concerted efforts to utilize digital technologies to make of the emotions and perceptual apparatus the object of a carefully controlled training regimen. In lieu of Eisenhower's "military-industrial complex," the past two decades have witnessed the emergence of "the military-entertainment complex," "militainment," "virtuous war," or "the military-industrial-media-entertainment network" (MIME-NET), as James Der Derian has labeled it. Leading military powers have poured billions of dollars into the development of synthetic environments and virtual reality (VR) war simulators such as *FlatWorld*, *Virtual Iraq*, and *Virtual Afghanistan* in close collaboration with the video game and film industry.[26] A milestone in this development was the founding of the Institute for Creative Technologies (ICT) at the University of Southern California (USC) in Los Angeles. In 1999, the Department of Defense (DoD) awarded the university an initial $45 million five-year contract to sponsor a University Affiliated Research Center working in collaboration with the U.S Army Research Laboratory. At the opening ceremony, the president of USC appeared next to the secretary of the US Army along with the CEO of Silicon Graphics, the president of the Motion Picture Association of America, the deputy mayor of Los Angeles, and the governor of California, Gray Davis, who was virtually present on a screen via satellite from Sacramento.[27] The purpose of this joint venture between the military, Hollywood, the game industry, and the political and educational institutions was and is, in their own words, to bring "film and game industry artists together with computer and social scientists to study and develop immersive media for military training, health therapies, education and more."[28] Celebrating its twenty-year anniversary in 2019, the ICT reflected on the DoD's choice of USC as its strategic partner and ascribed it to "the university's unique confluence of scientific capabilities, immersive creativity, and entertainment industry relationships [that] gives military subject matter experts the opportunity to work with scientists and artists, resulting in prototypes that successfully transition into the hands of warfighters."[29] In the interim, the ICT received contracts worth hundreds of millions of dollars, and the institute produced a large number of immersive media and synthetic environments—including sixty-five prototypes and 210 disclosures resulting in twenty-seven patents, which have been used to train more than 270,000 service members.[30]

One such project was the VR wargame *Full Spectrum Warrior*, developed in collaboration with the independent company Pandemic Studios and released in 2004. Given male teenagers' familiarity with video games, the ICT sought to leverage their knowledge and habits for the purpose of military training. *Full Spectrum Warrior* is a combat simulation intended to familiarize recruits with the war experience by immersing them in a virtual world in which they can train skills such as tactics, decision-making, coordination, and so on, without suffering the deleterious consequences of actual warfare. But such wargames also conduct a complex affective management. This becomes clear if we revisit Harun Farocki's video installation *Serious Games*. In the first video, *Serious Games I: Watson Is Down*, the left side of the split screen immerses the viewer in the training platform *Virtual Battle Simulation 2* (VBS2), while the right side shows the soldiers sitting in front of their computers playing the game.

As the platoon comes under attack, the soldiers' reactions are strangely subdued. In the background, other gamers are laughing, and they seem disengaged and emotionally detached from the virtual events unfolding in front of them. Several of the soldiers appear to be bored and stare coolly at the screen. When Watson's avatar is shot and killed and falls from the vehicle, Watson himself, the avatar's real-world counterpart, simply closes his eyes, sighs in annoyance, and pushes himself away

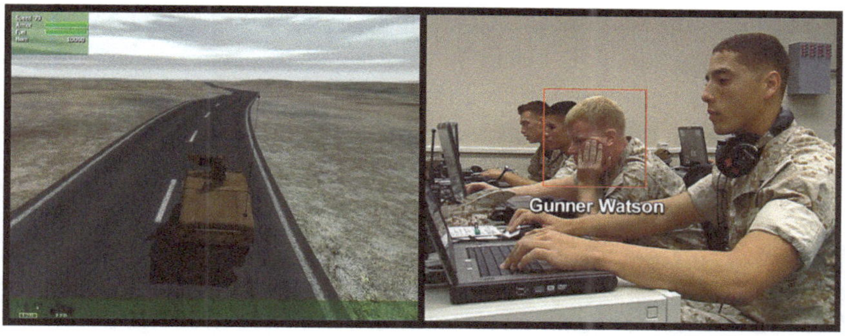

FIGURE 3.1. Watson, the gunner, staring at the screen shortly before his avatar is killed in a training scenario on the Virtual Battle Space platform. Source: Harun Farocki, *Serious Games I: Watson Is Down*. 2009–10. Courtesy of Harun Farocki GbR.

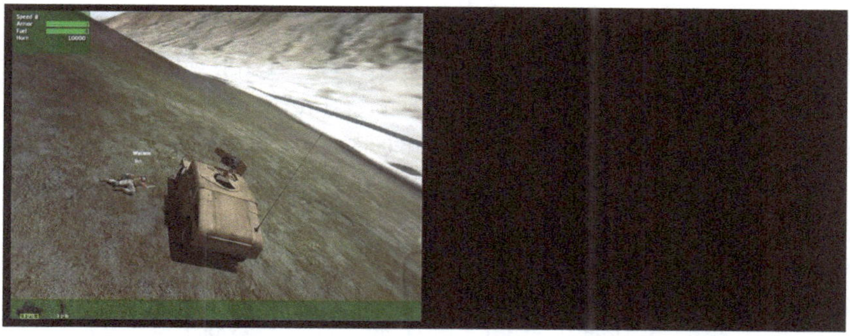

FIGURE 3.2. Watson is down. Source: Harun Farocki, *Serious Games I: Watson Is Down*. 2009–10. Courtesy of Harun Farocki GbR.

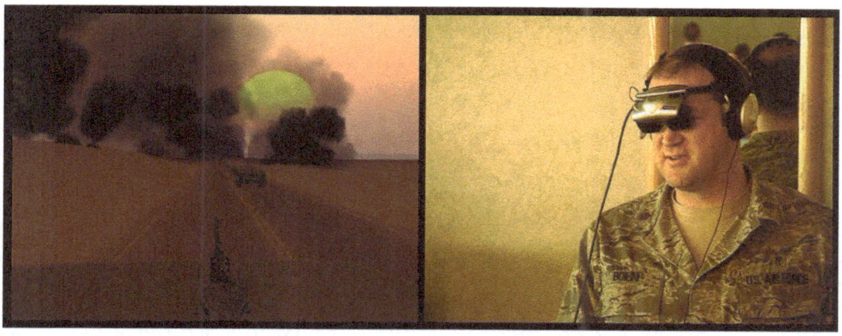

FIGURE 3.3. A demonstration of virtual reality exposure therapy (VRET). Source: Harun Farocki, *Serious Games III: Immersion*. 2009–10. Courtesy of Harun Farocki GbR.

from the computer console. Then the screen on the right, showing the still living Watson, goes black.

The reduction of emotional involvement is not happenstance but rather the effect of a carefully calibrated affective management system designed to protect not just the bodies but also the minds of US soldiers. Dr. Albert "Skip" Rizzo, a research professor at the ICT, has developed two projects that make use of immersive VR technology to manage and control human responses to the extreme experience of warfare. The first one, *Stress Resilience in Virtual Environments*, or *STRIVE*, is a VR training program that optimizes the psychological response to combat.

The program consists of six training scenarios that immerse its users in a virtual combat zone and exposes them, in a controlled fashion, to a traumatic incident such as the death of a child or the loss of a comrade. The scenarios are designed to offer an emotional inoculation based on the premise that pre-exposure to certain types and levels of stress may protect soldiers from being traumatized, and that systematic training will strengthen the soldiers' "resilience," or how quickly and efficiently they return to a normal psychological state after the stress of combat.[31] The emotional register and capabilities that the resilience training regime seeks to train includes, among others, "adaptability," "empathy," and "hardiness."[32]

The second project, virtual reality exposure therapy, or VRET—the subject of Farocki's third video, *Serious Games III: Immersion*—is designed for soldiers returning from war with PTSD.[33] Immersing soldiers in virtual Middle East–themed scenarios, prototypes such as *Virtual Iraq* or *Virtual Afghanistan* (or *Bravemind* in a later iteration) seek to reorder the relation between sensory input and emotional response to help soldiers overcome trauma.[34]

Indicating the degree of agitation on the Subjective Units of Disturbance Scale while reliving the traumatic experiences in the simulation, the soldier/patient is first resensitized in order to process the trauma. The multiple repetitions of the trauma then desensitize the soldier again to return the senses to a stable condition (allostasis).[35] In other words, the same immersive VR technology is now employed both before combat and afterward in an attempt to manage and control human responses to extreme experiences. The only difference, as Farocki dryly notes, is that the therapeutic trauma simulation features no shadows because the software program is slightly cheaper than the one running the combat training simulation.

The researchers at the ICT achieve this affective and sensory management by way of a creative aesthetics borrowed from the video game and film industry. The simulation and training branch of the US Army entered into a collaboration with the ICT in Los Angeles partly because the entertainment industry had far surpassed the military in the field of VR, simulations, and special effects. In the late 1990s, for example, STRICOM (the US Army Simulation, Training, and Instrumentation Command, today called PEO STRI, or the US Army Program Executive Office for Simulation, Training and Instrumentation)[36] used a wireless technology that had been developed by Hollywood ten years earlier for movies such as *Batman* and *Aliens.* Likewise, several of the simulations developed for the military have been based on commercially successful video games such as *Doom*, with the monsters replaced by enemy forces.[37] Thus Rizzo's VRET project at the ICT advanced traditional exposure therapy (the talking cure) by adding video game technology.

As the team puts it: "ICT researchers added to this therapy by leveraging virtual art assets that were originally built for the commercially successful X-Box game and combat tactical simulation scenario, *Full Spectrum Warrior.*"[38] Such virtual art assets, as the *STRIVE* project explains, include "advanced gaming development software, cinematically designed lighting and sound and narrative that maximizes character development and emotional engagement as well as clinical appropriateness."[39]

The ICT's immersive simulations, such as *Virtual Afghanistan*, *Virtual Iraq*, and *FlatWorld*, along with the digital games and platforms on which they are based, such as *Full Spectrum Warrior* and *Virtual Battle Space 2* (VBS2) and its recent iterations VBS3 and VBS4, exchange the boxes, boards, and maps of the old Prussian wargames with the liquid crystals of flat-panel screens. But they share the underlying logic of their analog predecessors. Only now the human sensorium has moved from the periphery to center stage as part of an elaborate emotional management system. The "fearlessness" that Opiz sought to cultivate with his early board game has evolved into an elaborate "stress resilience" program that targets an array of emotional states. In this way, the wargame, while operating directly on the senses and the emotions, subjects them to the same process of management and control that it imposed on the rational

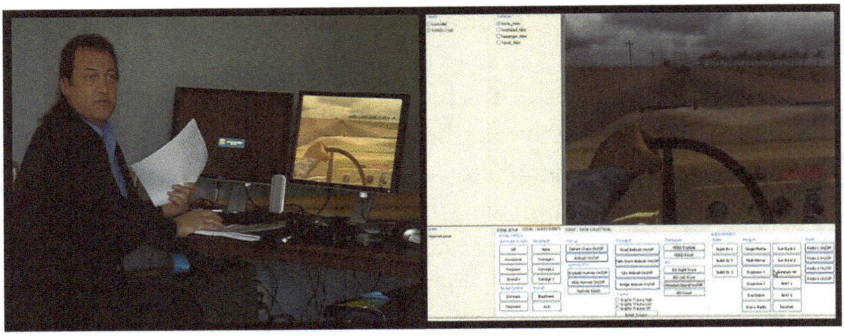

FIGURE 3.4. Dr. Albert "Skip" Rizzo, a research professor at the Institute for Creative Technologies, during a demonstration of virtual reality exposure therapy. Source: Harun Farocki, *Serious Games III: Immersion*. 2009–10. Courtesy of Harun Farocki GbR.

part of the mind. Both as a powerful psychological force to be evoked and as a potential danger to be quelled, sensations and emotions have entered into the military calculus as a central variable in a high-tech creative war apparatus. Unreal as it is, this technological war imaginary holds out an alluring promise to soldiers before their deployment: enter these fabricated worlds and you will receive the requisite martial skills by virtual means; you will obtain war experience in advance by aesthetic proxy. And should anything go wrong, the very same techno-aesthetic apparatus will fix your trauma—or so is the claim.

VIRTUAL AISTHESIS: THE MILITARY DISTRIBUTION OF THE SENSIBLE

Through these processes of interpellation, the contemporary war assemblage taps into the other main tradition of aesthetics. Although Moritz, Kant, and Schiller, among others, would quickly turn it into a theory of art, aesthetics was originally conceived as a theory of sensibility. When Alexander Baumgarten in 1750 founded the discipline of aesthetics with the publication of *Aesthetica*, he sought to recuperate the realm of sensibility for philosophical reflection. Instead of presenting a general theory of art, he made an argument for the expansion of the field of science to include and examine sensation and perception as mental faculties—lower and subordinate to the rational mind, to be sure, but independent and important faculties of knowledge in themselves. "Aesthetics," as he defines his subject, "is the science of sensory cognition."[40]

In the twenty-first century, Jacques Rancière has developed this tradition most forcefully. Reframing the relationship between politics and aesthetics, Rancière's influential theory claims that the common ground between these two fields consists in what he with a felicitous formulation calls the "distribution of the sensible"—that is, in the manner in which both political actors and works of art partition and organize forms of a shared sensorial experience. In this view, politics consists not primarily in the exercise of power or the struggle for power but in the way in which a specific space and time is configured materially and symbolically and in the choice of objects and people that populate this space. It is this primary act of configuration that for Rancière constitutes the "aesthetics of politics." Similarly, the "politics of aesthetics" does not reside in the theme or the political message of a given novel or film, nor in the representation of certain social groups, societal structures, or conflicts. The political force of aesthetics lies in the ways in which art reconfigures and suspends both the coordinates of ordinary sensory experience and the aesthetic forms instituted by the political ordering of the world. Art is inherently political because it institutes alternative ways of organizing the world that compete with the sensory order constructed by politics and thereby establish a space for dissent.[41] As Rancière himself notes, such a conception of aesthetics is at a far remove from Walter Benjamin's linkage of war, fascism, and aesthetics. To conceive of aesthetics in Rancière's terms is to attend to the production of a common world that precedes any overt aesthetic staging. It is to become aware of the strategic interests and effects that subtend the construction of an ordinary sensory world presented as given.[42]

Rancière focuses on the traditional field of art, and he has less to say about the production of sensibility not just of the industrial era but also of that of postindustrial, digital technologies.[43] But just as Pasi Väliaho has extended Rancière's insights into the realm of digital images and video art, we may similarly extend them to contemporary VR simulations. Doing so casts into relief the transformation of aesthetics effected by the military.[44] The collaboration between the entertainment industry, digital technology, and the institutions of war has developed a third category that conflates Rancière's distinction between the politics of aesthetics and the aesthetics of politics. In contemporary martial aesthetics, the political potential that Rancière finds in art has been co-opted by the military, thus transforming art into an engine of war. In serious wargames such as

Full Spectrum Warrior and the Virtual Battle Space series, the disjunction between the symbolic configuration of the world and the institutionalized, military one has been replaced by a mimetic relation. We should not think of this mimetic relation simply as military propaganda, even though that also plays a part.[45] Immersive VR wargames do indeed stage power and mobilize the masses—mostly male teenagers—but they should not primarily be regarded as an example of the aestheticization of politics in the Benjaminian sense. Rather, their force lies in the construction of a virtual world that configures and trains its users to see and sense the world in a certain way.

Consider Harun Farocki's installation once again. The specific mission played by the soldiers in *Serious Games I* and *IV*, for example, is called *Recognition of Combatants—Improvised Explosive Devices*. Farocki's video shows an instructor choosing different types of IED casings from a drop-down menu, such as cement blocks, soda cans, cardboard boxes, and animal carcasses ("dead dog 1" or "dead dog 2"), as well as various versions of enemy combatants—some unarmed, who appear to be civilians; some wearing military vests, hoods, and scarves.

In spite of the list of options and some degree of variability in the colors and size of the objects, the instructor can only choose from a fixed number of objects determined by the programmers of the simulation. The options inherent in the software program form the digital a priori of the world that can be constructed. Whether we call these stylized images stereotypes or schemas, their shape and design constitute the virtual world into which the soldiers are immersed. The functioning of the simulation as a training device is thus predicated on a reduction in perceptual complexity that establishes a set of mental schemas that can subsequently be applied in the field. As Lucy Suchman writes of the ICT's *FlatWorld* project, military simulations perform the realities they cite by creating the enemy as the performative effect of a regulatory ideal.[46] But the entire perception of war—what is seen, what is heard, what is felt—is a product of the way the simulation distributes the sensible objects and configures the immersive matrix, not just the enemy. Actions taken within the game must adhere to the affordances of the game program, what Claus Pias calls the "law code" of each game world, and every transgression of that law is punished by the symbolic death of the player.[47]

Moreover, because immersive VR wargames are not simply

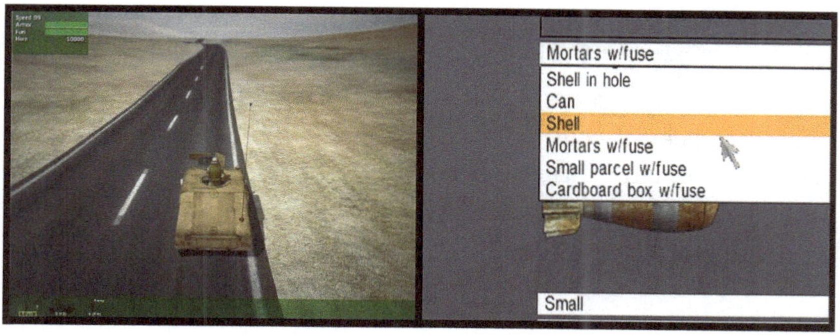

FIGURE 3.5. An instructor chooses and places explosive devices in the war simulation. Source: Harun Farocki, *Serious Games IV: A Sun with No Shadow*. 2009–10. Courtesy of Harun Farocki GbR.

representations to be more or less passively viewed but interactive simulations that demand participation, they impart their configuration of the world as well as its sensory experience in a more direct manner than other representations. For, as game theorists remind us, although the sights and sounds of the game may be virtual, the game play is real. A perceptual machine for reformatting the sensorium of the recruit for war, the game is built to actively inculcate its aesthetic and dynamic order through the soldier's decisions and actions with each new training session. Repeated again and again in the training center in Twentynine Palms, the virtual configuration of things in *FlatWorld* and *Full Spectrum Warrior* is designed to become an integral part of the soldiers' mental setup and muscle memory, until they are ready to implement this way of seeing and acting in the world on an actual battlefield. Indeed, the virtual training platform that is most widely used by Western militaries, the Virtual Battle Space series by Bohemia Interactive Simulations, now includes an "After-Action Review" feature "with timeline and editing capabilities" that allow the players to record, review, and replay their missions until everything goes smoothly.[48]

In his examination of the politics of aesthetics, Rancière is occupied with its potential, but he is less concerned with how potentially dissenting forms of aesthetics might be realized and actually make a difference in the way we organize the various dimensions of our common world. Wargames and synthetic training environments go a step further. The soldiers' active engagement with the fictional worlds lends their aesthetic reconfiguration a practical force. Generating a sensory experience of a certain configuration of the world and training soldiers to implement it, immersive VR scenarios halfway realize the latent potential power of aesthetics by changing its users' habitus. In other words, martial aesthetics does not correlate beauty and truth, to borrow from Keats, but simulation and effective force. The game is "serious" in the sense that it functions as a catalyst for real-world change. In its military adoption, aesthetics serves as a training device.

AESTHETIC TRAINING AND UGLY THINKING

The aesthetic training that takes place in modern wargames unwittingly follows a recommendation made over 270 years ago by Alexander Baumgarten. In the third section of his *Aesthetica*, Baumgarten recommends what he calls *exercitatio aesthetica*—aesthetical exercises to develop and calibrate the sensory apparatus:

> §47 The character of the happy aesthetician requires . . . ἄσχησις and AESTHETICAL EXERCISES, the frequent repetition of similar actions, such that a correspondence is established between the mind and the character . . . with regard to a given theme . . . more precisely with regard to only one object that is to be thought, only one thing, so the ability to think beautifully is gradually acquired.[49]

Beautiful thinking for Baumgarten consists in the formal correspondence between cognition and things, between the mental representation of an object and the object itself. Ugly thinking, by contrast, takes place when the correspondence is inadequate or lacking entirely. To become a *felix aestheticus*, you must engage in aesthetic exercises that train your mind to perceive the world properly. For Baumgarten, perception is not simply given but a skill that requires an aesthetic training.

Yet the exercises need not be perfect. He demands only that they display "a certain similarity," and he also accepts exercises that might corrupt the beautiful correspondence slightly. In certain cases, he even allows exercises whose ugliness is greater than their beauty—that is, exercises in which the mental representation has more inadequate correspondences than adequate ones. But Baumgarten will accept them only "if they are accompanied by the knowledge of their predominant ugliness."[50] And this, he claims, also pertains to the preparation for war.

Offering a military example, he states that the exercises soldiers perform before battle require less of them than battle itself. Here, too, a certain disanalogy between the exercise and the thing itself is allowed, but only if the soldiers are aware of the disanalogy.[51]

While aesthetic exercises have accompanied the fields of art and war from the beginning of the discipline of aesthetics, the contemporary martial aesthetic regime has transformed their character and function. On the one hand, the designers of modern wargames have unwittingly followed the precepts staked out in Baumgarten's aesthetic theory. VR wargames are aesthetic training devices that optimize the sensory apparatus to maximize lethality and increase the chances of survival. And the elaborate immersive virtual environments that private companies and military institutions have developed over the years purport to expose the recruits to situations that increasingly resemble the ones they will experience in the field. In this respect, they do in fact seek to demand as much as possible from the recruits during the exercise as during a subsequent battle.

On the other hand, VR wargames are designed to produce ugly thinking. The reduction of complexity and variety to a fixed set of stereotypes and forms that precedes the playing of the game establishes a set of mental schemas that prefigure what soldiers can perceive in the field. Instead of sensitizing the soldiers to seeing what Baumgarten calls *ubertas aesthetica*, the aesthetic richness of the world, the simulations train them in quick and dirty means of categorizing approaching objects.[52] Indeed, in spite of publicized claims, the ideal of the wargame lies not in high-fidelity mimesis but in the differences between the model and the real. The goal is not to create the most realistic wargame possible but to establish and inculcate a similar but significantly different model—the curated virtual images and the symbolic form of the game—that soldiers can subsequently apply to actual phenomena.[53] In other words, the goal is not merely to make simulations more realistic but also to make the awful reality of war less real. Affectively trained into a state of indifference, the soldiers can bring the images and the game mode with them on their missions, thus filtering the actual war experience through the schemas of a controlled fiction. Where Baumgarten seeks to cultivate the senses through aesthetic exercises, modern wargames instead control the senses and format them according to a suite of templates programmed into the software. Not only does the correlation between the invented worlds of synthetic training environments and actual warfighting remain uncertain; their promises of "realism" and "high fidelity" pave over the radical disjunction between an invented curated virtual world and the actual world it claims to model. The relation between the mind and the world that contemporary military technology establishes is, in this sense, ugly by design.

The aesthetic management by contemporary wargames thus resembles the process of recognition as defined by John Dewey. In *Art as Experience*, he distinguishes between perception and recognition in an attempt to understand the nature of the aesthetic in art and in life. Where aesthetics brings perception back to life from the slumber of automated processing and lets it develop freely to make us see and experience new and unexpected things, recognition, he claims, operates in reverse: novelty is fitted into a preexisting schema that reduces perception to the already known and eliminates the possibility of seeing something new. Recognition serves as a filter that only lets those things pass through to consciousness that are already there or that are close enough in appearance to match one of its templates. In his own words: "In recognition we fall back, as upon a stereotype, upon some previously formed scheme."[54] Instead of seeing fully what is there, perception is cut short by a specific purpose, such as, in Dewey's civilian example, whether we should greet or avoid a man we recognize on the street.

Recognizing the terrain, the temporality, the objects, the enemy, the particular operative logic of events in the field *as* those inculcated by the game, the soldiers have their aesthetic perception arrested and formatted to the templates in the software program. Afghanistan is filtered through its virtual counterpart, and the mission in Iraq or Syria or Pakistan is yet another repetition of the mission played through several times in the war simulator. In the martial aesthetic regime, aesthetics therefore takes on the opposite function as that assigned to it by Rancière, Baumgarten, and Dewey. Co-opting aesthetics and harnessing it for its own serious purposes, military simulations are designed to transform perception into recognition. Indeed, the recent introduction of artificial intelligence has increased the fidelity of the games to a degree that they now create sufficiently plausible universes that they may succeed in blunting the awareness of the disjunction between the game and the real. The original motto of the video game developer 3D Realms encapsulates this disregard of categorical difference: "Reality is our Game." The *felix aestheticus* in uniform is trained to think ugly without realizing it. Neutralizing the dissenting power of aesthetics to develop competing ways of describing and organizing the sensible world, military institutions have instead transformed it into an efficient tool to inculcate and implement a preprogrammed martial aesthetic regime: a particular configuration of the world, a tactical, militarized way of seeing, feeling, and acting.

In this way, martial aesthetics in the twenty-first century brings together the two main aesthetic traditions. On the one hand, virtual training scenarios constitute imaginary, self-contained, autonomous worlds that allow for projection and immersion in a 3D environment. On the other hand, this experience is generated by concrete images whose purpose is to effect a management and recalibration of the perceptual apparatus. This blend of *artifact* and *aisthesis* is discernible in inchoate form around 1800 when the inventors of analog wargames stress the importance of showing rather than telling, of visualizing, of *sinnlich darstellen* (i.e., representing for the senses), and of interpellating the emotions. What the current massive investments in synthetic training environments and other virtual training equipment reveal is the military's belief in just how powerful the merger of artifact and aisthesis can become in the contemporary digital ecology. If General Müffling's excitement at the presentation of Reisswitz's wargame in 1824 is emblematic of the incipient martial aesthetics at its origin, Watson's apathetic annoyance at his own death in Twentynine Palms encapsulates its full development in the twenty-first century. In this war assemblage, war emerges as a way of organizing an imaginary world and using this world to format the brains and bodies of its temporary inhabitants. War, in other words, has become inextricably tied up with the invention and institution of a specific ordering of sensible matter: the creation of a particular spatiotemporality, a particular logic of events, and a particular ontology.

But do contemporary war simulations actually perform as advertised? Do the operations that the scenarios perform on the players/soldiers indeed optimize tactical prowess, communication, or practical skills? Do they increase the soldiers' chances of survival, do they inoculate them against trauma, and do they surpass traditional treatments for PTSD? In other words, do they actually work? Given the increasing adoption of war simulations in Western militaries, there is a remarkable lack of evidence for their efficacy. A report of a clinical study undertaken by the US Army Research Laboratory, Advanced Training & Simulation Division, titled "Application of Virtual Environments for Infantry Soldier Skills Training: We Are Doing It Wrong," notes the need for thorough empirical studies to determine the actual military value of contemporary war simulations. In this pilot study, soldiers were tested using VBS3, the next iteration of the training platform used by Watson in Farocki's installation as well as by hundreds of thousands of army recruits. Although the soldiers were satisfied with the means of communication in the virtual platform, they were also confused by its user interface and dissatisfied with the unnaturalness of the locomotion interface, and they had difficulty discriminating between teammates and discerning the direction of fire.[55] A long report sponsored by the US Army Training and Doctrine Command and published by the RAND Corporation reviewed the available studies and concluded that in spite of the massive investment in virtual military equipment in the past decade, "the development of criteria for designing simulators lacks front-end analysis and fails to consider how users learn."[56] Given the military's focus on shining technology and graphic realism at the expense of pedagogy, synthetic training environments may well lead to "negative transfer," the inculcation of bad habits.[57] Similarly, even as virtual reality exposure therapy (VRET), pioneered by the ICT, is gaining traction, there is insufficient empirical data to back up its claims. The sample size of available clinical studies is too small to allow any meaningful conclusions, and results appear to be mixed. Some studies suggest that VRET may be as efficacious as or more efficacious than traditional treatments, but at the same time there is hardly any data about dropout rates or the potential negative effects of plunging traumatized individuals back into a virtual world of traumatic events.[58]

Even from the purely military point of view of optimization, then, the value of the large-scale project to use virtual artifacts to train the brains, the emotions, and the sensorium of future war fighters or veterans is steeped in uncertainty. Should the continued flow of funding into virtual training equipment eventually succeed in overcoming the manifest disjunctions between the model and real, however, this development will only enhance the more fundamental paradoxes of martial aesthetics. The danger of ugly thinking is one of them. But there are others. Let us turn to the further complications that beset these artifactual worlds: martial worldmaking and factitious futures.

MARTIAL WORLDMAKING

By co-opting and operationalizing several elements of traditional aesthetics—creativity, liminality, immersion, sensibility, and interpellation—contemporary military institutions have created war artifacts that are essentially about different ways of "worldmaking." As with the inventors of the first modern wargames around 1800, contemporary military officers and game designers build virtual autonomous worlds that impart a conception of war that is determined by the games' design. One way to conceptualize this operation is through the work of philosopher Nelson Goodman. In his modern classic *Ways of Worldmaking*, Goodman outlined a constructivist argument about the nature of knowledge: we make worlds of knowledge by remaking the elements of the actual world. "Knowing," he states, "is as much remaking as reporting. . . . Comprehension and creation go together."[59] Thus the task becomes to understand better "how worlds are made, tested, and known."[60] For Goodman, these worlds are made not only by theoretical discourse but also by art. By way of expression and exemplification, the versions of the world embodied in the formal configuration of matter in artworks are of equal significance. As he writes:

> Such worldmaking and such versions are my primary concern here; for a major thesis of this book is that the arts must be taken no less seriously than the sciences as modes of discovery, creation, and enlargement of knowledge in the broad sense of advancement of knowledge, and thus that the philosophy of art should be conceived as an integral part of metaphysics and epistemology.[61]

Artifactual martial worlds are ways of worldmaking not merely because they constitute an aesthetic object—an imaginary, fictional, autonomous construct—but also because the choices that inform their making determine the particular vision of the world, of what counts as relevant in it, of what is seen and what is not, of how people may act and how they are constrained. Violent, tactical, and agential, the artifactual martial world is constructed through processes and choices of composition, weighting, highlighting, omission, and supplementation that result in a particular configuration of sensuous environment, forms of hostility, knowledge order, possibilities for action, and objectives. The martial artifact thus constructs a particular "vision" of the world in competition with the worlds of other martial artifacts or with the nonartifactual worlds of ideology or politics.

Once this artifactual martial world has been made by the concerted efforts of programmers, game designers, psychologists, and military personnel, it in turn sets the parameters within which another form of worldmaking takes place. Playing and replaying the games, the soldiers build as many imaginary hypothetical worlds as needed to test and compare a range of tactical and strategic options as well as to prepare or repair the human sensorium. In some ways, this ludic method of gaming alternate possible worlds into being deviates from Goodman's concept of worldmaking. For Goodman, the worlds made by art are not (merely) possible worlds—that is, multiple hypothetical alternatives to the single actual world. The worldmaking of art is about *this* world. The worlds of fiction lie within the actual world and present versions of it "in much the same way as nonfiction."[62]

But Goodman is not alone in his dismissal of the purely imaginary. Martial worldmaking is ultimately about praxis, about remaking *this* world. Where a commercial wargame remains largely within the aesthetic realm, it becomes "serious" once it is plugged into the apparatus of military institutions. The former mirrors the worldmaking of Wallenstein cut off from any actual military engagement. The latter, however, makes the detour of the imaginary only to remake the actual world in the image of the imaginary one. The purpose is to realize the optimal artifactual world, to transform the *dunamis* of the artifact into the *energeia* of actual war. Evidently, this type of operational worldmaking goes far beyond Goodman's epistemological argument, but his concept of worldmaking points both to the creative element that pervades artifactual war in the twenty-first century and to the regulatory ideal as an operational force: as practical tools, their primary objective is to remake *this* world.

This conception of martial worldmaking may be seen as a complement and counterpoint to the framework of the creation and destruction of worlds developed by Elaine Scarry. In her influential study *The Body in Pain: The Making and Unmaking of the World*, Scarry opposes the destructive effects of war and torture with the creative capacities of the imagination. Unmaking the worlds of language and of the body by way of injury, war and torture find their counterpart in the making of mental and physical artifacts that restore sentience and project new sensibilities into the world. By linking war with torture, Scarry highlights physical harm as the central element of war. Defined as a "reciprocal activity of injuring,"[63] war is not merely a destructive phenomenon but the very antithesis of creativity: "'the structure of war' and 'the structure of unmaking' are not two subjects but one," as she writes.[64] Indeed, just as the event of torture and the event of the creation of an artifact can be seen as the negative and positive extremes of human potential, the same opposition applies to war and creation:

> If these two radically antithetical events are taken as models for the structure of creation on the one hand and as the deconstruction of the structure of creation on the other, then it is clear that war belongs on the same ground as torture, for here, too, what is "produced" is physical distress and bodily alteration rather than an artifact that eliminates pain.[65]

Scarry specifies this opposition of war and torture on the one hand and creation and sensibility on the other in two concrete arrangements: the "work-tool-artifact arrangement" operative in making is transformed into the "pain-weapon-power arrangement" operative in the unmaking of torture and war.[66] This perceptive analysis not only confirms long-standing beliefs about the destructive nature of warfare. Since its appearance in 1985, *The Body in Pain* has also opened new paths for the examination of the body in war as well as the nature of torture. But Scarry's framework also enables us to put into relief the particular character of martial aesthetics in the twenty-first century. Pitting destruction against creation, Scarry's framework establishes a sharp separation between the two and locates destruction in the realm of war and creation in the realm of the imagination. But it is precisely the neat separation of creativity and destruction, of the imaginary and the real, that the development of martial aesthetics has come to challenge. Merging these categories, the creative military artifact becomes instead the basis for real destructive capabilities. The militarization of aesthetics thereby results in a paradoxical form of creative destruction that brings together and transforms the two triadic arrangements identified by Scarry. The making of an imagined world in the form of a virtual scenario (a work-tool-artifact) is the precondition for the unmaking of the world in war (pain-weapon-power). Destructive unmaking becomes merely an extension of creative worldmaking.

Worldmaking thereby emerges as the central feature of the martial aesthetic assemblage. Building games and scenarios as immersive worlds, generating versions of each world by repeatedly playing them through, formatting emotions and perceptions, and operationalizing the scenarios and the habits that have been inculcated in order to change the actual world, "worldmaking" unites creation and destruction, the imaginary and the real, artifact and aisthesis into a phenomenon that is profoundly liminal but not ambiguous. Its character is not the either-or ambiguity of conventional games but the both-and of the serious game. Its measure is not mimetic fidelity to the actual world but efficiency and operational force—the degree to which the assemblage can transform the potential force of the virtual world into successful operations in reality. This liminality of artifactual warfare, the fact that it occupies both sides of numerous thresholds, stamps the actual operations with the imprint of the imaginary. But the reverse is also the case. Artifactual warfare infuses the imaginary with a direct transformational and violent force far beyond anything we have seen. It serves as a reminder that both fiction and fact derive from words that mean "to make": *fingere* and *facere*. What is *made up* in the military aesthetic assemblage can also be *made real*.[67] Here fiction does not stand in opposition to fact; the two have entered a close alliance that boosts the potential force of imaginary invention.

FACTITIOUS FUTURES

The worldmaking that characterizes the martial aesthetic assemblage reconfigures basic parameters of the military futurology of old. As we saw, Kepler disagreed with Wallenstein about the interpretation of his horoscope and the level of particularity and precision of his prediction, but they were in fundamental agreement about the astrological system that subtended the prediction of future events and guaranteed its overall validity. In this system, the dynamics of the celestial orbs largely determined events on the ground, but left open a window of opportunity for human agency. With the aid of horoscopes, star charts, and astrolabes, astrologers could predict future events, at least at a general level, and they could predict opportune moments for action. In both cases, astrological futures were therefore a matter of interpretation. The primary agency and cause of future events were to be found in the planetary movements in the superlunary realm, and because this celestial force could not be changed, the task of the astrologer was to read the stars and interpret the constellations to assess their impact in the terrestrial sphere. The military commander might navigate these forces by delaying a planned action or seizing an opportunity to carry it out, but he could not alter the basic tendencies. The problems of futurology in the astrological system therefore centered on questions of hermeneutics: What did a particular celestial alignment mean? How should the various interpretive elements be weighed against one another? Which general interpretive system was superior? As they waited for the future to arrive, astrologers read and debated both the signs and the sign systems that announced its coming.

In the martial aesthetic assemblage, however, the future does not simply arrive. As strategic instruments, military virtual scenarios build worlds that are inherently "of the future." Whether at their modern origin or in their contemporary development, these artifacts of war sever any transcendent links and function as immanent, practical tools to invent and compare possible futures. Astrologers looked at the stars as a text to be interpreted, but officers use wargames as a workspace where futures can be built and tested. Whereas the astrological future is a largely predetermined temporality whose arrival can only be awaited and dealt with, martial aesthetics seeks, in the present, to knead pieces of future time together and mold them into an ideal temporal structure, thereby building the future before it has a chance to arrive. Making strange loops in time, artifactual worlds construct a curious temporality that conflates past, present, and future. Borrowing from a series of imagined futures things *not* experienced, things *not* seen, and reflections *not* had, the VR simulation projects these imagined futures in order to generate actual behavioral patterns in the present that can subsequently be evoked in nonvirtual future settings. The link between the present of the simulation and the future of the subsequent operation is a recursive one, a temporal collapse in which the present merges with the future as both take place concurrently while the soldiers play the game. This looping of time means that according to the regulatory ideal of artifactual warfare, the future is not the natural arrival of the unknown but a repetition of a constructed future from the past—in other words, a repetition of something that has never taken place but has nevertheless already been made and played through multiple times.

The artifacts of war produce what we might call *factitious futures*. In contrast to the understanding of futurity as a natural phenomenon that marks the horizon of the unknown, factitious futures are, as the Latin term *facticius* indicates, "made by art" or "artificial." Manufactured inside analog and digital simulations and subsequently made real by the immersed players, factitious futures constitute a form of time that is made and designed rather than naturally appearing, awaited, and dealt with on arrival. In the production of factitious futures, once again, the imagined and the actual, fiction and fact, the artificial and the real do not stand as each other's opposites but are folded into each other as the players imagine, play, repeat, and implement.

This form of future-production makes the simulations into a particular kind of contingency medium. As tools to facilitate strategic thought and action under conditions of uncertainty, contingency media help to navigate and control the type of events known as future contingents. As we have seen, the older contingency media in the astrological war assemblage allowed for glimpses into the larger tendencies of events and offered the commander some possibility to prepare, but they also left significant room for uncertainty. As Kepler stated in his response to Wallenstein, it was an illusion to think that all terrestrial events "occur in accordance with concrete, calculated celestial events, and can therefore be predicted."[68] The military futurology inherent to contemporary VR simulations, however, encourages the belief that future military operations on the ground may indeed be calculated, made up, and made real. Producing factitious futures, these virtual scenarios suggest that the fundamental uncertainty inherent to future contingents can by and large be eliminated.

A key factor is the aesthetic nature of simulations. As full-fledged immersive worlds that offer a virtual experience of war, simulations give flesh to the future and impart it as a sensory fact. Analyzing the politics of the contemporary ecology of digital images, Pasi Väliaho puts it well: "Images incorporate the future in the present; they make the future a fact lived here and now in our bodies."[69] This visual experience is reinforced by the inclusion of other parts of the sensory apparatus. Training in haptic suits, soldiers may now experience virtually not just the visuals of war but also the smell, the sound, and the feel of war.[70] Such an aisthetic mode of presentation possesses a persuasive power that theoretical or discursive articulations do not. As one simulation designer puts it: "Previously, soldiers would rely on aerial photography, schematics, or 'word of mouth' before heading into danger. Now they'll be able to literally play through a mission over and over again with their squad mates until they feel they have everything down."[71] Discussing the VR simulations he filmed in *Serious Games*, Farocki states: "Somehow these images are very close to an ideal type. I think they are asking reality to be as calculable as these systems are. Of course there can be some contingencies and so on, but you know already, the ambush must be behind the bridge."[72] And indeed, when one of the traumatized soldiers undergoing virtual reality exposure therapy replays his actual mission in *Serious Games III*, his exclamation "It was so surreal" refers not to the technological setup in which he is immersed but to the actual unpredictable events that did not form a part of the future created by the simulations.

The experience that this virtual apparatus generates therefore suggests that as a contingency medium it does not so much manage future contingents as eradicate them. While current efforts to integrate AI into the architecture of synthetic training environments include programs with autonomous agents who will act independently and unpredictably rather than according to preprogrammed templates, the introduction of contingency into the training environment at the same time holds out the promise that contingency can be managed, subdued, or eliminated.[73] In a video presentation of a synthetic training environment developed at the ICT and sponsored by the US Army Research Laboratory, General Steven J. Townsend picks up a widely circulated statement by General Mattis—that soldiers should fight "twenty-five bloodless battles" before seeing combat. With the aid of the new immersive technology, Townsend says, "Our soldiers will become virtual veterans of twenty-five bloodless battles before the first round is ever fired in combat." The claim articulates well the strangely looping temporality of the simulations' factitious futures. Doing away with time as a naturally occurring phenomenon, the military inserts in its place an artifact that abolishes the future and the contingency it naturally harbors.[74]

VR simulations in the twenty-first century thereby suggest a new temporal model as compared to past futurologies. Louise Amoore has argued that within the fields of economy and security, the twenty-first century has seen a shift from "probability" to "possibility." In the nineteenth and twentieth centuries, the future was projected as a probabilistic phenomenon based on past occurrences; after 9/11, a complex of risk assessment, calculation, and algorithmic modeling emerged, not to predict the probable futures, but to handle the merely possible ones: "From terrorist attacks and cybercrime, to flood risk and the crisis of inadequately risk-priced finance, the idea that uncertain futures—however probabilistically unlikely—be mapped and acted upon as possibilities has captured the Zeitgeist."[75] The governing of such highly unlikely (but possible and threatening) events entails, as Brian Massumi has noted, a departure from older models of *deterrence* and *prevention* from the Cold War that were based on knowledge, perhaps limited, of specific threats, and the embrace of *preemption*: the elimination of a host of purely potential threats that may or may not ever transpire.[76] A radical uncertainty thus pervades the preemptive model of the merely possible. The future becomes the matrix of potential, inchoate, and emerging threats that only become knowable and fully existent the moment they are preempted. In the future envisioned by preemption, radical uncertainty and pervasive threat collapse.

Artifactual martial worlds harbor another temporal model. On the one hand, VR simulations and synthetic training environments, like earlier wargames, are contingency media that serve to guide action under conditions of uncertainty. As such they teach the soldiers to navigate the radical uncertainty of the preemptive model. On the other hand, the worldmaking of the aesthetic artifact risks impressing on the soldiers the experience that most contingencies can indeed be eliminated. Through the simulation, the future is given shape and form like an artifact and then experienced virtually in a kind of future anterior of the world to be. Instead of the potentiality of numerous unimagined and unimaginable threats of preemption, VR simulations offer the productive liminality of an artifactual world that has been designed, created, and experienced and just needs to cross a nearly invisible ontic threshold and step out into the real. Whereas *probability* envisions the future as an extrapolation of patterns from the past, and *preemption* envisions the future as a matrix of infinite possible threats, *martial worldmaking* casts the future as factitious—the actualization of an optimal world that has been creatively designed, carefully built, and already seen, heard, and touched.

The factitious future inherent to the artifact of war thereby ties in with a broader development in the field of futurology. Alongside traditional concepts of prediction, anticipation, planning, and others, a new idea has emerged that Nick Montfort labels "future-making."[77] As he defines it, the term "is meant to distinguish a potentially productive perspective on the future (let's build a better future) from a less productive one (let's predict what will happen, for instance, so that we can react quickly by anticipating it)."[78] As opposed to conventional concepts within future studies, futurology, and scenario planning that imply various degrees of uncertainty, "future-making" or "future building" takes charge of time by building the desired future. Instead of seeking to predict it—always having to measure the discrepancy between one's predictive model and the events that actually transpired—future-making creates a future world of its own and seeks to implement it. The condition of possibility for such a creative approach, Montfort suggests, is the development of digital media. With them emerge the possibility "to imagine the future systematically and in sufficient detail, [such] that one can share the imagination of the future with others, and that it is possible to work to develop specific innovations that are components of such a future."[79] In its military inflection, this shift toward future-making similarly relies on the *aisthetic* qualities of the simulated worlds of VR. Linking virtual aisthesis with strategic world-building, contemporary simulations install soldiers and inventors in the role of secular demiurges engaged in martial worldmaking, creating futures that are, in Montfort's words "not something to be predicted, but to be made."[80]

Operational aesthetics thereby emerges not only as the co-option of the imaginary as a practical tool uniting, once again, art with craft and utility; it also embodies the promise of a scalable factitious creation. According to the regulatory ideal inherent to the artifact, its generative force does not simply impact on the world; it creates the world and imparts its appearance, its dynamics, and its logic as a lived sensory experience. What began with the tentative experiments to merge war and aesthetics in a material artifact some 250 years ago has in the twenty-first century developed into a full-fledged digital regime of martial aesthetic worldmaking. That its regulatory ideal may be an illusion, that these artificial aesthetic worlds may instill a deceptive sense of control and safety, that they surreptitiously twist time into recursive temporal loops that banish contingency, the unforeseen, and the future itself—all this has no place in the military discourse or the tech companies' promotional material. But it haunts contemporary efforts to rethink war as the continuation of military technology with aesthetic means.

As we will see, however, the creative vision of war is not restricted to the games and simulations themselves. For while the military has developed a radical "operational aesthetics" with its advanced artifacts and with the often implicit set of ideas and principles that are folded into their concrete, material forms, these technological inventions have an explicit conceptual counterpart within military theory. This is the seductive idea that warfare is an art form.

4

THE WAR ARTISTS

On August 14, 2008, General James Norman Mattis issued a memorandum for US Joint Forces Command. It was titled *Assessment of Effects Based Operations*. The memorandum and the accompanying document *USJCOM Commander's Guidance for Effects-Based Operations* identified a number of problems with the existing conceptual frameworks guiding US military operations. Whether in the form of the so-called Effects-Based Operations (EBO), Operational Net Assessment (ONA), or System of Systems Analysis (SoSA), these frames, Mattis wrote, are underpinned by a number of faulty assumptions. They assume an unachievable level of predictability and an unattainable level of knowledge, and they disregard both the human dimension of warfare—passions, the imagination, willpower, and unpredictability—and warfare's inherent complexity. The conception of war inherent to these frames had resulted in unrealistic expectations of predictability in US headquarters and led to strategic planning that mechanistically attempted to provide certainty where none was to be had.[1]

In reaction to the experiences in Iraq and Afghanistan, Mattis instead promoted a new conception of war. War, he argued, is fundamentally unpredictable, uncertain, and chaotic. Military operations are characterized by the ubiquity of chance events, by the incursion of the unforeseen and unexpected, by limited or erroneous information, by emergent opportunities, and by the spiraling consequences of nondeterministic effects. War, for Mattis, is "fog, friction, and chaos."[2] Because Effects-Based Operations and associated concepts are fundamentally at odds with this understanding of war, Mattis proceeded to banish the effects-based paradigm from the US military mind:

> The underlying principles associated with EBO, ONA, and SoSA are fundamentally flawed and must be removed from our lexicon, training, and operations. . . . Effective immediately, USFJCOM will no longer use, sponsor, or export the terms and concepts related to EBO, ONA, and SoSA in our training, doctrine development, and support of JPME.[3]

Instead, Mattis outlines an alternative set of ideas to enable the US military to better handle the chaos and unpredictability of warfare. He now suggests, as a counterpart to the reframing of war itself, various new concepts for the skills and methods needed to manage it. Thus he emphasizes the importance of "initiative, pattern recognition, and decentralized decision-making" and, in particular, "creative campaign design." He does not, however, gather these notions into a larger operational concept or paradigm. Mindful of the real-world impact and potentially dire consequences of conceptual development within military doctrine, Mattis stresses the need for a careful evaluation of such frames, for "there is a cost in lives lost and mission failure when concepts are misapplied."[4]

A year later, on October 6, 2009, Mattis issued a new memorandum that significantly changed the way US military institutions understand warfare. In a document titled *Vision for a Joint Approach to Operational Design*, Mattis adopted and promoted "design" as a new framework able to meet the challenges posed by the complexities of contemporary warfare. The central component of this design frame is "creativity." As Mattis writes:

> Our current doctrinal approach to creativity is insufficient, but joint publication (JP) 3–0, *Joint Operations*, provides a foundation upon which we can build. JP 3–0 describes *operational art* as "The application of creative imagination by commanders and staffs—supported by their skill, knowledge and experience—to design strategies, campaigns and major operations and organize and employ military forces." *Operational design*—the conception and construction of the framework

> that underpins a campaign or major operation plan and its subsequent execution—provides a number of *design elements* to support operational art and the planning process.[5]

Creativity, the creative imagination, operational art, operational design, design elements—these citizens of the world of art and aesthetics now inhabit a central part of military thinking. Indeed, Mattis's promotion of "design" only marks the beginning of the emergence of a burgeoning discourse on military design whose precepts have been adopted by several Western military institutions in recent years. Not only in the US but also in the Netherlands, Canada, Germany, Israel, Poland, Sweden, Denmark, Great Britain, Australia, and elsewhere, military institutions have begun to speak the language of art and design.

In the previous chapters, martial aesthetics referred to the military media, technologies, and artifacts that have integrated art and aesthetics as tools of warfare. As I have shown, these artifacts include an implicit set of ideas about warfare folded into their material forms—ideas that needed to be unfolded and unpacked. But the role of aesthetics in warfare is not restricted to the technologies of war and the more or less subconscious ideas embedded inside them. As Mattis's statements amply show, the official concepts and theories of war are also explicitly informed by the language of art and aesthetics. This chapter will therefore bring us into the military brain itself. Military theory, doctrines, field manuals, and scholarly debates all give evidence of how the military thinks and theorizes. And in the twenty-first century, the military frequently thinks and theorizes about art. The discourse on design constitutes the theoretical component of a martial aesthetics that has until now only been described in its practical instantiations. Again, a historical perspective is critical, for the contemporary theoretical discourse reactivates a longer tradition of military thought that has framed warfare in terms of aesthetics.

In this chapter, I unearth the origins of the idea that war is an art form in its own right in the theories of a group of leading military thinkers from around 1800, and I trace some of the subsequent instantiations of this idea in the nineteenth and twentieth centuries. The arguments and developments of this tradition are both bizarre and deeply troubling, but they are also instructive. They enable us, in the final chapter, to better comprehend the current attraction to creativity, artistry, and genius in contemporary military circles. The chapter shows how military thought continues to adopt and deploy classical aesthetic concepts when the traditional theory of high art morphs into the broader contemporary discourse on design. The guiding questions throughout are: How did war become a work of art, and How were soldiers transformed into war artists?

THE ART–SCIENCE DEBATE

Is war an art or a science? This question forms the kernel of a long-standing discussion within military theory.[6] Since some of the earliest theoretical writings on war, the quest to establish warfare as a science—that is, as a field of knowledge with a set of laws that governs its practice—has been counterbalanced by the belief that the complexity and shape-shifting character of war allow no such formalization, that war can at best be regarded as an "art" and managed with know-how, intuition, judgment, experience, and practical *nous*. Already in the first century, the Roman general Frontinus wrote a now lost treatise on the *rei militaris scientia* (the science of war), but with his collection of historical examples of successful generalship published under the title *Strategemata*, Frontinus also juxtaposed the pretensions of *scientia* with the "*sollertia ducum facta*"—the clever deeds of generals who had relied on their off-the-cuff intuitions to devise their successful tactical stratagems.[7] The search for principles, rules, and laws of warfare peaked during the Enlightenment with the scientific revolution, when figures such as Newton, Boyle, and Euler laid the foundations of modern science and shaped the general patterns of thought that also came to dominate military thought. The complex geometries that grounded the science of fortification as developed by Vauban and Coehoorn, for example, became a model for the organization of the mobile architecture of troops in the field in the military theory of Puysegur.[8] Thus military thinkers considered not only the auxiliary individual branches of war—ballistics, fortification, mapping, metallurgy—as scientific endeavors that combined the already established sciences of, for example, mathematics and physics; they also believed that the larger collective effort that would soon be known by the term *strategy* had a scientific foundation and was subject to axioms, universal principles, and immutable laws. According to the Prussian officer Heinrich von Bülow, scientific progress proved that waging warfare successfully was not the prerogative of genius and that the principles of the "art of war" could soon be taught to everyone: "Then war will no longer be an art, it will only be a science."[9] The science of war, Bülow even believed, was so exact that it would make battle itself superfluous.

As Bülow's remarks suggest, however, the quest for a science of war runs up against a theoretical countercurrent that rejects the idea that war is subject to scientific analysis, universal laws, and predictive certainty. The "art of war" is the term that military thinkers often invoke to describe an understanding of warfare in clear opposition to the scientific pretensions of much military theory. The positive meaning of the term, however, is less clear. First of all, the terminological muddle that pervades much military theory blurs a distinct outline of the concept. Often theorists of war use the terms *art* and *science* interchangeably, sometimes even in the same sentence. From the Middle Ages via Napoleon to the US Joint Chiefs of Staff, leading thinkers and institutions have, for example, conceived of "strategy" sometimes as an art and sometimes as a science without any further clarification.[10] This terminological muddle led Carl von Clausewitz, in an essay titled "On the State of the Theory of the Art of War," to despair "that the theory of the art of war is very far behind in comparison to the development of other theories."[11]

Clausewitz's colleague, the fellow Prussian military thinker Otto August Rühle von Lilienstern, went even further. In an essay with a title similar to Clausewitz's—"On the Theory of the Art of War and the Division of the Military Sciences"—Rühle von Lilienstern notes the novelty of such a systematic inquiry:

> Since war has never truly been conceived and presented as an art by any writer, and the science of military theory is therefore in a miserable condition, then you should not raise your hopes to find anywhere even a merely passable indication of what might generally be understood by the terms the art of war and its theory. Either, and that is the most common and preferable case, the authors never touch on this topic, but immediately move on to the matter itself without making any further divisions, or they offer such cross-eyed and completely inadequate explanations that it would be a waste of time to rehearse them.[12]

To rectify this state of affairs, both Clausewitz and Rühle von Lilienstern took on the task of hashing out a more cohesive theory. The "art of war" as it emerges during the first few decades of the nineteenth century, however, is a rather complex concept. It invokes the practical skills of the artisan that the aesthetic philosophers had sought to separate from the concept of fine arts. But it also invokes the very concept of the fine arts themselves that the military thinkers now seek to reintegrate into the theory of warfare. Latching on to the aesthetic discourse on the work of art, the artist, and creativity that flourished during the late Enlightenment and the Romantic period, military theorists made use of the concepts that had only gained shape and clarity when the eighteenth-century philosophers had separated them from their mundane practical functions. Now these military theorists superimposed these concepts onto the world of military affairs as a frame to comprehend the nature of warfare. In the military theory of the time, the "art of war" became a multilayered theoretical construct that emerges out of the practical craft of the artisan but comes to approach the refined creativity of the artistic genius.

This conceptual operation takes place in different steps. The first step involves defining in more precise terms than did previous military theory the relation between the art and science of war. For Rühle von Lilienstern, the art of war, or "Kriegskunst," is first and foremost a praxeological concept—it denotes all "that is required for the exemplary realization both of the conduct of war itself and of the constant readiness for war."[13] Unlike "science," whose aim is the production of knowledge, the purpose of "art" lies beyond pure knowledge in the realm of action. As he puts it,

> What science is in the realm of knowledge, viz. the highest degree of perfection and the most sublime result of the activity of the mind, art is in the realm of action. Already the simple analysis of the word makes it clear that theone has to do with knowledge, the other with ability.[14]

While a certain portion of knowledge is necessary for all action, just as an element of skill is present in all science, both the etymology and the content of the term *Kriegskunst* highlight the elements of praxis, doing, action, and ability. The theory of the art of war is thus the systematic reflection on the nature of such practical activities. As a theory of action, the art of war invokes the craft of the artisan who also possesses a set of practical skills, but it departs from it in significant ways.

Indeed, for Rühle von Lilienstern, the art of war appears as a double articulation in opposition to science as well as to craft (*Handwerk*).[15]

For even as both the "artist" (*Künstler*) and the "craftsman" or "artisan" (*Handwerker*) produce "works," their skills differ markedly. The work of the artisan is characterized by routine, imitation, rote learning, and mechanical repetition. Against this form of "artisanal action" (*Handwerksmässiges Handeln*), Rühle pits what he calls "artistic action" (*künstlerisches Handeln*).[16] Artistic action is "the level-headed, orderly and unswerving pursuit of a particular goal, wisely choosing the most appropriate means and shrewdly assessing and cleverly managing all the competing circumstances."[17] In other words, artistic action is a more refined form of action and denotes a well-trained, highly skillful ability. Just as common knowledge relates to scientific knowledge, he continues in a series of analogies, so common action relates to artistic action, and craft to art.[18]

Rühle von Lilienstern's understanding of art as a subjective, highly developed practical skill involves a mental faculty that Immanuel Kant had placed at the center of intellectual discussions a few decades earlier—namely, the power of judgment. In his most sustained engagement with art and aesthetics, *Critique of the Power of Judgment*, Kant had established the power of judgment as the link between the categories of the understanding and the sense impressions provided by the imagination. Kant distinguished between two different ways that the power of judgment categorizes. If a general category of the understanding was given and the power of judgment sought to apply it to an empirical phenomenon at hand, Kant labeled it "determinate judgment." If only the empirical phenomenon was given and the mind sought to find the general category to which it belonged, Kant called it "reflexive judgment."

Steeped in this philosophical discourse, Rühle makes a very direct application of it to war. If warfare were merely a craft, he claims, then it would be possible for the commander in each tactical or strategic situation to search through the theoretical system as though it were a rule book or register to find the general rule to which the particular case belongs, which would then tell him what to do. In war, however, no such rule exists. The number of particular cases is "infinite," and any rule deduced from past wars will fail when it encounters the particularities of the next war.[19] In other words, the idiosyncrasy of each particular military situation thwarts any mechanical application of a rule system. War only allows for general rules of thumb, and to apply them properly, with the necessary modifications that the particularity of the situation demands, requires an acute mental activity. Unlike rote application, judgment in war consists of the "free use of general lessons," and as such it constitutes the "artistic transfer on to individual actions, i.e. an actual *art* in opposition to *craft*."[20]

The art of war thus involves a specifically artistic kind of judgment that exceeds mechanical application; that can gauge the relevance and applicability of general, guiding rules of thumb; and that even transgresses these rules when the particular case requires it. Indeed, this type of artistic judgment, Rühle claims, is the prerogative of "genius." Situations arise in war, he writes,

> when it is right and necessary to act against rules and prescriptions. To determine when these situations arise is the task of genius; to anticipate when success favors this necessary form of action and does not wreck the most prudent calculation due to later circumstances that cannot be calculated in advance; this is the heavenly ordained privilege of the rare human being who possesses an equal share of luck and genius.[21]

In an environment in flux, pervaded by uncertainty and unpredictable chance events, the only method is genius. This conception of the military commander as a "genius" derives from the general discourse on art and aesthetics that filled the air at the time. Once again, Kant had made an influential contribution to its theorizing. In the third critique, Kant defines genius as the inborn talent or mental disposition (*ingenium*) that does not merely follow an established rule but that itself sets a new rule. Since "fine art" can never be derived from an existing rule, Kant proceeds, "fine art is only possible as the product of genius."[22] Importing these ideas from the discourse on aesthetics to the phenomenon of war, Rühle von Lilienstern casts the military commander as a war artist who creates a new work of art on the battlefield:

> It becomes evident that the general objective, even and particularly in the critical moment of battle, can usually only be achieved when the generals, like genuine artists, forget all the rules they have studied and memorized and themselves create the new suitable rule. Precisely because war is a work of art and the conduct of war is an art form, only *artists*, i.e. those who move within their field with gracefulness and freedom, will emerge victorious.[23]

The concept of genius is so important to Rühle that he repeats it in several writings.[24] But as the preceding passage already indicates, Rühle proceeds to import not just the concept of genius but a whole series of associated concepts from the discourse on art and aesthetics into the theory of the art of war. As described in chapter 1, the conception of art that develops in the eighteenth century and reaches its high point with Schiller and Kant produced a new set of concepts in order to establish art as an autonomous realm. Originality, genius, creativity, freedom, expressivity, virtuosity, the unconscious, and the imagination—these terms from aesthetic theory now come to frame and characterize the subject of war. In a long and convoluted, but equally fascinating, sentence, we can trace the development from the vocabulary of art as praxis to the language of art as aesthetics. Rühle writes:

> Art, however, we primarily call those practical activities for whose exemplary conduct the exercise of the mind must be put into free enthusiastic play by our own volition and fresh air and the matter at hand, for which scientific knowledge alone will not suffice nor technical deftness nor mere intelligence, but which—because of the entanglement, the mutability, and the delicate treatment of the competing circumstances and conditions during the activity, because of the mediation of the conflict between living forces often required in the spur of the moment, because of the need to counteract the insufficiency of previous experience and the incomplete knowledge of the true nature and state of things with the presence of inner mental power and intuitive decisions—requires talent developed to the point of *virtuosity* instead of routine, *tact* instead of mere judgment, a *feeling* that seemingly rests on a *higher instinct* for everything right and fitting, an intuitive *creative power* instead of mere mediated knowledge, or, in a word: *genius*.[25]

Whereas games focus on the world of war, the merger of war and aesthetics in the theoretical discourse shifts emphasis to the individual who wages the war. The ideal commander is cast as a war artist whose display of artistry, virtuosity, creative powers, and instinctive genius is the sine qua non of managing and winning wars. The war artist may have another goal than the writer or the sculptor who seeks to produce beauty, yet the war artist must be equipped with the very same skills that characterize a true artist. The artistic raw material may differ, but the mental processes are the same. Indeed, just as the artist emerged as the essential figure of human prowess and creativity in Romantic discourse, Rühle sees the "artistic action" (*künstlerisches Handeln*) of the military commander as the highest form of subjectivity uniting all the "bodily, spiritual, and psychological powers of the human being" and displaying them in the highest degree of their development.[26]

Throughout Rühle's writings, then, aesthetics serves as the basic framework for understanding the nature of war. The "analogy between military action and artistic action" enables Rühle to regard war as an artistic practice and, in the end, "war as an art."[27] This theoretical gambit that unites a praxeological and an aesthetic understanding of the term *art* reaches its apogee in a final apotheosis of warfare as one of three essential phenomena to be inducted in the pantheon of the arts broadly conceived. With due deference to the muses, Rühle establishes a new superordinate category of "art as such," an umbrella term under which he subsumes the fine arts, the artisanal arts, and the art of war:

> Finally we wish to note that one might describe all the *practical* arts, which are directed toward living action and the attainment of elevated civic purposes and at whose summit, then, the art of war may boldly position itself, in contradistinction to the so-called *aesthetic* arts, which strive to produce beauty, and also from the so-called mechanical or *technical* arts, which have the cultivated production of all sorts of needs and the satisfaction of sensuous pleasures as their object, with the characteristic predicate of the noble arts in order thereby to ensure—without offending the *beautiful* arts of *Apollo and the Muses* or the useful arts of *Hermes*—that also the arts of *Pallas* may henceforth be secured a suitable place in the large domain of art as such.[28]

Not only does Rühle elevate the practical arts to the status of "noble arts," not only does he place warfare at the summit of these practical arts, but he also inscribes war into the broader category of art alongside the useful arts and the fine arts. The arts, then, come to designate a triumvirate of Apollo, Hermes, and Pallas, and the concept of "the art of war" evokes both Hermes and Apollo, both the praxeological and the aesthetic sense of the term *art*.

Thus, although the eighteenth-century philosophers of aesthetics developed their concepts in an attempt to separate art from craft, to establish art as an autonomous realm distinct and protected from the use value and pragmatics of worldly affairs, they also established an aesthetic vocabulary whose uses they could not control. The military theory that Rühle spurs on with his lectures and essays seizes these very terms and reapplies them to one of the most pragmatic of worldly affairs. This conceptual transfer retains many of the original aesthetic meanings, but it also gives them a new direction. Like the serious games invented at the time, the discourse of martial aesthetics breaks decidedly with the purity of the nonfunctional, autonomous artwork and with the speculative efforts of the artist. The theory of the art of war enlists aesthetics in an effort to develop a theory of praxis. It yokes aesthetics to practical military efforts, thereby operationalizing the theory of art.

CLAUSEWITZ: ON AESTHETICS

It is Rühle von Lilienstern who for the first time merges the discourse of aesthetics with the theory of warfare in extended reflections on their correspondences and overlaps. But it is his classmate and colleague at the War Academy in Berlin, Carl von Clausewitz, who would become famous for it. Indeed, a remarkable number of ideas that are today attributed to Clausewitz originate with Rühle. The perhaps single most famous idea, that war is the continuation of politics by other means, had long been accepted as a matter of course, and Rühle discusses it at length in several essays.[29] Moreover, the idea that war is a chaotic realm of uncertainty and contingency, a theme Clausewitz analyzes in detail in *On War* and elevates to one of the three constants alongside *enmity* and *politics* in his famous trinity of warfare, is central to Rühle's conception of war. Similarly, Rühle anticipates Clausewitz's extended reflections on the difference between science and knowledge on the one hand and art and praxis on the other.

It is therefore little surprise that the vocabulary of aesthetics also pervades Clausewitz's writings on war. In the third chapter of the first book of *On War*, titled "On Military Genius," Clausewitz picks up the Kantian understanding of genius as the creative individual who transgresses the existing rules and establishes a new rule. But he also offers a more elaborate psychological description of the mental profile that characterizes genius. Faced with the perplexing mass of events, contradictory information, and uncertainty, the commander relies on a series of mental abilities to discern and act on the best course of action: courage, resolve, presence of mind, levelheadedness, and the crucial skill Clausewitz calls the "tact of judgment"—the ability of the subconscious with lightning speed to evaluate all incoming information, to immediately discard the irrelevant and seize on the essential information. What distinguishes military genius, however, is both the presence and the mode of these abilities. First, they must relate to one another in a particular way. Clausewitz writes:

> for military genius consists precisely of this that it is not a singular force in one direction, as is, for example, courage, while other forces of the Understanding and the mind are lacking or have a direction that make them useless for war, but *that it is a harmonious union of forces*, in which the one or the other predominate, but none may go against the others.[30]

The mental faculties, in other words, must be balanced internally in a harmonious unity. Second, these well-balanced faculties must be developed far above average. They must reach a higher level and become an acute mental force that Clausewitz sums up as the "coup d'oeil," or eye of genius. An inner mental eye, more than a physical one, the coup d'oeil nevertheless indicates the key aspect of Clausewitz's conception of genius. Just as the purpose of theory for Clausewitz is to understand and serve praxis, so military genius, he repeatedly writes, is characterized not by great meditative power but by "a particular direction of the mind."[31] Genius, for Clausewitz, is operative. It is anything but separated and detached from the world, but rather is deeply enmeshed in the mutable empirical phenomena of war itself and dependent on courage and resolve to transform plans and opportunities into action. Indeed, for Clausewitz, mental operations are yoked so directly to action that they cannot be separated.

Clausewitz thereby at once adopts and transforms the prevalent conception of genius in aesthetics. Whereas the figure of the artistic genius in the philosophical and Romantic conception was the inward-looking recluse equipped with a powerful creative imagination, Clausewitz's military genius looks outward. The war artist is the one who successfully marshals both mind and emotions in order to transform the chaos of war into decisive action.

THE SENSE OF BEAUTY

Clausewitz may well have extrapolated from Rühle, but a curious circumstance may also have contributed to the aesthetic inflection of his theory of war. It is well known that aside from his theoretical writings—as embodied in his magnum opus, *On War*—Clausewitz also authored several tomes of military history. It is less known that concurrently with these war writings, he penned essays on aesthetics.[32] These essays display a genuine interest in the aesthetic discourse of his time, but aside from his ruminations on poetry, architecture, and painting as art forms worthy of study in their own right, his thoughts on aesthetics also serve as a frame for thinking about his main interest—warfare. Analyzing the character of the fine arts, Clausewitz finds several ideas that he proceeds to transfer to the analysis of war in a series of analogies both broad and more specific.

In the essay "On the Concept of Corporeal Beauty," Clausewitz tries to tackle one of the most fundamental concepts of aesthetic theory. He is particularly interested in the way sensuous beauty impacts the individual at both the (mostly) subconscious level of emotions and at the level of conscious or semiconscious ideas. What are the possibilities, he asks, of establishing *Kunstgesetze*, aesthetic laws of beauty, to better comprehend beauty's dual impact? Clausewitz picks two examples from architecture to show that the field itself is "infinite" and "irregular." At the same time, it is impossible to exclude any irregular or random architectural element from the discussion, as they all contribute to the overall aesthetic impression on the viewer.[33] Accordingly, the theory of art does not allow for any absolute laws that may never be transgressed. In Clausewitz's words, "So here we only find rules, but not laws. For a rule is only a guide."[34]

The field of art as an empirical phenomenon thereby emerges as an analog of warfare: both fields are infinitely varied in their appearances, and in neither case can one establish universally valid laws. But the analogy goes further. If art is infinitely varied, what is the criterion of artistic beauty? What makes art art? Clausewitz proceeds to ask. His answer: "*The combination of the elements into a whole*"[35] (italics in the original). The formalism of the answer is interesting. Beautiful art is a result of the proper combination of the individual parts that make up the whole. And if the artist shapes the artwork into a cohesive unity, then it will match the cognitive structures of the mind and bring about the pleasant effect of the beautiful:

> Thus the arts can serve the purpose of becoming useful, and it lies in the laws of our thinking and not in covetous habit, or in the need and misery of our meager nature, if we demand of each beautiful object that it must have a purpose that at least appears to be useful. This purpose forms for us the unity that the artwork strives toward and constitutes the bond that unites all the parts. For this mere thought suffices, reality adds nothing. Only the concept of a church is necessary to erect a beautiful building, not that it is used.[36]

Once again Clausewitz's Kantianism is evident. As we saw earlier, for Kant the artwork is characterized by its "purposiveness without purpose." In other words, even if the work of art is autonomous and only has itself as purpose, the formal organization of the elements that it comprises gives the appearance of an overall purposiveness. This inner, formal purpose lends the artwork a (beautiful) unity that in turn puts the mental faculties of the viewer into a state of free play, resulting in pleasure. Likewise, for Clausewitz, the "only apparently useful purpose" in the architectural example forms the formal unity of the artwork, activates our "sense of beauty," and produces "a pleasant effect of the whole."[37] A building with too many nonintegrated parts, by contrast, produces, according to Clausewitz, "the feeling of nonpurposiveness."[38]

Clausewitz's adoption of Kantian aesthetics suggests a correspondence between art and art theory on the one hand and war and military theory on the other. His invocation of the discourse on genius, the reference to commanders as "war artists," the comparison of generals to Mozart all indicate the analogous positions and abilities of the subjects of war and art.[39] As already indicated, however, Clausewitz's writings on aesthetics also point to a correspondence between the two objects: the work of art and the battle or the military campaign.

This is particularly evident in Clausewitz's essay "On Art and Art Theory." Discussing the differences between the various art forms, Clausewitz there defines the two central elements of any aesthetic phenomenon: means and purposes. He writes:

> The means very often constitute the difference between the arts. Music, poetry, and almost all *beautiful arts* have the same purpose, but they reach it in different ways. In one art the tones constitute the different elements, in another it is the colors, in the third the mental images.[40]

Whether with colors, tones, or mental images, the fine arts all employ a given material, but this material is shaped according to an overall unifying purpose. The relation between means and purpose is central to the artistic endeavor, and, Clausewitz specifies, the ability to unite them properly is the very definition of art:

> Both purpose and means must be there before the art, they cannot emerge from it; they are given to art and limit its domain on both sides. To unite purpose and means with one another is called *creation*. Art is the ability to create. . . . The whole creation of art consists of the combination of the purposes with the means.[41]

Clausewitz proceeds to define artistic genius as "a creative power," as the "ability to invent," and he writes that the genius exercises these innovative, creative powers by coming up with novel ways of uniting means and purpose.[42] This understanding of artistic creation that subtends the works of art made its way into *On War* when Clausewitz defines "creation and production" as the essence of art as opposed to the pure knowledge of science.[43] But, more important, this conception of artistic creation also comes to define his conception of strategy. The third book of *On War*, *On Strategy in General*, defines its topic in a straightforward fashion: "Strategy is the use of the engagement for the purpose of the war."[44] In the field of warfare, the means are no longer the sounds, the clay, or the images of the fine arts but violence; and the purpose is not the production of the beautiful work of art but the military victory and the political goals that this victory enforces.[45] The relation between means and ends, however, the shaping of the individual elements into a cohesive overall structure, is that of the work of art:

> Strategy is the use of the engagement for the purpose of the war; it must therefore set a goal for the whole act of war . . . it develops the plan of the war, and to this goal it ties a series of actions that should lead to it, i.e. it makes the plans for the individual campaigns and in each one it organizes the individual engagements.[46]

Organized into a unified whole (*ein Ganzes*) in which every violent action leads toward the overarching goal, war becomes a work (*Werk*) or, as he often writes, a work of art (*Kunstwerk*).[47] As a work of art built out of violence, the battle, at the tactical level, and the overall campaign, at the strategic level, merge the aesthetic conception of the formally unified work, the inner purposiveness of structure, with the operational praxis and an ultimate purpose in the world of war and politics. In other words, a brilliant commander's victorious campaign is the military equivalent of the beautiful work of art created by the aesthetic genius. Both the subjective and the objective parts of the analogy are clearly evident when Clausewitz continues his analysis of strategy:

> A sovereign or a commander, who knows how to carefully organize his war according to his purposes and means, who does neither too much nor too little, thereby offers the greatest proof of his genius. But the effects of this genius are revealed not just in new forms of action that immediately stand out, but also in the happy result of the whole. It is the correctness of the silent assumptions, it is the noiseless harmony of the entire action that we should admire and that is only heralded in the success of the whole."[48]

Genius reveals itself not only in the striking creativity of original actions but also in the quiet shaping of the multiple elements into a harmonious whole. The war that Clausewitz beholds and admires is war as a *Gesamtkunstwerk* of violence, the total military-political work of art created by the war artist from the violent means of battle for the overarching purpose of a political desideratum. Indeed, in his essay "On Art and Art Theory," Clausewitz goes so far as to regard the military work of art as the subjective expression of the commander's individual character. Distinguishing between "principles" and "laws," Clausewitz argues that the former have a more subjective character than the latter and continues:

> It is rarer to hear of the principles of art than of the principles of the artist; the term is also used very frequently in the art of war, but in this art, as is well known, the whole individual nature of the artist has such a tremendous influence on the artwork.[49]

As in the aesthetic discourse, but even more strongly, Clausewitz binds the subjective and the objective parts of creative violence closely together: the martial work of art is a direct expression of the subjective character of the war artist. Looking at a brilliant military campaign, then, we can admire in its formal totality the material traces of the creative strategic imagination that molded it into being. War, in this conception, emerges as the highest creative expression of genius.

FALSE ANALOGIES

The overlap between aesthetics, praxis, and war that pervades Clausewitz's writings is striking. Writing analytical treatises on both the fine arts and on war, Clausewitz proceeds to interweave the discourse on art and aesthetics with a praxeological approach to military theory. Given his subsequent fame, Clausewitz, rather than Rühle von Lilienstern, becomes the originating figure for a line of thought that merges aesthetics and war into a martial aesthetics or art form. Before turning to the further developments of this way of thinking, however, it is worth dwelling on a number of critical qualifications in Clausewitz's texts. In spite of his general adoption of aesthetics as a frame for thinking war, Clausewitz has several caveats. First of all, he is well aware that in the application of aesthetic concepts to the phenomenon of war, he is transforming the meaning of the concepts in a practical direction, thus breaking with the intentions of the aesthetic theorists. In a discussion of the distinction between art and craft, Clausewitz inserts a footnote to preempt attacks from disgruntled aestheticians: "How the aesthetician further wishes to define art and artist, does not concern us. We are already convinced that he will find the explanation given above too material."[50] The application of an aesthetic vocabulary to the praxis of war instead of to the fine arts, however, has a further consequence. Stressing the dialectical nature of warfare, that one always must contend with a thinking, strategizing, and acting enemy rather than an inert material, Clausewitz eventually comes down on neither side of the art–science debate. Even though, he claims, it is more fitting to speak of the *art* of war than the *science* of war given the practical nature of military operations, he eventually dissolves the debate with a new definition:

> We say, then, that war does not belong in the realm of the arts or the sciences, but in the realm of social life. It is a conflict of great interests, which is resolved with blood, and it only differs from other conflicts in that respect. Rather than comparing it with art, it could more accurately be compared with commerce, which is also a conflict of human interests and activities, and it is *much* closer to politics, which in turn

> is a form of commerce on a larger scale. Moreover, politics is the womb in which war develops.[51]

Clausewitz seeks to move beyond the art–science debate because the material of the artist and that of the commander are different in kind. War forms a part of social life and politics and therefore cannot be compared with the dead material of the mechanical arts, nor even with the living material of the "ideal" or fine arts—the human spirit and the emotions—because they remain passive objects shaped by the artist. The commander instead works with a "living, reacting material," which makes warfare into a dialectical relationship between equally active parts.[52] The agency of the object, along with the pervasive uncertainty of intelligence about the enemy's doings and plans, thwarts the seamless superimposition of the vocabulary of art onto warfare. Indeed, in a possible retort to Rühle von Lilienstern, Clausewitz states that the art–science debate has led the whole discussion in a false direction and has "caused an automatic equation of war with other art forms or sciences and a host of false analogies."[53]

As shown earlier, one of the analogies that Clausewitz himself frequently uses is the campaign as a work of art. But just as the reactive material of war differs from the passive material of art, so the genius's creative efforts lead to different products. Comparing the military campaign to the paintings of Raphael and Rubens, Clausewitz proceeds to underline their differences: the visual masterpieces of art can be taken in completely and in their totality, but war offers no such finished "artworks."[54] Given the incompleteness of historiography, events must be painstakingly reconstructed out of limited and often contradictory eyewitness accounts, dispatches, letters, and a range of other documents. The totality of a campaign, the "work" shaped by the strategic brilliance of the commander, will always remain a conjecture, a whole that is fuzzy not only at the edges but also at the very center. In other words, just as the material consists only of "mutable elements,"[55] so does the final result of the commander's creative endeavors.

These discrepancies reveal the uneasy relationship between art and aesthetics and warfare. Appealing and pervasive as the discourse of aesthetics is in his works, Clausewitz at once applies and disowns it. On the one hand, the fusion of the two vocabularies is made possible by the establishment of a series of basic analogies between the fields. The subject of art and the subject of war must be possessed of certain overlapping qualities and abilities—genius, creativity, originality—just as the objects correspond in their status as the end product of an artistic form-giving. On the other hand, these very analogies are undermined by the realization that the aesthetic frame does not quite fit the nature of the object to which it is applied. By fusing two understandings of art—the practical and the aesthetic—Clausewitz develops the concept of an art of war as a superior theoretical notion as compared to the scientistic theories that had governed eighteenth-century thought on war, but he insists that it remains an inadequate frame for understanding the nature of warfare. With Clausewitz, then, the theory that war is an art form is born alongside the counterargument that war is neither an artisanal art nor an aesthetic art, but something else entirely. As pervasive and suggestive as the aesthetic vocabulary is, it comes with the injunction that, in the end, it may well fail to properly grasp its object, that it misdescribes and misleads as much as it enlightens.

MARTIAL ETHICS AND AESTHETIC MARTIALISM

We will do well to keep in mind this uneasy relationship between aesthetics and war, poised between insight and error, when we consider the continued aesthetic tradition within military theory. Rühle, as we recall, did not hesitate to merge the two fields and eventually describes the apotheosis of war as an art form. This aesthetic understanding of military operations brings with it a value system that paves the way for a social and moral justification of war. Such arguments can be found already in Rühle's unsavory and deeply problematic "Apologia for War." Defending warfare there against philosophical critiques, primarily Kant's outline of a vision for an eternal peace, Rühle argues for the necessity of war, for its "inner moral sublimity and dignity."[56] The premise for this argument, which Rühle announces in the opening sentence, is that we must "rise to the idea of an *art of war*" and that we need to recognize war as "the sublime mother or sovereign of all other practical arts."[57] Once war is conceived as an art, and even as the most noble of all practical arts, the condition of possibility is established for the transfer of qualities and values from the one field to the other. Thus the eternal peace in Kant's speculative vision becomes in the "Apologia" a state of death and decay in which morals degenerate. For Rühle, society implodes because it lacks the "creative spirit" that manifests itself in warfare and lends it dignity and honor.[58]

Statements such as these form part of a broader discourse that Karma Nabulsi has labeled "martialism." An influential ideology articulated forcefully in Prussian military circles and later adopted among a wide swath of military and state thinkers, martialism denotes the belief that war "is the supreme instrument and ultimate realization of all human endeavor."[59] Instead of viewing war as an evil or, in the case of the realist school of thought, a necessary evil that should be limited and avoided whenever possible, the martialists glorified war. To realize the full potential of man's belligerent nature and the ultimate destiny of nation states, war was regarded as a necessary virtue, and martialists celebrated it and installed it at the top of their hierarchy of values.[60]

When Clausewitz and Rühle begin to merge military theory with the discourse on aesthetics, this theoretical move can be seen as the pinnacle—or abyss—of the broader martialist discourse. It marks the birth of an *aesthetic martialism*, a new martial ethics that invites a transfer of values from the fine arts to war. What are these values? With the rise of philosophical aesthetics in the eighteenth century and even more strongly with the discourse of Romanticism that pervaded the atmosphere of intellectual life in the first decades of the nineteenth century, the artist was installed as the quintessence of human achievement.[61] Against older ideals of mimesis, imitation, and skillful copying, the imagination, creativity, and originality were elevated as the noblest capacities of the human mind, even as the essence of the human. If the imagination, for example, as Jim Engell has shown, had been regarded since antiquity as a primitive reproductive faculty for the storage of images and was often associated with a dangerous irrationalism, the new aesthetic order recast the imagination as an advanced faculty that combined perceptual sensibility with a creative force that enabled the production of novelty.[62] As such it became both the mark and the precondition for genius. This is evident already in 1774 when Alexander Gerard in his *Essay on Genius* sought to define his subject—"GENIUS is properly the faculty of *invention*"[63]—and it continues in the nineteenth century when the figure of the artistic genius reached its apogee as a demigod of the secular religion of art both in the speculative aesthetic theories of Schelling, Hegel, and Schopenhauer and in the bourgeois conception of art as a reified realm of spirituality.

In other words, the division in the concept of art in the eighteenth century—the emergence of the fine arts as a separate, autonomous realm—also involved the establishment of a hierarchy of values. The concepts associated with the mechanical arts (utility, rule-following, rote repetition) were pushed to the bottom of the hierarchy, while the concepts associated with the fine arts (the imagination, creativity, freedom, autonomy) were placed at the top. Whereas the objects of craft were the result of a simple mechanical processing of the material at hand, the refinement of the fine arts was the result of a spiritual form-giving, of the transformation of matter into the objectification and manifestation of an idea.[64] And the primary subject and originator of these ideas was the genius. The figure of the genius, then, emerged as the embodiment and signifier of the highest values of humanity.

When Clausewitz and Rühle therefore channel the aesthetic currents of the period into their analyses of war, these valorizations often flow along with them. If war is at base an aesthetic phenomenon, an art form in its own right, then it enables the manifestation and display of the finest intellectual and emotional capacities of human beings. For Clausewitz this view is always tempered by a more sober assessment. Both in his historical writings and in his theory of war, he emphasizes the destructive elements of warfare. Thus his famed "trinity" of war comprises not only chance and political rationality but also "primordial violence, hatred, and enmity."[65] For Rühle, however, the aesthetic dimension of war becomes an integral part of the justification and even glorification of warfare.

If we trace the subsequent theories of the art of war, two different positions become clear. On the one hand, we find a prima facie "neutral" conceptualization of war as an art form; on the other hand, we find an explicit martial ethics that valorizes and justifies war based on its aesthetic character—aesthetic martialism. In both cases, Clausewitz's thought often serves as the silent or openly acknowledged background and origin for this conceptualization of war. In his numerous lectures and essays on military theory, for example, Helmuth von Moltke shows his debt to Clausewitz both when he describes the link between politics and warfare as well as the pervasive impact of chance and unforeseeable events, and also when he repeatedly casts war as a "free, practical, artistic activity" that cannot be grounded in a system of rules.[66] As he puts it:

"In war, as in art, we find no universal forms; in neither can a rule take the place of talent."[67]

In the same years that Moltke developed this conception of warfare, which had a profound impact on German military thought for decades,[68] his younger colleague, Max Jähns, took Clausewitz a step further. Jähns, who taught at the royal War Academy in Berlin for fourteen years and became a prolific and respected military historian and theorist, was not only interested in the impact of war on the civil and cultural sphere—as he sought to explicate in his work *On War, Peace and Culture* (*Über Krieg, Frieden und Kultur*) from 1893—but also in war as an art form in its own right.[69] This conception emerges powerfully already in 1874 in his essay "Die Kriegskunst als Kunst" (The art of war as an art). Traditionally, Jähns begins, the concept of "art" has been limited to the "fine arts," but theorists have failed to realize the wider ambit of the concept. Rehearsing the by now traditional tropes of the aesthetic conception of "art," such as creation, intuition, imagination, and genius, Jähns argues that these are the very terms that characterize the politician and, especially, the war commander. Indeed, like Rühle, he places the art of politics and the art of war at the top of the hierarchy of the arts. Politics and warfare, he writes, are

> the highest of all arts, because the material that they work with, viz. peoples and armies, is the most precious and fragile, because the art of their creative efforts is by far the most difficult given the impact of opposing enemy forces, and because their goal is the highest imaginable: the welfare of the state and victory![70]

In other words, war is not only an art form; it is the highest, the most demanding, and the most admirable among the arts. To argue his case, Jähns superimposes the fine arts and war in an elaborate analogy with music. Comparing the commander to a maestro conducting an orchestra in a performance of his own symphony, Jähns emphasizes both the similarities and the differences. Before the concert, the maestro has had ample time to work on the score; every note is in its proper place; every tempo, every crescendo is clearly marked. The general, however, can only offer an outline of the main motif that structures the overall strategy; as to the "pauses in combat," the "tempo of attack," and the "crescendo of defense"—these details can hardly ever be planned in advance.[71] The maestro holds practice sessions with the orchestra to ensure that all instruments are in tune, that the players know their parts and the details of the whole symphony. The general, by contrast, must make do without such practice sessions and is forced to bring "his out-of-tune instruments to the concert, worn out and tired from the march, excited and vibrating in the midst of danger."[72] As soon as the maestro raises the baton, the hall falls silent, and the complex rhythms and intertwined melodic lines are resolved in a harmony that was planned from the beginning. The general, however, is faced with a much more complex task before the chaotic elements of war can find their harmonious resolution. In a remarkable passage that also reveals the deep influence of Clausewitz, Jähns writes:

> But the moment the commander waives his baton, a horrific *foreign* music from the enemy roars against the thunder of his cannons. Every step is blocked; nothing is certain; every moment brings new events, demands new decisions. In front of the commander, the plans and dispositions of his opponent are covered in darkness. To decipher what the enemy, following the general principles of the art, could do, might do, to get a scent of the probable in the swarm of possibilities, to comprehend the inner nature of the constantly changing circumstances, to unite the endless abundance of appearances and exigencies in one viewpoint, to solve the intertwined combinations, to calculate time and space, mobile and hindering forces with unerring tact, to counter the power of chance with the force of self-reliance and presence of mind, to vanquish danger with courage, to assess correctly the characters of the participants, not least of the enemy officers, to see right through them, to inspire one's own comrades, to keep all of them dependent, loyal, and devoted, to put the right man in the right place and to leave him the appropriate freedom of action while leading him with a firm hand—*those are the tasks that the war artist must fulfill* if he wishes to enforce his plan, his motif, unfazed by the flow of events, if even the dispositions of the enemy are to become new means for the realization of his idea, if the terrifying whirl of wild dissonances that roar through the battle and the campaign in the end should lead to harmony, and the artwork thereby completes itself: in victory.[73]

War is a mass of actual and potential events that intersect in an entirely unpredictable way; it is the chaos of mobile and hindering forces that pervade time and space and throw them into a jumble. To manage this heterogeneous, malleable, and elusive material is the almost insurmountable task of the general. But equipped with a powerful artistic imagination, he is able to unify this mass of seemingly random elements into a single vision, to shape this material by infusing it with an idea. The artistic imagination thus becomes the intellectual force that transforms the chaos of matter into a harmonious work of art. Given the at once elusive and intractable nature of the material, the creative efforts of the war artist far exceed those of the maestro and or any other artist among the fine arts as traditionally conceived. Combining "inborn power of genius" with "masterful technique," the general becomes the very symbol of "an authentic, true *artist*."[74]

How, then, does a well-read Clausewitzian respond to his reservation that, in the end, war is neither an art nor a science but belongs to the realm of politics and social life? Jähns acknowledges Clausewitz's ultimate banishment of war from the realm of art, but he immediately overrules the judgment. Art, he argues, also springs from social life; it reflects and gives form to the experiences of social interaction. Likewise, the art of war forms part of the larger social fabric, and its development is bound up with the broader changes in the progression of human society. Thus war and art are not only part and parcel of the same field; the history of war is also a history of aesthetics. To prove this point, Jähns outlines a history of the art of war from the point of view of *style*. Just as there are changing styles in the fine arts—for example, in architecture—so there are particular aesthetic styles of war. And a historical analysis will show, he argues, "how closely they correspond with the equivalent phenomena of the fine arts."[75] Thus, from the formal features of the phalanx in ancient Greece via the virtuosity of the condottiere in the Renaissance to the mass warfare of Napoleon, Jähns traces a military history that he yokes directly to the stylistic features of art history: from the Doric columns of the Greek temples via the playfulness of the baroque and the ornaments of the rococo to the eclecticism, splendor, and opulence of the *style Empire*. And as in the other arts, these styles constitute the common denominator in different and competing aesthetic schools. As he puts it: "Just as with the architects, the sculptors, and the painters, formal schools were formed among the war artists."[76]

Whether by musical analogy or by the juxtaposition of war and art history, Jähns's argument is the same: warfare is an art among the fine arts. And not only can "martial creation" lay claim to the name "art";[77] given the intractability of his material, the war artist takes pride of place among artists—he is the emblem of artistic creation and genius. Jähns thereby argues for a conception of war that closely resembles that articulated by Rühle von Lilienstern. War is not only an art form; it also partakes of art's system of values. Like Rühle's induction of war into the pantheon of the arts, Jähns concludes his essay by crowning the war artist with the laurels of Apollo. This evidently signifies the transfer of the set of values associated with the fine arts to war, but Jähns goes further: the aesthetic conception of war shapes both the character and the ethics of war. Comparing the style of war during his own time with the contemporary architectural predilection for massive structures of iron and glass, he dismisses the suggestion that the equally expanded modern battlefields should be filled to the brim with masses of soldiers, for two closely related reasons: "for then the number of victims would rise to an unbearable number; and one of the noblest demands of any artwork—that it produces the ideal thought (in this case *victory*) in greatest purity and with the least exertion of external means—would not be met."[78] The ethics of avoiding unnecessary deaths is justified by reference to the rules of art: a work of art should express the idea of its creator in the purest and most economical way possible. Thus ethics becomes a matter of aesthetics. And while the aesthetic criterion of purity dictates the avoidance of unnecessary mass deaths because they would ruin the artwork, the artwork also requires a number of "necessary" deaths in order for the war artist to bring it into existence. In this manner, the aesthetic conception of war not only justifies violence and elevates it to an art on par with or even at the top of the fine arts; it transforms the very nature of violence into a thing of beauty. Moving beyond mere analogies, Jähns's military theory offers an aesthetic apologia for war: violence is the necessary means for the production of harmonious works of art.

ALL THAT YOU CAN BE

The merger of war and aesthetics in these texts of Prusso-German military theory, however, is pushed even further in US military thought. The most influential military theorist who had something to say about warfare as an art at the beginning of the twentieth century was A. T. Mahan. He taught at the US Naval College and published a number of his lectures in his widely read *Naval Strategy* in 1911. In a general reflection on the art–science debate, he comes down clearly on the side of war as an art. Pitting art against science, he casts the term in opposition to rigidity and the scientific ideal of absolute certainty. But art also takes on more aesthetic properties:

> Art, out of materials which it finds about it, creates new forms in endless variety. It is not bound down to a mechanical reproduction of similar effects, as is inanimate nature, but partakes of the freedom of the human mind in which it has its root. Art acknowledges principles and even rules; but these are not so much fetters, or bars, which compel its movements aright, as guides which warn when it is going wrong. In this living sense, the conduct of war is an art, having its spring in the mind of man, dealing with very various circumstances, admitting certain principles; but, beyond that, manifold in its manifestations, according to the genius of the artist and the temper of the materials with which he is dealing. To such an effort dogmatic prescription is unsuited; the best 300 of rules, when applied to it, cannot be rigid, but must have that free play which distinguishes a principle from a mere rule.[79]

Mahan invokes the free creative capacities of the human mind as the prerequisite for managing the variety of circumstances and the flux of events, and casts the general as an artist who gives shape to the raw material of his particular art form. By doing so, Mahan continues the line of thought we found in Clausewitz and Moltke. In spite of the aesthetic coloring of his concept of art, however, Mahan's rapprochement of war and aesthetics remains both abstract and brief and does not go far beyond the general outline quoted here.

An elaborate theory of the total merger of aesthetics with war, however, can be found in James Mrazek's *The Art of Winning Wars* from 1968. Mrazek, who served as a colonel in the 326th Glider Infantry Regiment in World War II and was subsequently on the faculty of the Command and General Staff College at Fort Leavenworth, expounds a full-fledged aesthetic theory of war that seeks to recuperate the force of artistic creativity for the optimization of US military capacities. Replete with references to Mozart, Rembrandt, Balzac, Poe, Stevenson, and Tolstoy, who was a pacifist, Mrazek argues for the recognition by the US military of artistic creativity as the most powerful but hitherto neglected weapon in the arsenal. Well aware of the apparent oddity of his assertion, Mrazek acknowledges its unconventionality but proceeds to stake his claim:

> At first it seems strange to think of creativity in the context of battle. But most significant military victories have been artistic masterpieces, owing more to insight than infantry. They are the result of an innovative idea emanating from the mind of the creative leader. The military might, formerly so often regarded as the sole cause of victory, is frequently only the midwife, as it were, assisting in the birth of a victory which has already been conceived. From a creative point of view, battlefield successes often compare in emotional impact and, incongruously, in a kind of beauty with the paintings of a Rembrandt or the vibrant symphonies of a Tchaikovsky.[80]

The ease with which Mrazek is able to ignore the incongruity of his argument—even as he himself notes it in passing—may be due to wider societal developments at the time. By the late 1960s and early 1970s, the ideal of creativity embodied by the artistic genius had expanded far beyond the confines of the fine arts and had been implanted into a range of nonaesthetic societal spheres. Luc Boltanski and Eve Chiapello have shown how in the 1970s and 1980s, work was restructured according to new ideals of creativity.[81] But the aestheticization of society went far beyond the workplace. Commercials, products, psychology, sports, and education, among other things, were all remodeled according to aesthetic imperatives.[82] Thus what Reckwitz calls the "aesthetic-creative complex," the co-option of aesthetic procedures, methods, and ideals by other societal fields, was in the process of being consolidated.[83] Observing these developments and clearly aware that creative phenomena were no longer merely "the province of a few inquisitive artists and philosophers" but were being studied and used much more widely, Mrazek issues his challenge to the military institution: How can it be, he asks, that in spite of the pervasive interest in art, aesthetics, and creativity, "Western military leaders, with few notable exceptions, fail to see war as an aesthetic exercise and, consequently, ignore creativity's vital role in it"?[84]

Answering the question himself, Mrazek identifies four general obstacles. First, military institutions generally regard war as a science rather than an art. Second, art is considered beautiful and creative, whereas war is grim and destructive. Third, art is aesthetic, (i.e., it is connected with great works of art); and fourth, creativity is a threat to military discipline. Instead of giving precise answers to these apparent discrepancies between war and art, Mrazek partly refutes and partly ignores them and proceeds to trace both art and war back to a fundamental human capacity and desire for creativity. Just as creativity is the source of great art, it is the source of military victories.[85] Guerrillas, for example, "are like artists experimenting and creating with paint and brush, using the jungles, the mountains, and the captured supplies to create weapon and war." In this conception, it is not the guerrillas themselves but the "the creative artist within the guerrillas [that] makes them the grim military problem they are to their enemies."[86] Mrazek cites Clausewitz and Mahan approvingly for their descriptions of the artistry of war, and he takes Jomini to task for mistakenly eulogizing "the military artisan instead of the artist" when he conceived of war as an art.[87] The shift from the artisanal and practical concept of art to an aesthetic conception of war as an art form is evident. But Mrazek also gives the theory of war a psychological inflection. Building on the self-growth psychology that flourished at the time, he regards war not only as a creative and aesthetic phenomenon; war also constitutes the means for creative self-development and self-realization. To understand how this might be, we need to fundamentally rethink the war environment—battle itself. Yes, the battlefield forms the stage on which raw violence meets massive uncertainty, but as a temporary zone in which the fetters of rules and laws lose their force and soldiers can experience a freedom of action unattainable in civilian life, war forms "an ideal environment for creativity."[88]

> War provides the commander with an ideal creative environment. This is particularly true in an environment where a breakthrough of the enemy lines has taken place. Having left the restrictive laws and traditions of his homeland, the creative leader now feels psychologically free to operate in what is for him a free environment.[89]

Only when the restrictive and coercive laws that normally hold people in check are gone can the true creative potential of the individual be developed. Even as he notes that the absence of restrictions and the disappearance of the threat of law often lead to violation, rape, and sheer barbarity, in the same breath Mrazek states that war "permits the soldier in the philosophical and psychological sense to realize himself. It provides a release of the unconscious—of the id, as psychologists have described it."[90] The absence or the transgression of established rules and norms of behavior that lead to barbarity and heinous crimes becomes the precondition for creative acts of military artistry. Only in an environment free from laws of any kind can the soldier experience "the exhilaration of an artist in the act of creation."[91] For the professional soldier who strives to become a creative artist, the true tragedy of war, Mrazek concludes, is that it must end.[92]

Merging war, individual self-realization, and creative artistry, Mrazek envisions war as the optimal environment for the realization of the creative potential of the human psyche. To fight a war is no longer a matter of violence, destruction, or self-sacrifice for a national cause. To fight a war is the best way to unleash the creative artist inside you and reach your full creative potential. This creative vision of war gives a spin to the renowned US Army recruiting slogan that Earl Carter would later coin for the US Army in 1980. "Be all you can be" interpellated the potential recruit as a subject whose latent capacities only needed the proper environment to come to fruition. For Mrazek, however, war is a self-development project that has the potential to transform everyone into artists. Not only the generals, commanders, and officers at the higher echelons but all soldiers at all levels and in every function may become creative artists. Whether they become "artists of the battlefield" or "artists of administration" or excel in "the artistic medium of tanks," for Mrazek all soldiers throughout the army are potential artists: "Each soldier is creative to some degree, with his creativeness higher in some fields than others. In some way, each is an artist."[93] This reframing of war from a military or political phenomenon to an artistic one not only trades on the set of values inherent in the aesthetic concepts and the roster of brilliant artists in the Western canon that Mrazek invokes; it also serves as an aesthetic justification both for war as such and for the transgressions and crimes that come along with it. Where Kant defined creative genius in the realm of art by the transgression of established rules, his ethics in the social realm was determined by the categorical imperative. Mrazek, however, regards the transgression of judicial laws, especially on enemy territory, in the form of rape and random killings as the unfortunate but necessary condition of unfettered freedom that must be in place for the soldiers' full creative potential to be realized. From the point of view of aesthetic martialism, creativity justifies any legal and ethical transgressions—indeed they become its prerequisite.

The theoretical merger of aesthetics with war, then, comes with a set of dire problems. From the very beginning, the transformation of warfare into an art form, battle into a work of art, and soldiers into artists leads to both epistemological and ethical pitfalls. When Rühle von Lilienstern and Clausewitz originate this line of thinking, Clausewitz is quick to flag the theoretical hazards of false analogies, while Rühle proceeds to invoke aesthetics as a justification for war. In the theory's later instantiations, the relationship between war and aesthetics remains carefully poised between attempts at objective analytical insights into the nature of war and an active militarism that justifies, promotes, and elevates warfare by way of aesthetic arguments. The co-option of aesthetics, then, results in a comprehensive reframing of the whole phenomenon of war that not only offers new insights but also—at times inadvertently, at times perversely—misrepresents and misleads as it transfigures coordinated violence into a realm of artistry and creative self-realization.

In 1968, Mrazek's version of a martial aesthetics was a vision only. His point of departure was precisely the lack of understanding within the US military of the aesthetic nature of warfare. His book is as much a call for military leadership to embrace creativity as a powerful resource that can be weaponized, as it is a theory of the aesthetic nature of warfare. For Mrazek, the "endeavor to harness creativity" is "a matter of national urgency" and would entail a complete change of praxis "in schools, doctrine, and thought."[94] The urgent appeal points to the fact that the aesthetic dimension of war did not form a part of official doctrine at the time. Indeed, the theoretical reflections on warfare as an art form might seem mere historical curiosities that are either bound up with their moment in time—as when Clausewitz and Rühle breathed the air of Kantianism and Romantic thought—or that are merely fringe developments with little impact on doctrine or even on debates or more broadly accepted ideas in the thinking of war. The memorandum issued by General Mattis on October 9, 2009, however, may be seen as the belated response to Mrazek's appeal. It signals the beginning of the adoption of many of the aesthetic concepts and perspectives outlined in this chapter. For in the twenty-first century, aesthetic martialism has resurfaced in a new guise and has come to shape both US doctrine as well as the wider field of military thought. The new form taken by the specter of art is the discourse on military design.

5

DESIGNING WAR

When General Mattis issued the memorandum *Vision for a Joint Approach to Operational Design* in October 2009, he presented a series of concepts that powerfully impacted Western military thought. In the past decade, the notion of "military design" has moved from a fringe phenomenon in academic journals, online debate forums, and a few courses at select military institutions to a global phenomenon that shapes the doctrines and curricula of numerous Western militaries from Australia via Israel and several European countries to Canada and various branches of the US military.[1] Perusing these military documents, one finds them peppered with concepts from art and aesthetics. Mattis's emphasis on "creativity" and the "creative imagination" is matched by a vocabulary of genius, artistry, aesthetic pleasure, and virtuosity. If you attend a workshop or a conference on military design, you are as likely to hear references to Picasso as to tanks and tactics.

Entering the military brain is already a strange experience. As a field of knowledge, modern military discourse is replete with gnomical abbreviations, euphemisms, and abstractions that make warfare seem like anything but war. But this abstract discourse offers more than practical instructions. Where field manuals (such as the Army FM-5.0 that Mattis references in his memorandum) focus more on the concrete how-to dimension of warfare, doctrine expounds the military's basic assumptions of how the world works. It articulates, both implicitly and explicitly, a particular vision of the martial world: of its structure, its logic, and its functioning. Military theory more broadly, but doctrine in particular, embodies various "onto-epistemological assumptions," as one proponent of design has put it—a set of beliefs about what the world looks like and what we can know about it.[2] Moreover, the practical nature of war means that military discourse has a practical component built into it. What war is and what we can know about war are tied directly to the question of how military forces may act efficiently given the circumstances. Ontology, epistemology, and praxeology—being, knowledge, and action—are tightly connected in this field. They form a trinity in which one part cannot be meaningfully conceived without the other two.

To some extent, all scientific discourse contains an implicit normative element. By setting the parameters, possibilities, limits, and expectations for thought and behavior, scientific claims inevitably police the borders of the so-called objectivity they describe. The descriptive language of military thought, however, is not merely implicitly normative. Military doctrine has an explicitly prescriptive function: it produces templates for action. In this sense, military discourse is radically performative. It builds a vision of a world to be, a conceptual model to be enacted and realized. In the ideal military world, the "desired system" or "friendly desired system" is the performative realization of a strategy developed within the basic worldview of the doctrine.[3] Military doctrine thereby includes descriptions of what it takes the world to be and how we may know the world, as well as prescriptions for the world it wants to create.

The language of military doctrine has an unusually powerful force. As the brain of the military body, doctrine connects directly to the individual branches—that is, it connects directly to its own enforcement. The transformative power of language is therefore more than an ideal or a purely linguistic operation. We are dealing with a discourse that, perhaps more than in any other field, contains an inherent force—at the end of its language there is an army attached to do the dirty work. This evidently raises the stakes tremendously. The vocabulary of doctrine, its understanding of the nature of war, and the particular version of the world it seeks to enforce have immediate real-world consequences. As Mattis warned, the price of misapplied concepts is paid in human lives.

The military's resurrection of the specter of art is a both strange and remarkable fact. Why do militaries in the twenty-first century seek recourse to aesthetic design concepts to tackle complex challenges of global warfare? The wider commercial and entrepreneurial investment in design in recent years and the fact that, as a concept, design is so broad that it can be applied as a tool in innumerable fields and contexts go some way to explain its appeal to military thinkers. But, as we shall see, "design" also designates a segue between traditional aesthetics and practical functionality. Design itself merges the autonomous realm of art with the world of praxis. From this point of view, the discourse on design seems ideally suited for military co-option. In this chapter, I examine the work that aesthetic design concepts perform once they are taken from their original habitat and released in the fields of military theory and doctrine. Evidently, the contemporary co-option of aesthetics by the military repeats and gives a new inflection to the problems that earlier aesthetic theories of war also encountered, as we saw in the previous chapter. But the character of these problems also takes its shape from the particular nature of design as a military discourse or even a field in its own right. Let us first look at how this field emerged and developed such that the concept of "design" could land on Mattis's desk and seem a desirable conceptual solution to the so-called wicked problems that beset the US military.

A BRIEF HISTORY OF MILITARY DESIGN

Military design is a curious bastard of systems theory and aesthetics, born in Israel and raised in the US.[4] In 1995, the retired brigadier general Shimon Naveh of the Israeli Defense Forces (IDF) founded a think tank, the Operational Theory Research Institute. Via this institution, Naveh propagated a new approach to warfare called Systemic Operational Design. Fearing that it would stifle creative discussion, Naveh was hesitant to publish his ideas. In early 2005, however, he taught his theory to a group of US and British officers prior to a war-gaming exercise. They in turn published their understanding of the theory later that year.[5] Here is their definition of Systemic Operational Design:

> Systemic Operational Design (SOD) is an application of systems theory to operational art. It is an attempt to rationalize complexity through systemic logic employing a holistic approach that translates strategic direction and policy into operational level designs.[6]

The goal of Systemic Operational Design, in other words, was to create a "holistic design" or frame for a military intervention or a war, which was in turn conceived as an open system of constantly evolving elements. An advanced form of problem solving, Systemic Operational Design emphasized reflection, inviting personnel to rethink and reset a given problem, rather than simply solving it by conventional methods. And as opposed to concrete planning, which Naveh conceived as a linear, mechanical process organized into a process of sequential steps, the holistic form of Systemic Operational Design stressed the elusive logic of the (war) system particularly in urban warfare: nonlinearity, emergent properties, change, and surprise were its constituent elements.

The intellectual pedigree of Systemic Operational Design was unusual to say the least. As Eyal Weizman has documented, Naveh borrowed several of his ideas from French postmodern philosophers such as Guy Debord, Gilles Deleuze and Félix Guattari, and the deconstructive architect Bernard Tschumi.[7] Importing concepts from *Difference and Repetition*, Deleuze's radical ontology of difference, and Deleuze and Guattari's *A Thousand Plateaus*, an antistate manifesto if ever there was one, the Israeli state adopted poststructuralist concepts such as deterritorialization, nomadic terrorists, smooth and striated space, and the war machine and brought them to the urban warfare with the Palestinians and Hezbollah. As Naveh puts it in an interview with Weizman:

> Several of the concepts in *A Thousand Plateaus* became instrumental for us [in the IDF] . . . allowing us to explain contemporary situations in a way that we could not have otherwise explained. . . . In the IDF we now often use the term "to smooth out space" when we want to refer to operation in a space in such a manner that borders do not affect us. . . . Rather than contain and organize our forces according to existing borders, we want to move through them.[8]

In the attack on the West Bank city of Nablus in 2002, French poststructuralist concepts were then quite literally blowing holes in the walls of civilian homes, as the Israeli military sought to deal with the contingency and unpredictability of urban warfare by avoiding the open streets and moving through the apartment walls of domestic interiors. Naveh's invention of Systemic Operational Design, then, co-opted philosophical concepts in the service of a spatial strategy. Armed with these concepts, Israeli military leadership transformed space from being merely the site of war to being the medium of war—a medium that through microtactical destructive acts could be reinterpreted, reorganized, and reshaped. The Israeli Defense Forces thereby imbued these theoretical concepts with a force that their originators in faraway France could only have dreamed of. But the Israeli Defense Forces also left behind an untheorized rubble, a trail of destruction through entire neighborhoods—the collateral damage of French theory gone to war.

The tactical success of Systemic Operational Design proved short-lived. During the 2006 Israel-Hezbollah War, the technical and at times abstruse language of poststructuralist theory that dominated leadership at the Operational Theory Research Institute proved incomprehensible to the soldiers on the ground. As Weizman recounts, one of the leading officers, Gal Hirsh, issued an instruction that among other things demanded the "systemic-spatial deconstruction of the enemy infrastructure."[9] The defeat not only led to his forced resignation; it also tainted Naveh's theory and gave the upper hand to more conservative, empirically minded officers within the Israeli Defense Forces who wanted nothing to do with Systemic Operational Design.

And yet the result of the Lebanese War and the closure of the Operational Theory Research Institute already some weeks before the war in May 2006 did not hinder the further development of design thinking—quite the contrary. Naveh's invitation to the US brought his ideas from the Israeli Defense Forces to new fertile grounds. In 2006, revised versions of joint publication (JP) 3–0 and 5–0 included sections on operational design, as did publications from the Marine Corps; the US Army Training and Doctrine Command, or TRADOC, also began discussing military design under the name "campaign design," as signaled by the pamphlet *Commander's Appreciation and Campaign Design* (CACD) published in early 2008. Soon SAMS, the US Army's School for Advanced Military Studies, was charged with developing design further. As part of what was, in Mattis's words, a "multi-year design initiative," SAMS developed a whole design curriculum with a twenty-four-lesson design course; it held twenty-five seminars on design and wrote monographs and articles to promote the theory. Indeed, as the director of the school put it, "Our graduates have taken it straight from the classroom to the battlefields in Iraq and Afghanistan."[10] By March 2010, the US Army formally incorporated design into its doctrine in the form of a simplified

Army Design Methodology, and the US Joint Forces Command began advocating for its adoption throughout the armed forces. As one military educator put it, "Operational design is perhaps the single most important transformation emerging in joint doctrine."[11] In the US, design theory has since burgeoned into the global phenomenon it has become today. In the past decade, a host of Western militaries, including NATO, have adopted the discourse of design in its various local forms.[12] Even if its claims are often vastly exaggerated—theorists, for example, speak of a "design revolution" and compare it to "the rise of scientific thinking" in preindustrial military societies—military design nevertheless has a significant and growing influence on Western militaries.[13]

Across this discourse, design emerges as the answer to a problematic shift in the character of war in the twenty-first century. In hindsight, the Cold War offered a relatively stable model of conflict, one that lent itself to prediction. Whether framed by cybernetics or systems analysis, the theory of war was governed by a scientific ideal which suggested that war as a linear and well-structured phenomenon could be fully controlled through modeling and detailed sequential planning. Although the numerous civil wars that followed in the aftermath of the Cold War put pressure on this conception of war, after the turn of the century the so-called revolution in military affairs revived the dream of total control through informational-technological superiority.[14] Yet the protracted, uncontrollable, and seemingly endless wars in Iraq and Afghanistan punctured such ideals. Concepts such as effects-based operations (EBO), operational net assessment (ONA), or system of systems analysis (SoSA) that assumed a high degree of predictability and a solid knowledge base proved inadequate to deal with the complexity of globalized war in the twenty-first century. When Mattis banished these concepts from US doctrine in 2008, it was because they no longer fit the changed character of war. The mesh of new technologies, mass media, competing ideologies, and nonstate actors had given rise to a new epistemology: war appeared as a profoundly uncertain phenomenon, pervaded by chance and shot through with unpredictable events. Moving on from the linearity of predictable causes and effects that dominated US military thought during the second half of the twentieth century, military institutions in the twenty-first century think of war in terms of nonlinearity, complexity, contingency, and chaos. As Antoine Bousquet has put it, war has become *chaoplexic*.[15]

How do you handle this complexity? As General David Barno notes, the erosion of traditional notions of war has left a conceptual gap: "In the aftermath of the relative certainty of doctrine, training, tactics, adversary, and known terrain of the Cold War, our military today is in a sense operating without a concept of war and is searching desperately for the new 'unified field theory' of conflict."[16] This is where design enters the picture. Faced with a complexity and a pervasive uncertainty that have rendered traditional concepts useless, military thinkers introduce design as a tool to manage the chaos of twenty-first-century warfare. Compared to Naveh's curious construct of systems theory and French philosophy, however, recent versions of design theory have developed the concept in a new direction. Even though Deleuze and Guattari's concept of the nomad still resonates in the military design community,[17] the current discourse on military design has downplayed the at times esoteric language of French philosophy for which Naveh was criticized and replaced it with a new and more accessible vocabulary from the field of art and aesthetics: intuition, imagination, and creativity are among the new skills required to deal with contingency and complexity. Mattis's invocation of the "creative imagination" is merely the tip of the iceberg. In spite of the dry, matter-of-fact style of official military discourse, one of the first official documents to adopt the language of design, TRADOC Pamphlet 525-5-500, *Commander's Appreciation and Campaign Design* (CACD), referenced creativity, intuition, and genius as key concepts as well as architects and industrial designers as models for the "operational artists" performing military design.[18] Over against simple, mechanical, linear problem solving, which the document associates with engineering and the "science of war," it inscribes design as an element in the "art of war"—an element that becomes the moniker for the creative, imaginative, rule-breaking skills that modern warfare requires. As the graphic shows, the opposition of art and science, designing and engineering is directly correlated with the new episteme of complexity.

The CACD thereby revives the old art–science debate and argues that the idea of war as a practical art must be reimplanted into military discourse after decades of modeling and detailed planning that followed a scientific ideal of complete knowledge and full control. But it also links war with the tradition of art and aesthetics. Already in this early official document, design comes to designate a process of artistic creation

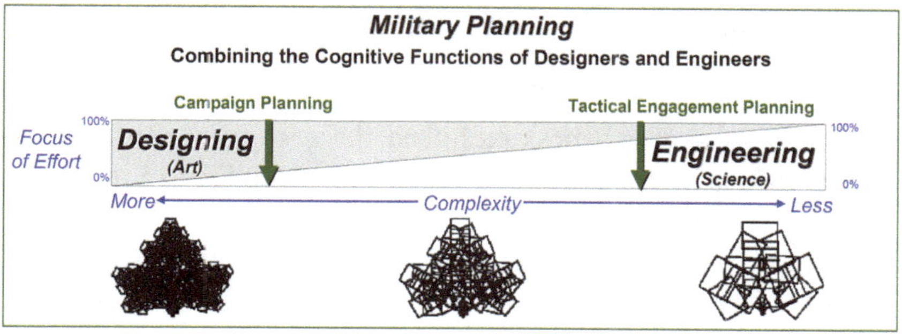

FIGURE 5.1. Military planning according to the United States Army Training and Doctrine Command. Source: US Army, TRADOC Pamphlet 525-5-500, *The U.S. Army Commander's Appreciation and Campaign Design*, 14.

analogous to that of creative artists. Here is how the document defines *design* in its glossary of key terms:

> As used in creative endeavors such as art and architecture, the act of working out the form of something (visualizing), requiring considerable research, thought, modeling, iterative adjustments and re-design to pull together the rational with the natural; intended to guide the making of something else. It is a basic scheme or pattern that affects and controls function or development; it reflects the purposeful or inventive arrangement of parts or details toward an intended purpose.[19]

In other words, the authors trace the meaning of "design" to the realm of the arts and define it as the creative process of making and remaking a given thing or phenomenon by giving it shape and form. In addition to systems theory, then, the background and key template on which the discourse of design is modeled is aesthetics. Waging war in the twenty-first century, according to the CACD, is a matter of inspired form-giving, of intuition, creativity, artistry, and play—it is a matter of design.[20]

THE INTELLECTUAL HISTORY OF DESIGN

Where do these ideas come from? Given the new episteme of uncertainty and complexity and the recourse to theories of war as an art both in the pragmatic and the aesthetic sense of the term, it is little surprise that Carl von Clausewitz has returned as the master thinker for proponents of military design. In his two memoranda, for example, General Mattis refers both to Clausewitz's "trinity of chance, uncertainty and chaos" and to his notion of "the commander's coup d'oeil," a key component in the Prussian's conception of genius.[21] Already in Clausewitz's *On War*, epistemology and aesthetics were linked: the episteme of war—the "empire of chance" as he labeled it—could only be handled by a theoretical framing of warfare as an art, drawing on both the pragmatic and the aesthetic understanding of the term.[22] Military discourse in the twenty-first century has revived this link as aesthetic concepts inherent to design are invoked as the answer to the contingency of contemporary warfare. When the CACD refers to "intuition" and "genius" as fundamental to the new focus on the *art* of war, the reference to the Prussian thinker is almost a matter of course.[23] The *Planner's Handbook for Operational Design* issued by the Joint Chiefs of Staff in 2011 stresses "the importance of the underlying creative process"[24] and of "the creative imagination"[25] to meet the unpredictable and uncontrollable nature of contemporary warfare. It defines operational design as "a methodology that extends operational art's creative thinking and intuition,"[26] and it proceeds to argue that "the commander should be the central figure of design"—once again with reference to Clausewitz and his notion of the genius's "coup d'oeil."[27] In this way, the handbook summons the military theory developed against the background of Napoleonic mass warfare and imbued with the discourse of aesthetics as the response to the challenges of twenty-first-century global warfare.

The invocation of design, however, comes with an intellectual baggage of its own. Design emerged in the first half of the twentieth century as a reaction against industrial production. The raw functionality of the objects and consumer goods mass-produced by industry was met with an increased focus on the aesthetic qualities of things. The Arts and Crafts movement, Russian constructivism, and Bauhaus shared a common interest in dissolving the borders that had been erected between work and art, between artisanal objects and artworks, between the practical and the aesthetic. The educational program in Bauhaus, for example, involved the training not only of artistic but also of artisanal and technical skills that from the outset established the conditions for the merger of the *ars liberales* and the *ars mechanicae*. In this way, the transfer of the aesthetic to everyday-use objects is key to the concept of design. As Reckwitz puts it: "It is not the artwork that is in focus but the aesthetically formed use object, not the autonomous ideal alternative world, but the aestheticization of the practical world of things."[28]

Whereas the emergence of design in the first half of the twentieth century focused on infusing concrete practical objects with an added aesthetic value, during the second half of the century, the aesthetic dimension became the key element. With the rise of the creative economy, the ambit of design expanded markedly as the basic value of an increasing number of products was no longer the practical function they performed but their aesthetic quality. As a result, the notion of design was generalized and abstracted into a master concept for a number of different fields. Delivering a nominal promise of creativity, beauty, pleasure, and craftsmanship, design has made inroads into everything from the service industry to management theory.[29] Today, design seems to be everywhere. Industrial design, business design, finance design, experience design—the list goes on. Colonizing these diverse fields, design has thereby detached itself from its original anchor in concrete objects and has become a general methodology that goes by the name of "design thinking." As such it can be applied virtually everywhere if only the argument can be made that traditional, staid, mechanical processes of thought should make room for an injection of creativity, innovation, and out-of-the-box thinking. The object of design is no longer an object, so to speak, but a much broader and more diffuse array of phenomena, processes, ensembles, relations, and experiences that can all be designed *as* an object.[30] One of the recent sprouts of design thinking, design management, for example, installs design as an ineluctable management technique for any company that wishes to succeed. In opposition to rigid, hierarchical bureaucratic structures, design management calls for teams of creative designers to devise innovative solutions to issues through creative thinking and imaginative experiments. In *The Art of Innovation: Lessons in Creativity from IDEO*, an influential book on design management, Tom Kelley argues that such innovative solutions emerge in collaborative settings that gather creative teams or "hot groups."[31] Modeled not on the individual artist but on the artist collective, the "hot group" profits from the combined creativity of the company workers to solve the problem. In this way, design management performs a double aestheticization. On the one hand, it aestheticizes the product the company delivers—be it a service, a function, or an experience—*as if* it were an object. Part of the appeal of the design discourse is that it seems to transform complex, functional, and often boring management activities into a slick aesthetic object. It turns a sales strategy for refrigerators from a messy array of numbers, Excel charts, and customer surveys into a thing of beauty. On the other hand, and at the same time, it recasts company workers as creative artists. The lone sales representative crunching numbers is enrolled in a collective of intuitive designers who express their unique talents as part of a creative process.

Design, then, aestheticizes objects and phenomena that are at the outset very far removed from the realm of aesthetics; it gives promises of strategic success and individual self-realization through creativity, intuition, and innovation; and it serves as a mediator between aesthetics and praxis. Through the discourse of design, the world of practical affairs is reframed as an art object to be shaped and molded on par with the work of the sculptor, the architect, the composer, the painter, or the writer. As one design theorist puts it, "I think of design as a kind of creative, imaginative authoring practice."[32]

These are the ideas that have come to shape the most recent field to be colonized by design thinking: war. Not only the CACD but also doctrines such as the joint publication 5–0, *Joint Operations Planning* and *Army Doctrine Publication (ADP) 5–0: The Operations Process*; manuals such the *Army FM 3–0* and *Field Manual 5–0* as well as *Army Design Methodology*; and textbook material such as *Art of Design Version 2.0, SAMS*, have all adopted the concepts and language of design. Surrounding these official documents, a wider discussion of military design has flourished in academic articles, books, online essays, and discussion forums. Some of these documents reflect more explicitly on the origins of design discourse and note the strangeness of its appearance within military theory. The Hague Center for Strategic Studies, for example, has issued the book *Designing Future Stabilization Efforts* in which its authors introduce strategic design in the following terms:

> Many readers may be surprised to see the term design associated with military planning. When most people think about military planning, they typically think of military staffs huddled over a set of maps to come up with an optimal course of action for an operation. When they think of design, they are much more likely to think of imaginative designers creating hip and cool designs for mobile phones, interior deco-

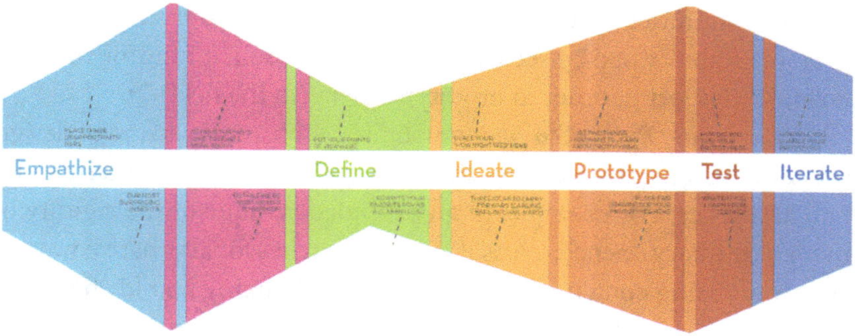

FIGURE 5.2. Design thinking according to the K12 Lab at Stanford Design School. Source: https://dschool-old.stanford.edu/groups/k12/wiki/6c04c/Visual_Resources.html. CC BY-SA 3.0. The image is reproduced in Stephan De Spiegeleire, Tim Sweijs, Peter Wijninga, and Joris Van Esch, *Designing Future Stabilisation Efforts* (The Hague: The Hague Center for Strategic Studies, 2014), 17.

> rating or architecture. And yet these two at first sight totally different terms have grown closer to each other over the past few years, even to the extent that the US Army now has an official Army Design Methodology that is used for operational planning purposes.[33]

Without giving further thought to the disjunctive relationship between war and design, however, the authors trace design thinking to Tim Brown's *Change by Design* and his consultancy IDEO, and they discuss different ways of conceiving the process of design thinking. This includes a brightly colored visualization developed by the Stanford Design School.

The illustration adorns the cover of the book and is juxtaposed with a drawing of the Sydney Opera House, Jørn Utzon's architectural design icon. The graphic visualizes the process of design thinking through a series of verbs from "empathize" via "ideate" to "iterate," and in the book itself the authors describe the process with reference to another designer, Jeanne Liedtka, and her book *Solving Problems with Design Thinking.* She boils the process down to four basic questions: "What is?" "What if?" "What wows?" "What works?" The authors then apply these ideas from design and business—including "the wow zone"—to war. In the process they cast the inhabitants of a war-torn country as the "end user" and "security customer" and speculate on crowdfunding security measures through "defense- or security-related Kickstarter-like websites where local communities in conflict zones could develop promising ideas that promote stability and/or security and then also solicit funding or other forms of support in order to prototype them (in the field)."[34]

In *Designing Future Stabilization Efforts*, a business version of design shapes how war is framed, but the more common influence is from art and aesthetics. For example, in an extended critique of the rigidity of modern military science, Chris Paparone searches for alternative ways of conceptualizing contemporary warfare.[35] Exchanging an old "modernist" paradigm based on positivistic science, predictability, modeling, and forecasting with military design, Paparone delves deep into the arts and humanities to explain the nature of the new paradigm. Military interventions should be interpreted as "artfully crafted and aesthetically pleasing." They are "artful actions" with "aesthetic qualities," and they involve creativity and "improvisation-in-action."[36] Because this general "move toward artistry"[37] involves a vocabulary that is lacking in the traditional military vocabulary, Paparone looks to the liberal arts and humanities for language that can be mined for useful concepts. In particular he turns to art metaphors. Describing war first through the prism of the "performing arts" and "dramaturgy," he proceeds to music.[38] Like that of Maximilian Jähns, Paparone's metaphor casts warfare as a traditional symphony, but also, to signal the new paradigm, in a more up-to-date version as a jazz improvisation:

> Should generals ORCHESTRATE operations (i.e. generals are CONDUCTORS, plans are SHEET MUSIC) or should they be more like JAZZ IMPROVISATIONALISTS who allow the MUSIC to FLOW more freely, permitting other MEMBERS OF THE BAND to assume the LEAD PLAYER where it feels right (i.e. military officers are JAZZ CLUB owners, who provide the ATMOSPHERE where MUSIC can FLOW)? . . . Leader activities in combat are like playing jazz: discovering goals, creating/changing procedures/rules, mixing the expected with the novel, and so forth.[39]

In this way, the US military intervention in Haiti in 1994 and the US Army's Ninth Infantry Division operations in the Mekong Delta during the Vietnam War become improvisations "from old concepts into jazz-like extensions."[40]

The extent to which military design is modeled directly on the fine arts is particularly evident when Paparone turns to the visual arts. Referring to two scholars who discuss the metaphorical potentials of painting, Paparone finds that their account fits so well with his conception of military design that he simply replaces the terms while quoting their article:

> The article continues, and I substitute "Military Design" terms here for "painting," "researchers," and "social scientists" (which, for all intents and purposes, are the alter egos of military designers): . . . "The painting metaphor lends a new vision to the argument that [designing] itself is a method of inquiry, a way of looking at worldmaking. If [Military Design is] part of how [military designers] "see" their phenomena, then methodology becomes central to the question of what [military designers] produce, and the painting metaphor, being a means of rendering methodologies visible, has an important role to play.[41]

Thus military design takes on the function of painting. The terms are fungible. Paparone, in his own words, explicitly mines the "creative processes of painting, composing, music, poetry" in order to seize hold of "aesthetic metaphor[s] borrowed from the humanities and fine arts" and use these metaphors to establish the new paradigm of military design.[42] Such metaphors are more than simple linguistic turns of phrase. They are cognitive devices that structure the discourse of design at a fundamental level. Thus, as Paparone puts it, "art [is] a mainstay of Military Design."[43] Indeed, he cites John Dewey's analysis of the nature of aesthetics in *Art as Experience* in order to explain the unique aesthetic quality of military action.[44] In the end, the whole theoretical exercise is about transforming military leadership into "an art form."[45]

SUBJECTIVE DESIGN

The books, articles, pamphlets, and doctrinal statements on military design reveal the contours of a sometimes implicit but most often explicit aesthetic theory of war. Ostensibly a method for disrupting traditional habits of thinking and solving complex problems that cannot be handled with the standard repertoire of planning and prediction, military design frames war as an art form, an aesthetic phenomenon to be understood and managed with the conceptual tools offered by the fine arts. But as an aesthetic theory of war, military design comes in two conflicting versions: on the one hand, it theorizes the subjects of war—generals, officers, soldiers; and on the other, it theorizes the object of war—the strategy or campaign. In other words, the war artist versus the work of art.

Subjective design, as we might call the former component, is directly linked to the Clausewitzian epistemology of contingency and chaos. Detailed, analytic sequential planning is seen as pointless when everything in flux. The world will look different already after the first step has been taken, and thus the very parameters and foundations the whole plan was built on will have shifted. Military designers therefore take note of a warning articulated by Hannah Arendt. In *On Violence,* Arendt (herself a good Clausewitzian) writes:

> Predictions of the future are never anything but projections of present automatic processes and procedures, that is, of occurrences that are likely to come to pass if men do not act and if nothing unexpected happens; every action, for better or worse, and every accident necessarily destroys the whole pattern in whose frame the prediction moves and where it finds its evidence.[46]

Within such a logic of events pervaded by volatility, uncertainty, complexity, and ambiguity (high VUCA), military design responds with the notion of "artistry." To act and react in the chaotic, nonlinear environment of twenty-first-century warfare, soldiers must cultivate the intuitive, creative skills of an artist. As described in Richard Swain's *Fundamentals of Operational Design*,

> The function of design in operational art is to produce the skills that [James J.] Schneider, referring to U.S. Grant, lists for operational artists: the "unified and holistic approach in the design, execution, and sustainment of their campaigns. They have had that intuitive ability to render incomplete and ambiguous information into a meaningful impression of the true state of affairs in their theater of operations."[47]

One of the explicit goals of *Army Design Methodology* is also to set the stage for the development of these skills, helping soldiers "'break their frame'" to "encourage creative thinking."[48] The checklist of desired skills and characteristics of the members of a design team includes the following:

✓ Having an open mind and room for new ideas
✓ Having an inquisitive mindset; being curious and eager for knowledge

✓ Being comfortable with ambiguity
✓ Possessing creative—and innovative—thinking skills.[49]

Army Design Methodology further speaks of the importance of having a "creative" on the team.[50] As Dan Öberg has rightly put it, "The ideal military designer is characterized by a spirit of free thinking, creativity, and artistry. He or she is taken to display unique vision, to embrace chaos, and to look for root causes of military problems without being locked into rigid and linear thinking."[51]

Military design is framed as an ongoing artistic process—the repeated creative acts of inventing radically new solutions to the wicked problems that continue to emerge from the chaos of contemporary war. In this subjective conception, "the art of design," as two proponents put it, "is a way of thinking,"[52] and "designing," as the textbook written at SAMS states, "is a form of artistry."[53] In these attempts to reframe military activities as an artistic process, the frame of art often comes to block out the actual phenomenon it frames. The somber discussion of how to mete out violence through armed force is dissolved by or even transformed into the vocabulary of creativity, intuition, art, and artistry, as when Paparone concludes his chapter on artistic metaphors by encouraging fellow design theorists "to generate and explore exciting metaphors and invent breathtakingly rich eloquence in postinstitutional Military Design."[54] In this way, the wholesale transformation of soldiers and military thinkers into "designers" and "artists" is simply a natural extension of the aesthetic frame. Seeking to persuade the Swedish military leadership to adopt military design, for example, Ben Zweibelson—the program director of design thinking at US Special Operations Commands Joint Special Operations University—along with three centrally placed Swedish military officers and researchers, encourage the leaders to join "the design revolution" and "grow a small yet influential group of Swedish designers."[55]

It is perhaps little surprise, then, that the design theorists explicitly model themselves on artistic movements and figures. In the quest to introduce design into Western military institutions, they position themselves as forming a disruptive intellectual avant-garde within the military establishment,[56] an avant-garde that is at once "visionary" and "ostracized" if not "punished" due to its radical ideas.[57] As three officers put it, military design has for decades formed "an underground movement comprised of heretics, outsiders and trouble-makers," but the future will prove that military design is like other avant-garde movements that were "later revered by subsequent generations that benefited from their willingness to challenge the system at great personal sacrifice."[58]

At the same time, military designers model themselves on the Romantic figure of the creative genius. Although military design is often organized in collective group sessions, the image of the inspired individual artist keeps appearing. Zweibelson, again, offers his theory:

> Creativity is, in my opinion something often occurring individually instead of in group settings. This is based on a lifetime of being an artist, plus four-and-a-half years of college education as a graphic designer and fine arts major, along with my over 18 years in the military. One might enjoy inspiration in a group setting, but for me, creativity is an internal function of intelligence, experimentation, visualization, inspiration, and creation and destruction.[59]

Zweibelson relates his experience of a design exercise at the US Army School of Advanced Military Studies (SAMS) and how he felt the need to break away from his assigned group to think for himself. Only then did he reach "creative discoveries"[60] and—the following day—even a "creative breakthrough,"[61] which he in turn shared with the group. Zweibelson sums up the design process like this:

> In the end, it was a journey where I wandered into the fog, made observations and created things, and walked "back to base camp" to talk by the fire with my fellow travelers. They helped me make sense of whether I was on the right track, but then I went back out into the mist, alone, to continue to create.[62]

With reference to Jacques Rancière's *The Ignorant Schoolmaster*, Zweibelson argues that it is key for military design to acknowledge "the creativity that exists within all humans."[63] Ultimately, the goal of military design is for soldiers to get "in touch with their true creative potential."[64] Indeed, in the broader design community, Naveh is credited as the originator of an "intellectual emancipatory project" that enables officers to transgress their own biases and prejudices in order "to be liberated" and to "reach individual and professional potentials more fully."[65]

The discourse of military design thus inscribes itself into the longer tradition of aesthetic theories of war from Rühle and Clausewitz via Mahan and Jähns to Mrazek. Ostensibly a method for solving complex problems, it consistently evokes the skills of intuition, creativity, imagination, rule-breaking, and genius associated since the eighteenth century with the artist and claims them for the military designer. The subject of war is reframed as a war artist who has the opportunity to unleash his or her creative potential when freed from the constraints of rigid military bureaucracy, discipline, and regimentation of thought. The figure of the liberated artist becomes the model par excellence for modern soldiers. Indeed, through this transfiguration of violence into artistry, warfare, as in some of the earlier aesthetic theories of war from the nineteenth and twentieth centuries, is seen as a realm of creative self-realization—"a journey of discovery" and "an intellectual, emotional, and emancipatory experience."[66] With Play-Doh, cardboard, tape, Legos, Post-it notes, Tinkertoys, and other tools of modern creatives, military design invites everyone to truly be all you can be—an artist.

OBJECTIVE DESIGN

Artists produce works of art. While military design frames the subjects of war—generals, officers, and soldiers—as war artists, the curious combination of systems theory and aesthetics also reframes the object of their design efforts: the nature of war itself. Once again the premise for this reframing is the onto-epistemology of contingency and chaos. For the war artist, artistry and creative design were the necessary answers to handle the pervasive uncertainties of an environment in flux. But for military designers, the chaos of twenty-first-century warfare also presents an opportunity. Across doctrines, manuals, and the wider discourse on design, war is frequently conceived as the imposition of a distinct form on a fluctuating, but pliable and uniform, material. Enemy territories, armies, populations, infrastructure, and interests are atomized into an indistinguishable mass. The repeated invocation of "chaos" does not merely denote an epistemological problem—the difficulty of obtaining secure, validated knowledge—but a state of being in the biblical sense: a formless mass, a pure matter that precedes and awaits creation by a form-giving power. This is where military design steps in. In addition to designating a (creative) process, military design involves the production of a thing, a conceptual object, often represented graphically, variously called a "campaign design," a "design concept," or simply "the Design."[67] The purpose of this conceptual object, as two military design theorists put it, is to "organize interventions as patterns in space and time."[68] Or, as another theorist puts it, "Design is all about helping the commander to create his or her vision of a future campaign or operation," and this entails developing an "operation framing" that "stipulates the form, as a pattern of actions in space and time, to be performed in a particular ensemble, to transform the existing situation into the desired state."[69] The accompanying references to architects and the Sydney Opera House are echoed by a student of military design who summarizes its purpose thus: "When applying military design you become the architect of your own battlespace."[70]

Within this frame, the military emerges as a secular creator who—following a formalist aesthetic—imposes abstract patterns on the pliable, atomized, fluctuating matter and shapes it into a stable form. Out of chaos, the "operational artist" fashions a work of art.[71] The abstract formalism of this way of conceiving warfare is evident in the diagrams that often supplement the theorizing. The figure here illustrates the various "elements of design" that designers may avail themselves of in order to shape and bring into being the "desired state" of the system.

The aesthetic formalism underlying these endeavors has two corollaries. First, the design view of war as the imposition of ordered patterns and forms onto a chaotic matter signals a vision of autonomy and control. Curiously, by atomizing war into pure chaos, what is resistant and intractable is flattened into a uniform, passive material that lends itself to, almost invites, free creative form-giving. As Banach and Ryan put it: "Designers determine their own purpose; therefore they set their own problems."[72] This belief in the freedom and autonomy of the military designer to set their own tasks is at odds with the rationale behind subjective design—specifically, the idea that the complexity of contemporary warfare allows only creative reactions to unpredictable developments that the military cannot plan for. Objective design, however, transforms this open-ended process into a self-contained product. Indeed, design becomes the conceptual tool to shape chaos into an artifact. By constructing war as a conceptual artifact, military design discourse invents a linguistic analog to the technological artifacts of VR simulations and other training scenarios we saw earlier.[73] In this way, design serves as a conceptual

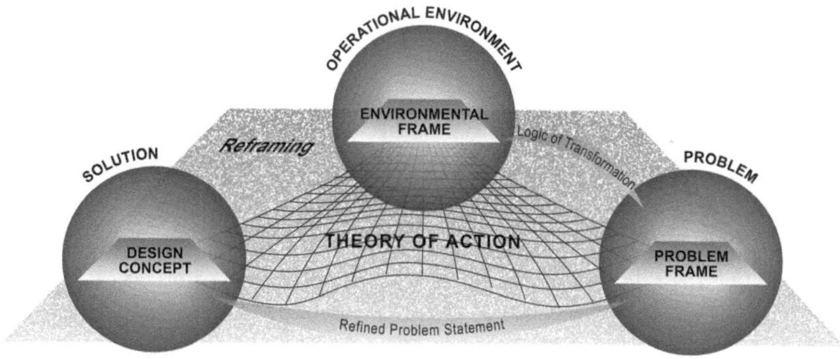

FIGURE 5.3. Warfare according to military design. Source: Stefan J. Banach and Alex Ryan, "The Art of Design. A Design Methodology," *Military Review* (March-April 2009), 114.

contingency medium. Earlier, horoscopes, maps, and wargames served as material contingency media to enable strategic thought and action under conditions of uncertainty. With "design," however, the military has developed a linguistic tool to handle a world perceived as radically contingent. But if subjective design invoked artistry, creativity, and intuition to help navigate an ocean of contingency, objective design seeks to abolish contingency altogether. Shaping the raw material of chaos into a well-ordered artifact of coherent patterns and forms, design reclaims the control it had relinquished to its onto-epistemology of contingency and flux. With artistry and creativity, military design shapes the "fog, friction, and chaos," which Mattis diagnosed as the essence of modern warfare, into a work of art.[74]

The aesthetic formalism of military design in turn has a second corollary. Once the artifact of design has emerged from the imposition of forms and patterns on the chaos of matter, it serves as a form of *prescriptive worldmaking.* The design serves as the blueprint for a world to be realized or "implemented."[75] As Banach and Ryan put it, "Whereas scientists describe how the world is, designers suggest how it might be."[76] Design, in other words, creates models of future worlds, and, ideally, it serves as a catalyst to transform a martial imaginary into actuality. In this, the discourse of design is once again the conceptual analog of the technological artifacts of simulations and wargames. Like them, design is engaged in a form of worldmaking whose task is to imagine how the actual world might be different, to build a new version as an imaginary martial artifact and to realize it.

This is the point where design takes traditional aesthetics one step further. Unlike the autonomous imaginary worlds of the fine arts, military design is committed to the real. Its vision of generative worldmaking undoes the distinctions that the aesthetic philosophers were at pains to establish, and it deploys the vocabulary of aesthetics for practical purposes. The broader frame of design is indeed well suited to effect this shift, for, as we saw, from the very beginning design has merged aesthetics and functionality.[77] But the generative vision of martial worldmaking inherent to military design also trades on more recent ideas within design thinking. In 2005, the term *design fiction* was coined by Bruce Sterling in his book *Shaping Things*, and a few years later, in 2009, it was firmly established by Julian Bleecker in his influential "Design Fiction. A Short Essay on Design, Science, Fact and Fiction."[78] Using fiction in a broad sense to designate any kind of medium that can build an imaginary world, Bleecker examines how such fictions can be adopted and paired with design practices in order to imagine and realize created futures: "How can design participate in shaping possible near future worlds? How can the integration of story telling, technology, art and design provide opportunities to re-imagine how the world may be in the future?"[79] This integration of elements results in a curious hybrid state of being, a mode that hovers between the imaginary and the actual, the present and the future. While the products of design fiction are material and real, they are also imaginative models for a future yet to be realized. A hybrid phenomenon, design fiction thus operates "in a murky middle ground between ideas and their materialization."[80] This liminality, however, is precisely regarded as the particular advantage of design fiction. Through its fictional worlds, it functions as an imaginative matrix for the gestation of actual worlds to be. Or, to put it differently, design fiction is a tool for transforming fictions of the future into facts of the present. "Fiction," as Bleecker writes, "has real, material consequences."[81]

Harnessing the power of the imaginary, design fiction explicitly sets itself apart from futurologies based on predictive models of current behavior. For Bleecker, prediction of how events will unfold is beside the point. What matters is "a willfulness to create different worlds";[82] it is a matter of using fiction creatively to help bring about a future you have yourself designed. What matters is not what the world is or might develop into but how we want it to be. Like Nick Montfort's notion of "future-making," the overarching aim of design fiction is that of "imagining and materializing future habitable worlds."[83]

These ideas from the broader field of design thinking also pervade twenty-first-century warfare. Whether in the technological form of contemporary simulations and wargames operating in the liminal realm between fiction and fact or in the conceptual form of military design, war is construed as a generative worldmaking activity, as the creative design of an imaginary future that can subsequently be implemented. Like the technologies, the discourse of design thus establishes a particular vision of being and time. Building *factitious futures* with concepts rather than with high-tech media, military design similarly relies on an aesthetic onto-temporality according to which future worlds can be invented and realized by present creative fictions. Where the wargame emerged as a self-contained artifact that united autonomy, emotions, creativity, and play to generate an imaginary experiential world "of the future" to be implemented, design offers the theory of generative worldmaking that subtends it. The martial aesthetics of twenty-first-century warfare, then, involves both technology and ideas, co-opting aesthetic artifacts as practical tools and aesthetic theory as a new conceptual frame for military worldmaking.

MARTIAL AESTHETICS AND ONTOGENETIC WARFARE

Martial aesthetics thereby links up with a both wider and deeper political and military conception of war. This is the view that war is a productive political and social force that creates stability, order, and peace. Rather than a medium of destruction and suffering, war is installed as an obscure but potent and necessary force for the establishment of states, institutions, and national identities. Jens Bartelson has unearthed the historical trajectory of this view, which he summarizes in the following terms:

> [The] widespread belief in the destructiveness of war has been allowed to overshadow the existence of another way of viewing war that may help us understand why war came to be seen as a natural part of the human condition in the first place. This is the belief that war is a productive force in human affairs that ought to be harnessed for the right political purposes, such as the creation of order and peace . . . for want of a better term, I will henceforth refer to this view as ontogenetic war.[84]

At once a primordial force and the source of structure and meaning, war becomes "a means of imposing order onto chaos,"[85] a productive power that generates political order and stable, peaceful societies. Harking back to antiquity, the ontogenetic view of war was revived in the early modern period and dominated political thought in the modern period, during which it became widely accepted as a matter of course. Only with the invention of nuclear weapons after World War II did the productive view of war seem obsolete given the expected massive destruction of a thermonuclear attack.

In Bartelson's account, however, ontogenetic war has made a strong comeback since the end of the Cold War. Against the background of globalization, theorists have increasingly justified humanitarian interventions and processes of nation building in weak or failed states. Particularly in the wake of 9/11 and the ensuing war against terrorism, strategies emerged to rebuild failed states. The humanitarian discourse of the "lesser evil" bolstered such efforts with the moral argument that military intervention was not only allowed but a moral obligation in order to protect citizens of states unfit to take care of their own.[86] As part of the justification for military intervention and the transgression of national sovereignty, the ontogenetic view of war was revived. To remove the preconditions of violence and systemic failure, states must be "rebuilt more or less from scratch."[87] Behind the projects of state building and nation building we find once again the generative view of war as a productive force that imposes order and fashions stability and peace out of the chaos of violence into which failed states have degenerated.

In the political imaginary, ontogenetic war thus overlaps with the creative worldmaking of martial aesthetics. Indeed, we may regard the aesthetic frame of military design as a theoretical extension and reinforcement of the productive view of war. War is an obscure, impersonal, generative force, yes, but it does not produce a new sociopolitical order all by itself. For military designers, the force of war must be wielded properly, and to do so is a difficult art that requires original, creative, intuitive thinking. Supplementing the productive view of war with an aesthetic dimension, the design discourse installs soldiers and officers as the subjects of this force—the war artists—whose creative efforts in turn elevate the world they make into a carefully crafted work of art. Adding both a creative subject and an artfully crafted object to the theory of the generative force of war, military design functions as its aesthetic extension and enhancement.

Military design thereby takes ontogenetic war to a new level. For while the ontogenetic view of war is invoked to both explain and justify military efforts with reference to the responsibility to protect, martial aesthetics justifies war as an art form. As it transfigures violence into artistic matter, military design frames war not as a brutal act of military force and a means of last resort but as a virtuous and even desirable activity to be pursued for its own sake. Even if military design does not espouse the explicit aesthetic martialism of nineteenth- and twentieth-century military thinkers, its specter haunts the discourse. As Dan Öberg writes, military design "participates in creating an imaginary that risks justifying future wars as transgressive design projects."[88] Such projects, further, may not only invent new creative forms of violence hitherto unseen but also lead to vast imbalances between Western and non-Western militaries and skew the casualties and destruction they cause. When the Israeli military reinterpreted space according to early design theory during Operation Defensive Shield in the West Bank in spring 2002, Israel had four casualties, according to the UN, while the Palestinians counted 497 casualties. The Palestinian cities, Nablus in particular, suffered massive destruction of civilian buildings, leaving more than seventeen thousand people homeless.[89] The efforts to creatively optimize the war machine have so far shown little acknowledgment of the human lives at the end of the design experiments and little promise for a reduction of violence.

In a historical perspective, military design is merely the latest incarnation of the idea of war as an art form. As Rühle von Lilienstern some two hundred years ago inducted warfare into the temple of the arts and crowned it as the highest among them, military design lends war the noble, even auratic qualities of art. Where humanitarian warfare argues for war by reference to a calculus of deaths and the argument for the "lesser evil," creative warfare appears to eliminate evil entirely by transfiguring death and destruction into a productive, noble, even admirable activity. In this way, the praxeological understanding of the art of war yields to an aesthetic understanding of war as a fine art and its associated value system. Fueled by intuition, originality, and creativity, war is considered a subjectivizing and emancipatory force that makes artists out of soldiers and art out of violence. As an aesthetic phenomenon, war, it is thought, does not merely produce peace, stability, and order; these desiderata display a crafted beauty whose aura outshines the violent means that went into their creation. While several earlier theoretical attempts to merge war and art articulated an explicit justification for active military intervention, military design contains an implicit but pervasive aesthetic apologia for war.

Tracing the emergence, development, and current manifestations of martial aesthetics is an equally strange and troubling experience. On the one hand, the aesthetic dimension of warfare is a historical fact, as witnessed by the technologies and ideas that have shaped, and continue to shape, both military practice and military thought. This history has revealed that war has long been pervaded by imaginary worlds and aesthetic concepts, and it has shown that such "airy nothings" contain a powerful force of real-world change once they are harnessed to the military apparatus. Curiously, by mining aesthetics for its imaginary power, the military—of all institutions—reveals the sheer transformative power of the aesthetic imaginary when it eschews the traditional notions of autonomy and self-sufficiency and takes aesthetics into the wild.

At the same time, the militarization of aesthetics displays an obscene perversity, for all these attempts, historical and contemporary, to transmute destruction into creation and violence into art do not in any way change the fundamentals of war. In the end, none of the technologies or ideas of martial aesthetics sweep away the principles, logics, and effects of violent force, coercion, and destruction. If we even briefly connect the theoretical abstractions with the grim realities on the ground, we are faced with a truly monstrous artwork shaped out of the blood and the bones, the traumas and the nightmares of men, women, and children, of soldiers and civilians alike. While repeatedly quoting Clausewitz on the art of war, military designers uniformly ignore his critical caveat—that the comparison of warfare to an art form leads to a series of false analogies and that, in the end, it should be abandoned. As he writes: "It is futile, even wrong, to try to turn a blind eye to the brutality of war because of unwillingness to accept its true nature."[90]

If we insist on framing war as an art form, however, and follow through with the analogy, the abstract illustrations that accompany military design with their curious blend of systems theory and aesthetics find

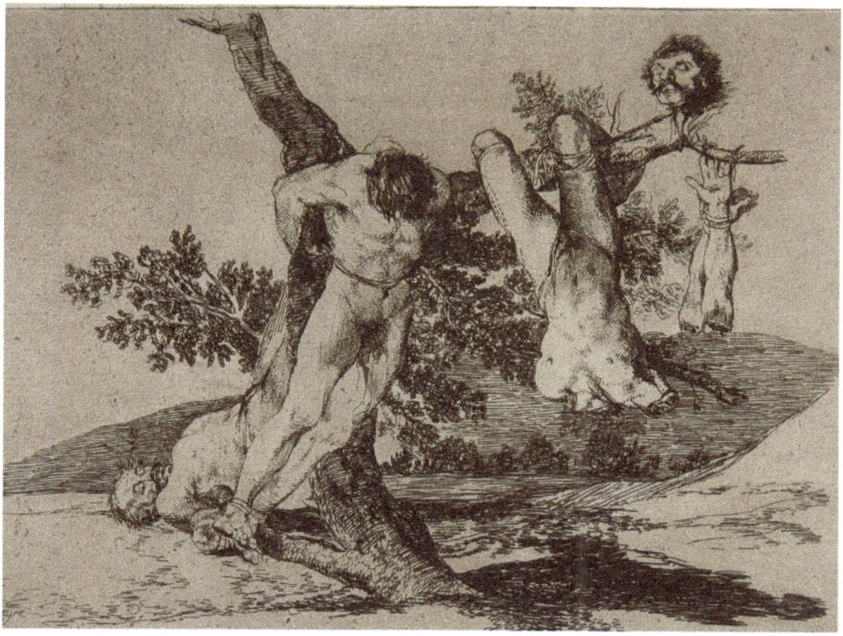

FIGURE 5.4. Francisco de Goya. *Grande hazaña! Con muertos!* (A Heroic Feat! With Dead Men!) – from *Los desastres de la guerra* (The Disasters of War), plate no. 39 (1863). Courtesy of Yale University Art Gallery.

their counterpart in a different series of images that better captures the hidden monstrosity of martial aesthetics. Between around 1810 and 1820, just as the idea that war could be conceived as an art form first emerged, Francisco Jose de Goya y Lucientes made a series of eighty etchings that was later given the title *The Disasters of War.* In unsparing detail, these etchings document the excessive violence of the Napoleonic Wars in Spain. In this kaleidoscope of horrors, one image stands out. Plate 39 is titled *Grande hazaña! Con muertos!—Great deeds! With the dead!*

The sheer brutality of the image makes it difficult not to avert one's eyes. But there is a deeper horror that lies not in the dead bodies themselves but in their postmortem desecration. Decapitated and dismembered, the human form of one of the men has been destroyed only to be creatively rearranged and put on display on the tree. Going beyond the violence of killing, the perpetrators have reduced the enemy to a physical material that can be taken apart, reordered, and rearranged into a new shape, thereby transforming the corpse into a macabre and gruesome work of art in an exhibition of a violence that knows no bounds. In Goya's image, the disjunctive merger of war and aesthetics leads only to pure monstrosity—a monstrosity that must, however, be acknowledged and seen. The ethical demand made by the etching is precisely that we do not avert our eyes but rather look at it without flinching. Goya's close-up of this macabre work of art may stand as the emblematic counterpoint to the abstract romanticizing of military design, as a glimpse into the shadows cast by the seductive theory of war as an art form.

EPILOGUE

Failures of Imagination

When the US withdrew its troops from Afghanistan after a protracted twenty-year war, the Hamid Karzai International Airport in Kabul was a scene of chaos. Tens of thousands of Americans, Afghans, and other foreign nationals struggled to be airlifted to security. Footage from the runways showed people hanging on to planes as they took off, in a desperate measure to leave the country. In the highly volatile situation, the Eighty-Second Airborne Division was deployed to secure the airport. Unlike the National Guard and two battalions from the Marines also present on the ground, the soldiers from the Eighty-Second Airborne Division wielded a new spatial technology that delivered a 3D representation of the airport. According to the US Army Futures Command, the virtual visualization provided a more accurate and detailed representation of the area and enabled commanders to understand crowd flows and identify potential vulnerabilities.[1]

The new technology utilized in Kabul offers a glimpse into the future of martial aesthetics. It is called One World Terrain, and it forms the basis of a virtual dream that the US Army Futures Command is currently trying to realize: a global war simulation. The military has contracted with the private company Maxar Technologies, which specializes in space and imaging technologies, and it is currently developing the project in collaboration with, among others, the Institute for Creative Technologies and Bohemia Interactive Simulations. One World Terrain is a vast database that aggregates imagery from satellites, airplanes, drones, OpenStreetMap, and other sources to enable a comprehensive 3D simulation of the entire globe, including building interiors and subterranean and suboceanic space. A military Google Earth, One World Terrain offers the most detailed and most extensive terrain data of the world to date and presents it in a georeferenced 3D ellipsoid representation of the planet.

Unlike Google Earth, however, the One World Terrain database is set to form the geospatial foundation for all synthetic training environments and simulation trainers in the US military. At present, many simulation trainers are not compatible with one another, but One World Terrain is supposed to form "a single, global planetary engine to drive the training and simulation requirements."[2] Through the army network, US soldiers will then be able to access the cloud-based service wherever they are at the so-called point of need. By clicking on the simulated globe, soldiers will immediately be transported to any locality on the planet that has been identified as a potential battlespace in order to train their mission in a seemingly exact digital replica of the real environment. Moreover, the database not only supports training systems but also, increasingly, the US Army's operational systems. As Brigadier General William Glaser, who directs the army's synthetic training environment efforts, put it, "It really just started off as an idea within the simulations community, but it's expanded out significantly into the operational community. When we can converge the training and operational community into one, that's very clearly a win."[3] Phase 1 of Maxar Technologies' contract focused on simulation and training; phase 2 extends these technologies to support multidomain operations and mission command systems. In other words, training for war and waging war will integrate fully and take place on the same digital platform. While at present only portions of the global simulation dataset have been constructed, it is expected to reach full operative capability during 2023, with significant funds allocated by the Department of Defense for its further development over the coming years.[4]

It is perhaps fitting that the end of a war that helped fuel the expansion of martial aesthetics in the first two decades of the twenty-first century also served as a trial run for its future evolution. With One World Terrain and the synthetic training environment that it enables, the militarization

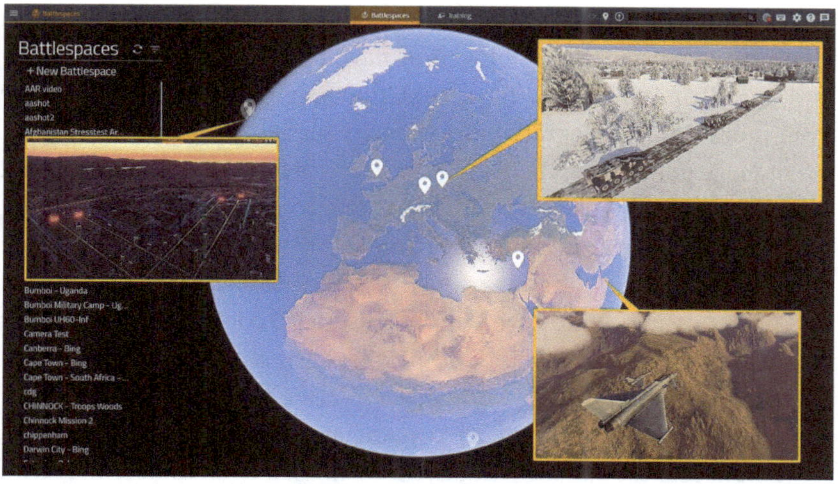

FIGURE 6.1. Bohemia Interactive Simulations is integrating its Virtual Battle Space series with One World Terrain to allow the creation of battlefields for training and deployment around the globe. Source: Bohemia Interactive Simulations.

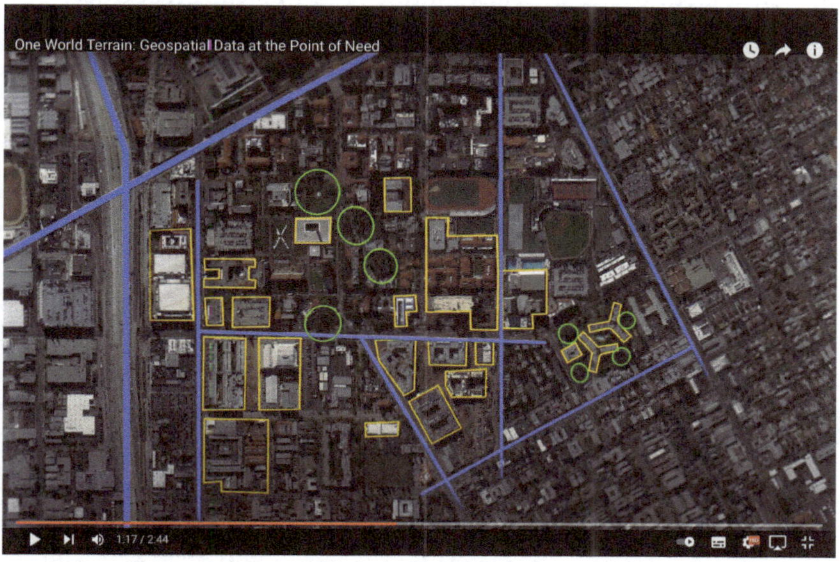

FIGURE 6.2. Identifying structures, vegetation, and other terrain features, users process the raw data in One World Terrain to develop a functional simulation. Source: Institute for Creative Technologies, "One World Terrain: Geospatial Data at the Point of Need." *YouTube*. https://www.youtube.com/watch?v=6Avi4CiZ-CU.

and operationalization of aesthetics that began some 250 years ago with a handful of Prussian analog games have reached a global scale. Play and war, the potential and the actual, the imagined and the real will be even more tightly integrated as the entire planet is transformed into a single large potential battlefield. With every site a potential "operational environment," and every "operational environment" a virtual testing ground for repeated mission rehearsal, we will very soon all live inside a fully operational global war simulation. If Leibniz's God created the best of all possible worlds, with all the miseries it contains, the military's techno-aesthetic apparatus is in the process of creating its negative image: a global war zone, a sinister world of destruction that measures its degree of perfection in the most efficient organization of violence.

In light of these ongoing efforts, the technologies on display in Harun Farocki's *Serious Games* now seem almost primitive and obsolete. But the problems Farocki's installation raises remain in place. Propagating a fantasy of security and control through the techno-aesthetic creation of violent factitious futures just waiting to be implemented, One World Terrain generates a strange form of hallucinatory anesthesia. Immersed in a world that they hone to perfection through multiple repetitions in a closed circuit on digital home turf, soldiers will, for good or ill, hallucinate an imaginary world of their own making. At the same time, the hallucination works by dulling the perception of the realities it leaves out. Flatlining soldiers' emotions and recalibrating their sensory apparatus in a synthetic training environment, martial aesthetics is designed to induce a selective anesthesia, a resilient numbness to the brute realities of warfare. The continued production of such preemptively secured, anesthetized futures on a global scale cannot but blunt the awareness of what Clausewitz called the "raw element" of war, the real, brutal physical violence and the havoc it wreaks on individuals, societies, and cultures.[5] Viable nonmilitary futures may then more easily be pushed aside, making the military option, whose success can already be verified by numerous rehearsals in the One World Terrain simulation, preferable to the unpredictable, slow, and cumbersome back-and-forth of diplomatic negotiations.

This hallucinatory anesthesia also marks the limits of the martial creative imagination. Despite their co-option of aesthetic technologies and aesthetic concepts, US military institutions have time and again displayed a profound failure of the imagination when it comes to understanding their adversaries. The 9/11 Commission famously concluded that the main reason for the attacks that sparked two decades of protracted warfare was a "failure of imagination" to properly understand the threat.[6] Reductive military scenario building, however, is not the answer. Even as extensive theorizing has argued that the power of aesthetics to generate "empathy"—in the sense of "the ability to understand the thoughts and feelings of another"—is among its main characteristics and prime strengths, martial aesthetics, both as a range of media technologies and as a set of ideas, consistently ignores the autonomy, the beliefs, and the broader cultures of opponents. It reduces foreign populations to a threat to be eliminated or a material to be redesigned—or it simply disregards them.

A recent literary work by a veteran of the Iraq War illustrates well this failure of imagination. Following his award-winning collection of short stories *Redeployment*—one of the finest pieces of writing to emerge from the US-led wars in the twenty-first century—Phil Klay published his first novel, *Missionaries*, in 2020. It outlines the worldwide, interconnected, technological form of warfare that silently rages around the globe and continues to do so even after the return of great-power politics with the Russian invasion of Ukraine in 2022. One of its central characters is a man by the name of Juan Pablo, a Colombian mercenary trained by American special forces. Moving across the globe and from one digital battlefield to the next, he flies to the United Arab Emirates to work in a targeting cell and improve the precision of the Emirati missile strikes against the Houthis in Yemen. After yet another lethal attack, Juan Pablo begins to reflect on the people he is killing:

> He didn't know what a Muslim funeral was like. Were they the same? Or did Yemenis have particular customs? In all his time watching Yemenis die on video screens, he had not once talked to a single Yemeni, or even seen one in person. They were a notional people to him, defined not by experience but by a few articles he'd read, by talk among his fellow mercenaries, and by a few opinion polls he'd sought out to learn about their retrograde beliefs.
>
> Were they as motivated by primitivism as he thought? Was this war of attrition they were fighting grinding down their resistance, or would

> it spawn pockets of resistance, deep enmities, nonnegotiable hatred? What were they like? He didn't know. It wasn't necessary to know for a campaign like this, which was one half war and one half extermination.[7]

A missionary of war, Juan Pablo travels the globe converting life into death without giving a second thought to the people at the receiving end of the sophisticated technical apparatus he wields or to the larger consequences of his actions. Klay's novel exposes the primitivism of this mode of thinking. The convergence of warfare, advanced global targeting technology, and willful ignorance marks the point where civilization reverts to barbarism.

The same may be said of the military's techno-aesthetic apparatus when it transforms the globe into a vast potential war zone and of the theoretical efforts by military designers to frame the enemy as an artistic material they can violently shape into a "friendly desired system." With at best only the most rudimentary notion of the other, the military's efforts perform an obscene perversion of the traditional field of aesthetics. They transform the ability to creatively imagine other minds, beliefs, cultures, and civilizations into a highly truncated martial imaginary governed by a one-sided operational logic of tactical and strategic efficacy. Empathy is replaced by a calculated apathy and a projected hallucination of preconceived ideas. Such a reformatting of aesthetics may or may not serve as a useful anesthetic to protect the minds and bodies of the soldiers carrying out the grim work in the field, but in any case the merger of war and aesthetics is increasingly blurring the line between civilization and barbarism.

One World Terrain offers a preview of the techno-aesthetic world to come. In the realm of ideas, however, there are also new developments on the horizon. Curiously, they involve the co-option of a much more traditional medium—literature. In 2015, Peter Warren Singer, a widely read nonfiction author, analyst, and military consultant, and August Cole, also a military consultant and a former journalist, published the novel *Ghost Fleet: A Novel of the Next World War*. Set in an unspecified but not-too-distant future, the novel imagines how World War III might play out as a great-power conflict between the US and China. In this, the novel does not differ from the dictates of the genre. From H. G. Wells's

The War of the Worlds via John Hackett's *The Third World War* to Tom Clancy's Jack Ryan series, popular war science fiction is an established entertainment subgenre. Aside from the unnatural dialogue, inept plotting, and shallow characters, who seem mere appendages to the fancy technological devices the novel revels in, *Ghost Fleet* fits seamlessly into the tradition.

But the novel stands out in two respects: in its reception in the military sphere and in its curious experimentation with genres. After its publication, Singer and Cole began to receive numerous invitations to established military institutions in the US and among its allies around the globe. More than seventy-five military and governmental organizations including the White House, the CIA, the Pentagon, the NSA, NATO, the Royal Air Force, and the Australian Parliament were all curious to hear more about the futuristic dystopian scenario the two consultants had painted with all the lurid colors a literary techno-thriller allows.[8] In other words, like Reisswitz's wargame in 1824, Singer and Cole's novel was quickly plugged into the powerful apparatus of leading military institutions. Indeed, the book led to policy changes and triggered multiple governmental investigations to fix security issues the narrative had uncovered.[9]

That a novel can attract such interest among politicians, generals, and US and international military institutions is unusual to say the least. To be sure, war novels have had a political impact before. In 1871, Sir George Tomkyns Chesney caused a sensation with his short story "The Battle of Dorking: Reminiscences of a Volunteer," which sparked a debate over England's defensive capabilities. And Tom Clancy's *The Hunt for Red October* and *Red Storm Rising* were favorites of Ronald Reagan.[10] The main reason established military institutions took Singer and Cole's novel seriously, however, was the curious mixed genre of the novel. In contrast to much science fiction literature, *Ghost Fleet* is based on years of extensive research, and the futuristic technologies presented in the novel are all realistic insofar as they already exist as prototypes or are in development. Moreover, the science out of which the text weaves its yarn is copiously documented by over two hundred footnotes at the end of the novel.

By operationalizing war literature, Singer and Cole have invented a new literary genre—the martial novel.[11] They themselves call it "useful fiction" or FICINT—a shorthand for "fictional intelligence." In their own words, useful fiction is neither a "techno-thriller" nor a "nonfiction current-affairs book" but both combined.[12] And they highlight the composite genre as the key to its efficacy. White papers, research articles, or PowerPoint presentations may present accurate facts, but few people bother to read them. A science fiction fantasy may find an audience, but it remains implausible speculation. But useful fiction, they claim, unites the virtues of fact-based scholarship with the appeal of narrative satisfaction and plausible imaginary experimentation. The genre is, as they put it, "a deliberate fusion of narrative's power with real-world research's utility."[13] Thus the novel *Burn-In*, their sequel on the future of artificial intelligence and robotics published in 2020, is, according to Singer, a "package" that conveys "exactly 300 researched insights."[14]

The militarization of the novel is an example of the same operational aesthetics that governs "serious games." What the inventors did to the game of chess around 1800, Singer and Cole are now doing to literature. As then, the co-option of aesthetics is about leveraging the force of a creative imaginary world for military purposes. Unwittingly rehearsing the arguments of the early wargame inventors, Singer and Cole argue that useful fiction offers "simulated versions of our world," that it generates a virtual "synthetic experience," and that it primes the readers "to act" by engaging their emotions.[15] Even their injunction that useful fiction must be governed by an aesthetic of realism—"the rules of the real"—mirrors the ideal of "realism" or "fidelity" in wargames and synthetic training environments.[16]

But useful fiction also continues the discourse on war as an art form. With *Ghost Fleet*, *Burn-In*, and their invention of the martial novel, Singer and Cole have quite literally transformed military thought and strategy into an art form, a literary genre in its own right. As founders and managing partners of the company Useful Fiction, they sell in-person and online courses to military leaders to help them become creative writers of martial literature. Through collaborations with the US Marine Corps Warfighting Lab and the think tank the Atlantic Council, August Cole has also participated in writing contests that invite soldiers to apply their creativity to write plausible stories of the military future in order to augment the Marine Corps' security environment forecast, *Futures 2030–45*.[17]

This attempt to recruit literature and transform it into an operational military tool seems to be catching on. In 2016, NATO's Allied Command Transformation provided a group of futurist authors with information from its Strategic Foresight Analysis and its Technology Trends Survey, as well as other data-based prognostications, and asked them to envision the future in fictional stories, resulting in the literary anthology *Visions of Warfare 2036*.[18] In 2017, the Army Cyber Institute at West Point and the Threatcasting Lab at Arizona State University began producing a series of "science fiction prototypes" in the form of graphic novels, with titles ranging from *Quantum Winter* to *Invisible Force: Information Warfare and the Future of Conflict*.[19] And in 2020, the August issue of the US Naval Institute's journal, *Proceedings*, featured an article that packaged ideas about a future crisis with China in a fictional wrapping. The story was written by Admiral James A. Winnefeld, former commander of NORAD, and Michael J. Morrell, former head of the CIA.[20] While war is framed *as if* it were an art in the long history of war as an art form from Clausewitz and Rühle von Lilienstern to military design, soldiers from the bottom to the top of the security echelon are now literally becoming war authors—a martial-aesthetic avant-garde exploring the uncharted territories of a new literary genre.

Unlike military designers, however, who seek to shape the enemy into a "friendly desired system," the military authors frequently imagine a darker vision of the future. As Lt. Colonel Natalie Vanatta of the US Army Cyber Institute puts it in her introduction to *Quantum Winter*, "Our story does not shy away from a dystopian vision of tomorrow. Exploring these dark regions inspires us to build a better, stronger, and more secure future for our Armed Forces."[21] In this way, martial literature performs a curious inversion of the Leibnizian logic that informs the martial techno-aesthetic apparatus. Instead of training the best of all possible wars into existence, martial literature imagines the worst of all possible worlds. Generating fear and anxiety, it is designed to spur readers to act preemptively to avoid the projected imaginary catastrophe.

The recent emergence of martial literature would seem to mark a new phase in the longer history of martial aesthetics. As soldiers become creative writers and published authors, the co-option of aesthetics appears to reach its ne plus ultra: the actual takeover of a classical aesthetic medium, the fusion of strategic thought and imaginative literature, the becoming-author of the soldier. Yet martial literature also marks a serious failure of the creative imagination. The failure is less the abuse of literature it regularly performs through its didacticism and seemingly unlimited supply of clichés, and more that the "useful" stories and novels of the violence to come remain trapped within their own limited horizon of strategic interests and high-tech gadgets. Securitizing the present through the projection of future threats, martial literature is a not-too-subtle propaganda tool for increased militarization, and it suggests technological and violent solutions to difficult problems that arise from the tight entwinement of complex political, social, and cultural spheres. Extracting from literature the power of invention, narrative, and emotional engagement and putting them to use to promote military technology, this curious new brand of fiction is unable break free from its own limited assumptions. It fails to imagine a complex human environment in any credible detail, it fails to imagine the nefarious consequences of increased militarization, and it fails to imagine solutions and logics other than war and the development of even more advanced military technology. Because of these failures of imagination, the genre of useful fiction makes of literature a seductive aesthetic instrument to promote martialism through a mixture of fear, entertainment, and techno-fetishism. If trend lines continue, a wide array of martial short stories, novels, and graphic novels will soon become fixtures on the reading lists of military institutions and among the wider reading public.

As these recent examples indicate, there is little to suggest that martial aesthetics will come undone anytime soon. To the contrary, the logic of militarization and the still unrealized military potential of aesthetics only signal the steady expansion of its reach. As we look further into the twenty-first century, the techno-aesthetic apparatus is on course to transform the planet into a global war simulation, while aesthetic ideas are colonizing all our possible futures with skeletal visions of never-ending warfare. And this, ultimately, may be the greatest failure of imagination: for all its futures, for all its artistry, and for all its creative projections, martial aesthetics has not imagined a single world one would like to inhabit.

ACKNOWLEDGMENTS

As any writer knows, books owe their existence to a large but often invisible collective of colleagues, friends, and family. Over the past five years, I have had the tremendous fortune to benefit from the discussions with my wonderful research group consisting of Jens Bjering, Solveig Gade, and Christine Strandmose Toft. Our research project on the aesthetics of war, lavishly sponsored by the Carlsberg Foundation and the Velux Foundations, enabled us to bring several old and new friends to Denmark, whose ideas and comments inform the book: Louise Amoore, Ryan Bishop, Christopher Coker, Mark Danner, James Der Derian, Anthony Downey, Mark B. Hansen, Caroline Holmqvist, Vivienne Jabri, Caren Kaplan, Phil Klay, Kate McLoughlin, Elaine Scarry, Joseph Vogl, and Arkadi Zaides.

At the University of Southern Denmark, I have had the pleasure of directing the War and Culture group and thank Martin Beck, Thomas Ærvold Bjerre, Naja Bjørnsson, Andreas Graae, Clara Juncker, Hans Christian Post, and Anders Bo Rasmussen for our many events, sessions, and discussions. The Center for War Studies has once again proven a lively forum for interdisciplinary inquiry, and I especially thank Trine Flockhart, Chiara de Franco, Martin Mennecke, and Olivier Schmitt for our dialogues and collaborations.

In the past years, I have been fortunate to be invited to present some of the material in the book at several events and venues. In Denmark I thank Johannes Lang and Helle Malmvig at the Danish Institute for International Studies, Lene Hansen at the Department of Political Science in Copenhagen, Mette Mortensen at the Department of Media Studies in Copenhagen, and Anders Djurslev and Christian Lollike at Sort/Hvid. Abroad I extend my gratitude to Luc Boltanski and Arnaud Esquerre at the EHESS in Paris, to Paul Bové in Pittsburgh, to Om Dwivedi in Surat, and to Alice König and Nicolas Wiater at St. Andrews. In March 2019, at the very last minute, I had to cancel what promised to be a stimulating interdisciplinary discussion with Tarak Barkawi and Antoine Bousquet at the London School of Economics due to the pandemic. I suppose it can be excused with *force majeure*, but I still feel bad and hope to make up for it down the line.

I am particularly grateful to a number of individuals who generously took time out of their busy schedules to read the manuscript in part or in full. In addition to the members of my research group, this includes Ryan Bishop, Tobias Nanz, Jussi Parikka, Trevor Perri, Neil Ramsey, Dominique Routhier, Oliver Simons, and Casper Sylvest. Along with two astute external readers, they offered invaluable critique and suggestions, and, as they will see, their advice can be detected throughout. Needless to say, all errors and shortcomings are my sole responsibility.

At Stanford University Press, I have had the luck of working with two superb editors, whose patience, encouragement, and insights I truly appreciate: Emily-Jane Cohen, who took on the project, and Erica Wetter, who helped me bring it to completion. During the early stages of the project, a *Sapere Aude* prize from the Danish Council for Independent Research enabled a research stay at Columbia University, where I was hosted by the ever generous Oliver Simons and also benefited from conversations with Jonathan Crary and the late Thomas Elsaesser. As always, I had productive disagreements with Dennis Yi Tenen that usually continued into the early hours. During the final stages of the project, I profited from the research time bestowed on me by the magnificent Elite Research Prize from the Danish Ministry of Higher Education and Science.

Portions of my reading of Harun Farocki's work were originally published as "Technologies of Experience: Harun Farocki's *Serious Games* and Military Aesthetics" in *boundary 2* 44, no. 4 (November 1, 2017): 155–78. Antje Ehmann has once again been exceptionally helpful with images from Harun Farocki's archive, and I thank Christine Strandmose Toft for all her efforts to procure several of the other images. A part of chapter 1 appeared as a separate article titled "Wallenstein's Contingency Media," in *Romanticism* 24, no. 3 (2018): 231–44.

My deepest gratitude is to my wife, Kristine, and to the life-affirming craziness of our two children, Benjamin and Ingrid. I couldn't have written the book without them.

But the book also owes its existence to someone who is no longer with us. In early 2014, Mette Teilmann Nielsen traveled to Kabul on behalf of the Danish Ministry of Foreign Affairs. It was the second time she was in Afghanistan working with the civilian population to build a better and more secure society through collaboration, education, and human rights. On a January evening, only two weeks after her arrival, her life was brutally cut short. Since then, I have been haunted and encouraged in equal measure by her indefatigable, contagious optimism. This book is dedicated to her memory, to her bravery, and to her dream to slowly but steadily work toward a more peaceful world with nonviolent means.

NOTES

INTRODUCTION

1. James Norman Mattis, *Memorandum for U.S. Joint Forces Command: Assessment of Effects Based Operations*, August 14, 2008. https://smallwarsjournal.com/documents/usjfcomebomemo.pdf; *Memorandum for U.S. Joint Forces Command: Vision for a Joint Approach to Operational Design*, October 6, 2009. http://www.jfcom.mil/newslink/storyarchive/2009/aod_2009.pdf.

2. Mark Foster Gage, introduction to *Aesthetics Equals Politics: New Discourses across Art, Architecture, and Philosophy*, ed. Mark Foster Gage (Cambridge, MA: MIT Press, 2019), 3–8, 7.

3. There is widespread scholarly agreement that the influential treatise is a compilation of texts that was composed by several different authors during the second half of the fourth century and the beginning of the third century BCE and later ascribed to an obscure individual who lived at the turn of the fifth century BCE called Sun Wu (Master Sun). A more faithful translation of the Chinese title, *Sunzi bingfa*, would read *Master Sun's Military Methods* or, more loosely, *Master Sun's How-To Book about Armies*. I thank Haun Saussy for this latter suggestion. See further the discussion by Victor H. Mair in Sun Zi, *The Art of War: Sun Zi's Military Methods*, trans. Victor H. Mair (New York: Columbia University Press, 2007). See also Huiwen Helen Zhang and Haun Saussy, "War and Chinese Culture," in *War and Literary Studies*, ed. Anders Engberg-Pedersen and Neil Ramsey (Cambridge: Cambridge University Press, 2023).

4. Filippo Tommaso Marinetti, "Estetica Futurista della Guerra," *Stile Futurista*, nos. 13–14 (November 1935). See also Walter Benjamin, "The Work of Art in the Age of Its Technological Reproducibility," in *Selected Writings*, vol. 3, *1935–1938*, ed. Howard Eiland and Michael W. Jennings, 101–33 (Cambridge, MA: Harvard University Press, 2006).

5. Benjamin, "Work of Art," 122.

6. Among the phenomena that lie just outside the purview of the present

investigation are the more immediately military forms of propaganda material and recruitment videos whose allure and efficiency they to a large extent owe their aesthetic elements. See, for example, Helle Malmvig, "Soundscapes of War: The Audio-Visual Performance of War by Shi'a Militias in Iraq and Syria," *International Affairs* 96, no. 3 (2020): 649–66. In this connection, it is also worth recalling the development of camouflage in the early years of the twentieth century. During World War I, the invention of the "razzle dazzle" painting technique whose striking angular designs were applied to warships in order to confuse the enemy's targeting efforts also saw several artists at work for the military. Among them were cubist painters as well as Lucien-Victor Guirand de Scévola, who coined the term *camouflage* in 1914. Although these artists did not invent full-fledged imaginary worlds, they did go well beyond the traditional propagandistic work of recruited artists. See Hanna Rose Shell, *Hide and Seek: Camouflage, Photography, and the Media of Reconnaissance* (New York: Zone Books, 2012); and Antoine Bousquet, *The Eye of War: Military Perception from the Telescope to the Drone* (Minneapolis: University of Minnesota Press, 2018).

7. Among several excellent studies, see Santanu Das, *Touch and Intimacy in First World War Literature* (Cambridge: Cambridge University Press, 2005); Mary Favret, *War at a Distance: Romanticism and the Making of Modern Wartime* (Princeton, NJ: Princeton University Press, 2010); Kate McLoughlin, *Authoring War: The Literary Representation of War from the Iliad to Iraq* (Cambridge: Cambridge University Press, 2011), and *Veteran Poetics: British Literature in the Age of Mass Warfare, 1790–2015* (Cambridge: Cambridge University Press, 2018); Jan Mieszkowski, *Watching War* (Stanford, CA: Stanford University Press, 2012); Stacey Peebles, *Welcome to the Suck: Narrating the American Soldier's Experience in Iraq* (Ithaca, NY: Cornell University Press, 2016); Christine Strandmose Toft, "'This Isn't a Real War': The Wars in Iraq and Afghanistan in Fiction" (unpublished dissertation, 2021); and Neil Ramsey, *Romanticism and the Biopolitics of Modern War Writing* (Cambridge: Cambridge University Press, 2022).

8. Paul Virilio, *War and Cinema: The Logistics of Perception* (London: Verso, 1989).

9. Bousquet, *Eye of War.*

10. The clearest articulation of these ideas is found in Friedrich Kittler, *Gramophone, Film, Typewriter* (Stanford, CA: Stanford University Press, 1999). See also Friedrich Kittler, *Optical Media: Berlin Lectures*, trans. Anthony Enns (Cambridge: Polity Press, 2010); Friedrich Kittler, *Operation Valhalla: Writings on War, Weapons, and Media*, ed. Geoffrey Winthrop-Young, Michael Wutz, and Ilinca Iurascu (Durham, NC: Duke University Press, 2021); and Geoffrey Winthrop-Young, "Drill and Distraction in the Yellow Submarine: On the

Dominance of War in Friedrich Kittler's Media Theory," *Critical Inquiry* 28, no. 4 (Summer 2002): 825–54.

11. Evidently Virilio was concerned with similar questions, but even as he describes the co-emergence of cinema and (military) aviation and thus examines "the osmosis between industrialized warfare and cinema," the point of comparison and his main focus remain the camera as a technology rather than cinema as an art form. Similarly, his reflections on the rise of simulations rarely touch on their aesthetic nature. *War and Cinema*, 73. A fascinating exception is Caren Kaplan's account of how military technologies of aerial imagery overlap with a wide array of other disciplines, including aesthetics. See *Aerial Aftermaths: Wartime from Above* (Durham, NC: Duke University Press, 2018).

12. Geoffrey Winthrop-Young has recently pointed out that Kittler's view of the relation between war and media tilts back and forth between the "martial a priori of media" and the "medial a priori of war." While the first vision inserts war as the origin of technology and in the second, new technical innovations enable and expand the field of war, Kittler also suggests that war is the ultimate purpose and end goal of human–machine interactions. See Geoffrey Winthrop-Young, "Introduction: The Wars of Friedrich Kittler," in *Operation Valhalla*, 1–48, 23. For a broader discussion of the martial temptations of media studies, see Geoffrey Winthrop-Young, "War and Media Studies," in *War and Literary Studies*, ed. Anders Engberg-Pedersen and Neil Ramsey (Cambridge: Cambridge University Press, 2023).

13. Karl-Heinz Stockhausen, "Huuuh! Das Pressegespräch am 16. September 2001 im Senatszimmer des Hotel Atlantic in Hamburg," *MusikTexte* 91 (2002): 69–77, 76–77.

14. One notable exception is Dan Öberg's article "Warfare as Design: Transgressive Creativity and Reductive Operational Planning," *Security Dialogue* 49, no. 6 (December 2018): 493–509.

15. Eyal Weizman, *Hollow Land: Israel's Architecture of Occupation* (London: Verso, 2012), and *The Least of All Possible Evils* (London: Verso, 2011).

16. Jonathan Crary, *Techniques of the Observer: On Vision and Modernity in the Nineteenth Century* (Cambridge, MA: MIT Press, 1992), 8; Hans Belting, *An Anthropology of Images: Picture, Medium, Body*, trans. Thomas Dunlap (Princeton, NJ: Princeton University Press, 2011); Pasi Vähliaho, *Biopolitical Screens: Image, Power, and the Neoliberal Brain* (Cambridge, MA: MIT Press, 2014).

17. Ryan Bishop and John Phillips, *Modernist Avant-Garde Aesthetics and Contemporary Military Technology: Technicities of Perception* (Edinburgh: Edinburgh University Press, 2010).

18. In the broader political environment of corporate liberalism during the Cold War, the neo avant-garde of the 1960s also ran afoul of the emerging

military-industrial ideology. Inspired by the earlier artistic avant-gardes, the postwar art-and-technology movement brought together artists and engineers in a series of remarkable collaborations during the late 1960s. The collaborative efforts were driven by a shared belief in creativity, innovation, and experimentation and involved, among others, MIT, Bell Laboratories, and the Los Angeles County Museum of Art. The movement eventually foundered due to the disjunction between the progressive ethos of the artists and the corporate, commercial, and military concerns of think tanks, private companies, and government institutions. See John Beck and Ryan Bishop, *Technocrats of the Imagination: Art, Technology, and the Military-Industrial Avant-Garde* (Durham, NC, and London: Duke University Press, 2020); and Pamela M. Lee, *Think Tank Aesthetics: Midcentury Modernism, the Cold War, and the Neoliberal Present* (Cambridge, MA: MIT Press, 2020).

19. See Joseph Vogl, *Kalkül und Leidenschaft* (Berlin: Diaphanes, 2007); *The Specter of Capital* (Stanford, CA: Stanford University Press, 2014); *The Ascendency of Finance* (Cambridge: Polity Press, 2017); and *Kapital und Ressentiment: Eine kurze Theorie der Gegenwart* (Munich: C. H. Beck, 2021).

CHAPTER 1

1. Johannes Kepler, *Die Astrologie des Johannes Kepler: Eine Auswahl aus seinen Schriften*, ed. H. A. Strauss and S. Strauss-Kloebe (Fellbach, Germany: Verlag Adolf Bonz, 1981), 225.

2. Angelika Geiger, *Wallensteins Astrologie: Eine kritische Überprüfung der Überlieferung nach dem gegenwärtigen Quellenbestand* (Graz, Austria: Akademische Druck- und Verlagsanstalt, 1983), 96–97.

3. Kepler, *Astrologie*, 239.

4. Kepler, 256.

5. Friedrich Schiller, *Wallenstein* (Frankfurt am Main: Deutscher Klassiker Verlag, 2005), 175. Here and elsewhere I have occasionally made use of F. J. Lamport's fluent translation. Unless otherwise noted, all translations are my own. See Friedrich Schiller, *The Robbers and Wallenstein*, trans. F. J. Lamport (London: Penguin, 1979), 345.

6. Nicholas Campion, *A History of Western Astrology*, vol. 1, *The Ancient World* (London and New York: Bloomsbury Academic, 2008), 71.

7. Nicholas Campion notes the functional similarity to modern military technology when he writes that "the observation of Jupiter's movements prior to Sargon's campaign offered intelligence of a similar character to that provided by modern satellites in preparing for military action." Campion, "Astrology in Babylonia" in *Encyclopaedia of the History of Science, Technology, and Medicine in Non-Western Cultures*, ed. Helaine Selin (Dordrecht: Springer, 2016), 616.

8. Aristotle, *The Basic Works of Aristotle*, ed. Richard McKeon (New York: Modern Library, 2001), 47.

9. Schiller, *Wallenstein*, 19.

10. Schiller, 39–40.

11. For a persuasive analysis of the game metaphor, see the chapter "Ein Spiel vom Spiel—und vom Nichtspieler" by Karl S. Guthke in his book *Schillers Dramen: Idealismus und Skepsis* (Tübingen, Germany: Francke, 1994), 165–207. The scholarship on Wallenstein is vast. Readings have focused on different versions of the dichotomy between calculation and imagination or reason and the subconscious; see, for example, Ritchie Robertson, "*Wallenstein*," in *Friedrich Schiller: Playwright, Poet, Philosopher, Historian*, ed. Paul E. Kerry (Bern: Peter Lang, 2007), 251–73, and Uffe Hansen, "Schiller und die Persönlichkeitspsychologie des animalischen Magnetismus," *Jahrbuch der deutschen Schillergesellschaft* 39 (1995): 195–229. On the genre of tragedy and Schiller's philosophy of history, see Lydia Moland, "An Unrelieved Heart: Hegel, Tragedy, and Schiller's Wallenstein," *New German Critique* 113, vol. 38, no. 2 (Summer 2011): 1–23. On Schiller's stance toward Wallenstein as an artist vis-à-vis his stance as a historian, see Steffan Davies, *The Wallenstein Figure in German Literature and Historiography 1790–1920* (Leeds, United Kingdom: Maney Publishing, 2011). Among the many readings of the play, three general approaches are of immediate relevance for this chapter: analyses of the function of astrology in the play, of the historical development of astrology, and of *Wallenstein* as a war play. From G. A. Wells's thematic reading via Maria Wolf's analysis of the political import of the stars to Klaus F. Gille's historico-philosophical reading and Dieter Borchmeyer's prism of the four temperaments that casts Wallenstein as a melancholic, the stars have been linked with several of the general themes that structure the play. See G. A. Wells, "Astrology in Schiller's 'Wallenstein,'" *Journal of English and Germanic Philology* 68, no. 1 (1969): 100–15; Maria Wolf, "Der politische Himmel: Zum astrologischen Motiv in Schillers 'Wallenstein,'" in *Schiller und die höfische Welt*, ed. Achim Aurnhammer, Klaus Manger, and Friedrich Starck (Tübingen, Germany: Max Niemeyer Verlag, 1990), 223–32; Klaus F. Gille, "Das Astrologische Motiv in Schillers *Wallenstein*," *Amsterdamer Beiträge zur neueren Germanistik* 1 (1972): 103–18; and Dieter Borchmeyer, *Macht und Melancholie: Schillers Wallenstein* (Frankfurt am Main: Athenäum, 1988). Rarely, however, are the media of astrology and their role as a tool of war considered in themselves. Although Joseph Vogl has analyzed the category of the "event" and argued that the play with its complex temporalities produces a radical contingency that even infects the ontology of the protagonist, he skirts the theme of astrology and the medial substratum of the event structure of the play. See Joseph Vogl, *Über das Zaudern* (Zürich: Diaphanes, 2008).

The more historical approaches have sought to situate the Duke of Friedland within the astrological thought of his time—for example, Angelika Geiger's meticulous excavation of the documents pertaining to Wallenstein's astrological beliefs, and Hadravová and Hadrava's analysis of the astrological motifs in the frescoes in Wallenstein's palace in Prague. See Geiger, *Wallensteins Astrologie*; and Alena Hadravová and Petr Hadrava, "Science in Contact with Art: Astronomical Symbolics of the Wallenstein Palace in Prague," in *Science in Contact at the Beginning of Scientific Revolution*, ed. Jitka Zamrzlová, 173–210 (Prague: National Technical Museum, 2004). Although they present useful information, these studies offer little insight into the larger historical constellation of institutions, epistemology, and practices that allowed astrological representations to function as media, nor do they consider the role these media played in the competing theories on the manageability of future contingents. This focus, finally, brings my chapter into the orbit of more recent studies that examine *Wallenstein* as a war play. Elizabeth Krimmer points to the ambivalent status of war as both a source of transcendental aspirations and national politics on the one hand, and as an engine of destruction on the other. Elizabeth Krimmer, "Transcendental Soldiers: Warfare in Schiller's *Wallenstein* and *Die Jungfrau von Orleans*," *Eighteenth Century Fiction* 19, nos. 1 and 2 (Fall 2009): 99–121. Jan Mieszkowski's deconstructive reading argues for the uncontainable force of the language of war, a force that always exceeds the speakers' strategic designs and takes on an uncontrollable agency of its own. Jan Mieszkowski, "The Pace of the Attack: Military Experience in Schiller's *Wallenstein* and *Die Jungfrau von Orleans*," *Goethe Yearbook* 16 (2009): 29–46. The focus on the medium of language, however, may be broadened to a whole range of media that have been specifically designed to produce contingency in order to contain it. Schiller's play, I argue, points not just to a general predicament of language, a predicament that is exacerbated in warfare, but also to two historically specific moments when the problem of contingency was handled with different war media.

12. Schiller, *Wallenstein*, 94.

13. Schiller, *Wallenstein*, 255.

14. The connection between games and astrology in *Wallenstein* is underlined by the rediscovery, in 1983, of an astrological dice game: "Ein Spiel mit Würffln." Three consecutive rolls of a single die would produce a sequence of three numbers that was in turn linked with a series of predictions, one for each sequence. It had been designed by an unnamed German astrologer, and Wallenstein had used it "wann Er zurkünfttiger sachen hat wisßen wollen" (when he wanted to know future matters). See Geiger, *Wallensteins Astrologie*, 135–45.

15. Schiller, *Wallenstein*, 110, 281.

16. As Bernhard Siegert puts it, "There is no subject area, no ontologically

identifiable domain that could be called 'media.'" *Cultural Techniques: Grids, Filters, Doors, and Other Articulations of the Real*, trans. Geoffrey Winthrop-Young (New York: Fordham University Press, 2015), 3.

17. Eva Horn, "Editor's Introduction: There Are No Media," *Grey Room* 29 (Winter 2008): 10.

18. See Joseph Vogl, "Becoming-Media: Galileo's Telescope," *Grey Room* 29 (Winter 2008): 14–25. The quotation is from Horn, "Editor's Introduction" (10). There are several overlaps between this conception of media and the more recent theoretical frame of "cultural techniques." See Bernhard Siegert, "Cultural Techniques: Or the End of the Intellectual Postwar Era in German Media Theory," *Theory, Culture & Society* 30, no. 6 (2013): 48–65; and *Cultural Techniques*. For a critical appraisal of the close ties that the field of media studies has long maintained with warfare, see Geoffrey Winthrop-Young, "War and Media Studies," in *War and Literary Studies*, ed. Anders Engberg-Pedersen and Neil Ramsey (Cambridge: Cambridge University Press, 2023).

19. Ptolemy, *Tetrabiblos*, ed. and trans. F. E. Robbins (Cambridge, MA: Harvard University Press, 1940), 221.

20. Ptolemy, *Tetrabiblos*, 225.

21. The basis that ensured the validity of the correspondence between the superlunary and sublunary realms was a cosmological world picture in which the universe was considered a single entity with all elements connected, from the celestial spheres to human beings, animals, the botanical and mineral realms. For the classic explication of the "cosmic order" in the Elizabethan period, see E.M.W. Tillyard, *The Elizabethan World Picture* (New York: Vintage Books, 1959).

22. See Nicolas Campion, *A History of Western Astrology*, vol. 2, *The Medieval and Modern Worlds* (London and New York: Continuum, 2009), 132.

23. See Christian Heitzmann, ed., *Die Sterne lügen nicht: Astrologie und Astronomie im Mittelalter und in der Frühen Neuzeit. Katalog zur Ausstellung in der Herzog August Bibliothek Wolfenbüttel* (Wiesbaden, Germany: Harrassowitz, 2008), 29–30, 57–58.

24. Quoted in Heitzmann, *Die Sterne lügen nicht*, 89.

25. "Sollten die Sterne nicht genausogut wirken in utero als extra uterum? Was meint ihr, dass die Sterne fragen nach einem kleinen Häutlein, das über dem Bauch des Weibes ist . . . ?" Quoted in Heitzmann, *Die Sterne lügen nicht*, 91.

26. Kepler, *Astrologie*, 244–45.

27. Kepler, 233.

28. Kepler, 238–39.

29. Kepler, 233. Kepler's ambivalence and critique are symptomatic of the larger demise of the astrological world picture. Already in 1572 Tycho Brahe

had observed the *Stella Nova* in Cassiopeia—a celestial event that contradicted basic tenets of Aristotelian cosmology. See Nick Kanas, *Star Maps: History, Artistry, and Cartography* (New York: Springer, 2012), 96.

30. Kepler, 239. Already in 1598, in an engaged deconstruction of the predictions of other astrologers, Kepler had explicitly stated "that in all of nature, none such specific prediction of future matters can be had as some demand of astrology, and therefore one cannot rely on its practices." See his "Schrieb-Kalendar auf das Jahr nach des Herrn Christi unsers Erlösers Geburt MDXCVIII," in Kepler, *Astrologie*, 54.

31. See Dan Edelstein, "Introduction to the Super-Enlightenment," in *The Super-Enlightenment: Daring to Know Too Much*, ed. Dan Edelstein, 1–35 (Oxford: Voltaire Foundation, 2010), 33. See also David Bates's essay "Super-Epistemology" in the same volume. The persistence in Kepler's thought of astrological themes such as the *harmonia mundi*, the analogy of macro- and microcosmos, can be seen even in his mathematical calculations. See Hania Siebenpfeiffer, "Astrologie," in *Futurologien: Ordnungen des Zukunftswissens*, ed. Benjamin Bühler and Stefan Willer, 379–92 (Paderborn, Germany: Wilhlem Fink, 2016), 385. See also Andreas Bähr, *Der Grausame Komet: Himmelszeichen und Weltgeschehen im Dreißigjährigen Krieg* (Reinbek, Germany: Rowohlt, 2017), 38–50.

32. Schiller, *Wallenstein*, 213. "Die Sterne lügen nicht, *das* aber ist / Geschehen wider Sternenlauf und Schicksal. / Die Kunst ist redlich, doch dies falsche Herz / Bringt Lug und Trug in den wahrhaft'gen Himmel. / Nur auf der Wahrheit ruht die Wahrsagung, / Wo die Natur aus ihren Grenzen wanket, da irret alle Wissenschaft."

33. Schiller, 87.

34. Schiller, 155.

35. Schiller, 155, 175. In 1623, the historical Wallenstein commissioned Italian artists to decorate the twenty-one-meter-long "Astrological Corridor" in his palace with frescoes that depict the seven known planets personified as ancient gods along with the signs of the zodiac. See Alena Hadravová and Petr Hadrava, "Science in Contact with Art," 181–84.

36. See, for example, the reading by Joseph Vogl in *Über das Zaudern*. Stefan Willer aptly notes that while Wallenstein would appear to be not only a deficient commander but also a deficient dramatic subject, his lack of action precisely marks the modernity of his character on the stage. See Stefan Willer, "Stratege," in *Futurologien*, 245–56, 247.

37. See Paul Oskar Kristeller, "The Modern System of the Arts," in *Problems in Aesthetics*, ed. Morris Weitz, 2nd ed. (New York: Macmillan, 1970). He sums up his view: "The grouping together of the visual arts with poetry and music into the system of the fine arts with which we are familiar did not exist in

classical antiquity, in the Middle Ages or in the Renaissance. However, the ancients contributed to the modern system the comparison between poetry and painting, and the theory of imitation that established a kind of link between painting and sculpture, poetry and music. The Renaissance brought about the emancipation of the three major visual arts from the crafts, it multiplied the comparisons between the various arts, especially between painting and poetry, and it laid the ground for an amateur interest in the different arts that tended to bring them together from the point of view of the reader, spectator and listener rather than of the artist. The seventeenth century witnessed the emancipation of the natural sciences and thus prepared the way for a clearer separation between the arts and the sciences. Only the early eighteenth century, especially in England and France, produced elaborate treatises written by and for amateurs in which the various fine arts were grouped together, compared with each other and combined in a systematic scheme based on common principles" (160–61). The essay was originally published in two parts in 1951 and 1952 in *Journal of the History of Ideas* 12:496–527 and 13:17–46.

38. Larry Shiner, *The Invention of Art: A Cultural History* (Chicago and London: University of Chicago Press, 2001), 99.

39. Shiner, 83–84.

40. Shiner, 111.

41. For a critique of Kristeller and Shiner, see Paul Guyer, *A History of Modern Aesthetics*, vol. 1, *The Eighteenth Century* (Cambridge: Cambridge University Press, 2014), 28–29; and James I. Porter, "Is Art Modern? Kristeller's 'Modern System of the Arts' Reconsidered," *British Journal of Aesthetics* 49 (2009): 1–24. The term *essentially contested concepts* was coined by W. B. Gallie. See Gallie, "Essentially Contested Concepts," *Proceedings of the Aristotelian Society* 56 (1955): 167–98.

42. J. J. Bodmer, "Anklagung des verderbten Geschmacks," in J. J. Bodmer and J. J. Breitinger, *Schriften zur Literatur* (Stuttgart: Reclam, 1980), 39. See also Elsa Jaubert, "Johann Jakob Bodmer (1698–1783) et Johann Jakob Breitinger (1701–1776)," in *Aux Sources de l'esthétique: Les débuts de l'esthétique en Allemagne*, ed. Jean-François Goubet and Gérard Raulet, 245–82 (Paris: Éditions de la Maison des Sciences de l'Homme, 2005), 13.

43. J. J. Breitinger, "Critische Dichtkunst," in J. J. Bodmer and J. J. Breitinger, *Schriften zur Literatur*, 86.

44. Leibniz, *Essais de theodicée sur la bonté de Dieu, la liberté de l'homme et l'origine du mal* in *Oeuvres Philosophiques de Leibniz*, ed. Paul Janet (Paris: F. Alcan, 1900), 2:347.

45. See also Hans Blumenberg, "Nachahmung der Natur: Zur Vorgeschichte

der Idee des schöpferischen Menschen," in *Ästhetische und metaphorologische Schriften* (Frankfurt am Main: Suhrkamp, 2001), 9–46.

46. Karl Philipp Moritz, "Versuch einer Vereinigung aller schönen Künste und Wissenschaften unter dem Begriff des in sich selbst Vollendeten," in *Schriften zur Ästhetik und Poetik*, ed. Hans Joachim Schrimpf (Berlin and Boston: De Gruyter, 1962), 3–9.

47. Martha Woodmannsee situates Moritz's contribution vis-à-vis his immediate predecessors in the tradition of German aesthetics and Moritz's religious pietism. See Martha Woodmannsee, "The Interests of Disinterestedness: Karl Philipp Moritz and the Emergence of the Theory of Aesthetic Autonomy in Eighteenth-Century Germany," *Modern Language Notes* 45, no. 1 (1984): 5–28.

48. Moritz, "Versuch," 3.

49. Moritz, 3.

50. Moritz, 6.

51. Kant, *Kritik der Urteilskraft* (Hamburg: Felix Meiner Verlag, 2001), 187–89.

52. Kant, 79.

53. As Kant writes: "Only where the Imagination in its freedom awakens the Understanding and is put by it into regular play without the aid of concepts, does the representation communicate itself, not as a thought, but as an internal feeling of a purposive state of the mind." Kant, *Kritik der Urteilskraft*, 177.

54. Kant, 190.

55. Schiller only began writing *Wallenstein* in the fall of 1796, but he had already conceived the plan for the play in 1791, some eight years before it was eventually published in 1799.

56. Friedrich Schiller, *Über die ästhetische Erziehung des Menschen in einer Reihe von Briefen* (Stuttgart: Reclam, 2000), 61–62. See also Guthke, *Schillers Dramen*, 167–68.

57. Schiller, *Über die ästhetische Erziehung*, 58.

58. Schiller, 85.

59. Schiller, 61.

60. Schiller, 120.

61. Schiller, 123.

62. Schiller, 110.

63. Schiller, 111.

64. Schiller, 160.

65. Schiller, 159.

66. For discussions of Aristotle's conception of *dunamis*, see Ekaterina Haskins, "On the Term 'Dunamis' in Aristotle's Definition of Rhetoric,"

Philosophy and Rhetoric 46, no. 2 (2013): 234–40; Thomas M. Olshewsky, "The Dynamics of *Dunamis*," *Review of Metaphysics* 71 (March 2018): 501–16; Andreas Anagnostopoulos, "Senses of 'Dunamis' and the Structure of Aristotle's 'Metaphysics,'" *Phronesis* 56, no. 4 (2011): 388–425; and Hartmut Böhme, "Einleitung," in *Contingentia: Transformationen des Zufalls*, ed. Hartmut Böhme, Werner Röcke, and Ulrike C. A. Stephan (Berlin and Boston: De Gruyter, 2016), 22.

67. Aristotle, *Basic Works*, 766.

68. Aristotle, 821.

69. See Haskins, "On the Term 'Dunamis,'" 238–39.

70. Aristotle opposes potentiality not just to *energeia* but also to *entelecheia* or *entelechy*, but he often used them interchangeably. *Entelecheia* is here translated as "complete reality."

71. Aristotle, *Basic Works*, 823.

72. Aristotle, 827.

73. Schiller, *Wallenstein*, 160.

74. Schiller, 86.

75. Vogl, *Über das Zaudern*, 51–55.

76. Schiller, *Wallenstein*, 112.

77. Schiller, 150.

78. Schiller, 63.

79. Schiller, 197.

80. Schiller, 255. The idea is formulated in an almost identical manner earlier in the play when Buttler compares his own trajectory to that of Wallenstein: "From humble duties in the stable rose / By skill in war to rank and eminence, / A lucky plaything of capricious fate. / Wallenstein too is wilful Fortune's child; / I love to see a path that's like my own." Schiller, *Wallenstein*, 126. The passage is here rendered in Lamport's translation, p. 292.

CHAPTER 2

1. Ernst Heinrich Dannhauer, "Das Reißwitzsche Kriegsspiel von seinem Beginn bis zum Tode des Erfinders 1827," *Militair-Wochenblatt* nr. 56 (1874): 529.

2. Aside from Dannhauer, see, for example, Peter P. Perla, *The Art of Wargaming* (Annapolis, MD: US Naval Institute, 1990); Philipp von Hilgers, *Kriegsspiele: Eine Geschichte der Ausnahmezustände und Unberechenbarkeiten* (Munich: Wilhelm Fink Verlag, 2008); Philip Sabin, *Simulating War: Studying Conflict through Simulation Games* (London and New York: Continuum, 2014); Jorit Wintjes, "Europe's Earliest *Kriegsspiel*? Book Seven of Reinhard Graf zu Solms' *Kriegsregierung* and the 'Prehistory' of Professional War Gaming,"

British Journal for Military History 2, no. 1 (2015); Anders Engberg-Pedersen, *Empire of Chance: The Napoleonic Wars and the Disorder of Things* (Cambridge, MA: Harvard University Press, 2015); Pat Harrigan and Matthew G. Kirschenbaum, eds., *Zones of Control* (Cambridge, MA: MIT Press, 2016); and Paul Schuurman, "Models of War 1770–1830: The Birth of Wargames and the Trade-Off between Realism and Simplicity," *History of European Ideas* 43, no. 2 (2017): 442–55.

3. See Claus Pias, *Computer Spiel Welten* (Munich: sequenzia, 2002), 173. The attempts to balance realism with playability often erred in one direction or the other. Commenting on a wargame by Venturini, the Prussian major and later field marshal Colmar Freiherr von der Goltz would later comment: "The whole thing resembles very closely the postal board game in vogue some years ago, in which, if you made an unlucky throw of the dice, you would tumble into a swamp, break an axle, or experience similar mishaps. . . . This wargame is a terrible outgrowth of the refined erudition of the military education during this period, which piled up so many difficulties that it was incapable of taking a single step forward." Colmar Freiherr von der Goltz, *Roßbach und Jena: Studien über die Zustände und das geistige Leben in der Preussischen Armee während der Uebergang vom XVIII. zum XIX. Jahrhundert* (Berlin: Mittler und Sohn, 1883), 219.

4. Johan Huizinga, *Homo Ludens: A Study of the Play-Element in Culture* (London: Routledge and Kegan Paul, 1944), 10.

5. Jesper Juul, *Half-Real: Video Games between Real Rules and Fictional Worlds* (Cambridge, MA: MIT Press, 2005), 1.

6. Juul, *Half-Real*, 133.

7. Georg Venturini, *Beschreibung und Regeln eines neuen Krieges-Spiels, zum Nutzen und Vergnügen, besonders aber zum Gebrauch in Militair-Schulen* (Schleswig, Germany: bey J. G. Röhß, 1797), xvi–xvii.

8. Johann Christian Ludwig Hellwig, *Versuch eines aufs Schachspiel gebaueten taktischen Spiels von zwey und mehreren Personen zu Spielen* (Leipzig: Siegfried Lebrecht Crusius, 1780), 144.

9. Georg Venturini, *Darstellung eines neuen Kriegesspiels zum Gebrauch für Offiziere und in Militärschulen* (Leipzig: bey Johann Conrad Hinrichs, 1804), 1–2. The demiurgic element of game design has since become a commonplace, as evidenced by the early computer game company Infocom, which in 1985 published a spoof on Genesis titled "THE CREATION," in which the world is programmed into existence in seven days by the programmer-as-player-as-God. See http://www.infocom-if.org/creation.html. See also Pias, *Computer*, 150–51.

10. Pias, *Computer*, 150.

11. Gottfried Wilhelm Leibniz, *La Monadologie*, in *Oeuvres Philosophiques de Leibniz*, ed. Paul Janet (Paris: F. Alcan, 1900), 1:715, 1:722, and passim.

12. Gottfried Wilhelm Leibniz, *Essais de theodicée sur la bonté de Dieu, la liberté de l'homme et l'origine du mal* in *Oeuvres Philosophiques de Leibniz*, ed. Paul Janet (Paris: F. Alcan, 1900), 2:236.

13. Leibniz, *Theodicée*, 226.

14. Leibniz, 345.

15. Leibniz, 346.

16. Leibniz, 346–7.

17. Leibniz, 345.

18. Gottfried Wilhelm Leibniz, *Gedanken zum Entwurf der teutschen Kriegsverfassung*, in *Sämtliche Schriften und Briefe*, series 4 (Berlin: Akademie der Wissenschaften, 1984), 2:589. See also Philipp von Hilgers, "Vom Einbruch des Spiels in die Epoche der Verunft," in *Visuele Argumentationen: Die Mysterien der Repräsentation und die Berechenbarkeit der Welt*, ed. Horst Bredekamp and Pablo Schneider, 205–23 (Munich: Wilhelm Fink, 2006), 221.

19. See von Hilgers, "Vom Einbruch," 205–23.

20. Hellwig writes, "Der Endzweck eines taktischen Spiels ist, die vornehmsten und wichtigsten Auftritte des Kriegs sinnlich zu machen." I here translate *sinnlich machen* as "visualize." A more literal translation would be "to represent for the senses." Johann Christian Ludwig Hellwig, *Versuch eines aufs Schachspiel gebaueten taktischen Spiels von zwey und mehreren Personen zu Spielen* (Leipzig: Siegfried Lebrecht Crusius, 1780), xi.

21. Johann Christian Ludwig Hellwig, *Das Kriegsspiel: ein Versuch die Wahrheit verschiedener Regeln der Kriegskunst in einem unterhaltenden Spiele anschaulich zu machen* (Braunschweig, Germany: bei Karl Reichard, 1803).

22. Hellwig, *Das Kriegsspiel*, 1–2.

23. For a more detailed account of the shift in the epistemology of war around 1800, see my earlier work *Empire of Chance*.

24. Johann Ferdinand Opiz, *Das Opiz'sche Kriegsspiel, ein Beitrag zur Bildung künftiger und zur Unterhaltung selbst der erfahrensten Taktiker* (Halle, Germany: Hendels Verlag, 1806), 13–15.

25. Opiz, *Das Opiz'sche Kriegsspiel*, 23.

26. As Jesper Juul has discussed, pain itself is often one of the attractions of playing games. See Jesper Juul, *The Art of Failure: An Essay on the Pain of Playing Video Games* (Cambridge, MA: MIT Press, 2013).

27. See, for example, Perla, *Art of Wargaming*; Philipp von Hilgers, *Kriegsspiele: Eine Geschichte der Ausnahmezustände und Unberechenbarkeiten* (Munich: Wilhelm Fink Verlag, 2008); Harrigan and Kirschenbaum, *Zones of Control*.

28. See Harrigan and Kirschenbaum, *Zones of Control*, xvii.

29. Harrigan and Kirschenbaum, xxvii.

30. Christian Jacob, *The Sovereign Map: Theoretical Approaches in Cartography throughout History*, trans. Tom Conley, ed. Edward H. Dahl (Chicago and London: University of Chicago Press, 2006), 21.

31. Hans Belting, *An Anthropology of Images: Picture, Medium, Body*, trans. Thomas Dunlap (Princeton, NJ: Princeton University Press, 2011), 27.

32. Belting, *Anthropology*, 28.

33. Venturini, *Beschreibung und Regeln*, xiv–xv.

34. Wilhelm Freiherr von Aretin, *Strategonon: Versuch, die Kriegführung durch ein Spiel anschaulich darzustellen* (Ansbach, Germany: Dollfuß, 1803), xi–xii.

35. Ludwig Freiherr von Welden, *Entwurf für die Verfertigung und Benützung der Plane zur praktischen Erläuterung mehrerer Theorien der Kriegskunst* (Vienna: Anton Strauß, 1825), 6.

36. Welden, *Entwurf*, 13.

37. Related ideas can be found in Otto August Rühle von Lilienstern's *Aufsätze über Gegenstände und Ereignisse aus dem Gebiete des Kriegswesens* (Berlin: Ernst Siegfried Mittler, 1818), and in the work of Heinrich von Kleist, in particular the play *Der Prinz von Homburg*. For an examination of the role of the emotions in Clausewitz's thought, see Ulrike Kleemeier, "Moral Forces in War," in *Clausewitz in the Twenty-First Century*, ed. Hew Strachan and Andreas Herberg-Rothe, 107–22 (Oxford: Oxford University Press, 2007).

38. Carl von Clausewitz, *Vom Kriege* (Bonn: Dümmler, 1980), 213; see also 208.

39. Clausewitz, *Vom Kriege*, 208.

40. See in particular *Vom Kriege*, book 1, chaps. 3 and 7.

41. Clausewitz, *Vom Kriege*, 1176.

42. Clausewitz, "Historische Briefe über die großen Kriegsereignisse 1806, 1807," in *Verstreute kleine Schriften*, ed. Werner Hahlweg (Osnabrück, Germany: Biblio Verlag, 1979), 116; Clausewitz, "Bemerkungen über die reine und angewandte Strategie des Herrn von Bülow oder Kritik der darin enthaltenen Ansichten," in *Verstreute kleine Schriften*, 82.

43. See Carl von Clausewitz, *Schriften, Aufsätze, Studien, Briefe*, part 2, ed. Werner Hahlweg (Göttingen: Vandenhoeck & Ruprecht, 1966/1990), 2:655–56.

44. Clausewitz, *Vom Kriege*, 369. For the importance of preparing soldiers for the experience of war, see also 265–66.

45. See also my more detailed account of the epistemology of Opiz's wargame in *Empire of Chance*, 127–33.

46. Opiz, *Das Opiz'sche Kriegsspiel*, 22–23.

47. Opiz, footnote on pp. 22–23.

48. Clausewitz, *Vom Kriege*, 254.

49. Aretin, *Strategonon*, xxxii.

50. Aristotle, *The Basic Works of Aristotle*, ed. Richard McKeon (New York: Modern Library, 2001), 1460.

51. Franz von Zychlinski, *Geschichte des 24sten Infanterie-Regiments, Zweiter Teil* (Berlin: Mittler's Sortiments-Buchhandlung, 1857), 196.

52. The "general merriment" (199) that did ensue had nothing to do with Reisswitz's game, but with the fact that the officers found the alcohol in the adjacent kitchen more interesting than the simulation of war.

CHAPTER 3

1. See Jeremiah Rozman, "The Synthetic Training Environment," the Association of the United States Army, December 2020, https://www.ausa.org/publications/synthetic-training-environment; and Ivan Martinez, "SFC Paul Ray Smith Simulation and Training Technology Center Overview," DEVCOM, 2021, https://www.trainingsystems.org/-/media/sites/ntsa/events/2021/11to/presentations/thu-17-june/17-june_1125-1_martinez_sttc-overview.ashx.

2. In an essay on video games, Patrick Crogan has also used the term *operational aesthetics* to theorize the interface between games and players. For Crogan, the term marks the link between "user input and preprogrammed responses." See Crogan, "Video Games, War, and Operational Aesthetics," in *War and Art: A Visual History of Modern Conflict*, ed. Joanna Bourke (London: Reaktion Books, 2017), 324–30, 424. As I use the term, however, operational aesthetics designates not merely an interface but the larger process of operationalizing aesthetic phenomena for the specific military purpose of waging war. In his fascinating book, *Operational Images*, Jussi Parikka develops Farocki's notion of the "operational image" into a broad analytical category that signals the transformation of the visual into action and connects images with data sets, platforms, and models. Going beyond war, Parikka discusses operational images across a large swath of domains in which images work to transform seeing into calculating and predicting. As part of this investigation, Parikka speaks of an "operational aesthetic." Even though my own term "operational aesthetics" is more general than Crogan's, it is more specific than Parikka's. His is a heuristic term that links technical imaging with operationality more broadly. But there are many overlaps and resonances with Parikka's media archaeological concept: training, sensation, control, and prediction are all central to both. See Jussi Parikka, *Operational Images* (Minneapolis: University of Minnesota Press, 2023).

3. See, for example, Martin van Creveld, *Wargames: From Gladiators to*

Gigabytes (Cambridge: Cambridge University Press, 2013); Pat Harrigan and Matthew G. Kirschenbaum, eds., *Zones of Control* (Cambridge, MA: MIT Press, 2016); Philip Sabin, *Simulating War: Studying Conflict through Simulation Games* (London and New York: Continuum, 2014); Philipp von Hilgers, *Kriegsspiele: Eine Geschichte der Ausnahmezustände und Unberechenbarkeiten* (Munich: Wilhelm Fink Verlag, 2008); and Peter P. Perla, *The Art of Wargaming* (Annapolis, MD: US Naval Institute, 1990).

4. Johann Ferdinand Opiz, *Das Opiz'sche Kriegsspiel, ein Beitrag zur Bildung künftiger und zur Unterhaltung selbst der erfahrensten Taktiker* (Halle, Germany: Hendels Verlag, 1806), 5.

5. Opiz, *Das Opiz'sche Kriegsspiel,* 5–6.

6. Georg Heinrich Rudolf Johann Freiheer von Reisswitz, *Taktisches Kriegs-Spiel* (Berlin: Gädicke, 1812), 1.

7. Clark C. Abt, *Serious Games* (Lanham, MD: University Press of America, 1987), 11–12.

8. See Parikka, *Operational Images*, chap. 2.

9. Rita Felski, *Uses of Literature* (Malden, MA: Blackwell, 2008), 8.

10. Felski, *Uses of Literature*, 8–9.

11. Quoted in Brian Sutton-Smith, *The Ambiguity of Play* (Cambridge, MA: Harvard University Press, 2001), 1.

12. See Henning Eichberg, *Questioning Play: What Play Can Tell Us about Social Life* (New York: Routledge, 2016), 139.

13. Johan Huizinga, *Homo Ludens: A Study of the Play-Element in Culture* (London: Routledge and Kegan Paul, 1980), 5, 9.

14. See Huizinga, chap. 5, "Play and War."

15. Huizinga, *Homo Ludens*, 61.

16. Huizinga, 18–19.

17. See Ryan Bishop, ed., "Baudrillard, Death, and Cold War Theory," in *Baudrillard Now: Current Perspectives in Baudrillard Studies* (Cambridge: Polity Press, 2009), 48; Rens van Munster and Casper Sylvest, *Nuclear Realism: Global Political Thought during the Thermonuclear Revolution* (London and New York: Routledge, 2016),120–21; and Tobias Nanz and Johannes Pause, "Das Undenkbare filmen. Einleitung," in *Das Undenkbare filmen: Atomkrieg im Kino*, ed. Tobias Nanz and Johannes Pause (Bielefeld, Germany: transcript Verlag, 2013), 7–24.

18. Herman Kahn, *On Escalation: Metaphors and Scenarios* (New Brunswick, NJ: Transaction Publishers, 2010), 39.

19. Sharon Gamari-Tabrizi, *The Worlds of Herman Kahn: The Intuitive Science of Thermonuclear War* (Cambridge, MA: Harvard University Press, 2005), 49.

20. Jean Baudrillard, *Simulacra and Simulation*, trans. Sheila Faria Glaser (Ann Arbor: University of Michigan Press, 1994), 31.

21. Sharon Ghamari-Tabrizi, "Simulating the Unthinkable: Gaming Future War in the 1950s and 1960s," *Social Studies of Science* 30 (2000): 164–222, 192–93.

22. Sharon Gamari-Tabrizi, "Wargames as Writing Systems," in *Zones of Control*, ed. Harrigan and Kirschenbaum, 337.

23. A. Scott Glancy, "The 'I' in Team. War and Combat in Tabletop Role-Playing Games," in *Zones of Control*, ed. Harrigan and Kirschenbaum, 71–80.

24. See Glancy, "The 'I' in Team." Many of these games include maps of the fictional world the player moves around in and, as Stephan Günzel has noted, thereby bring together in a single representation the two main modes of spatial representation in the history of European imagery: perspective and map projection. See Stephan Günzel, *Egoshooter: Das Raumbild des Computerspiels* (Frankfurt am Main: Campus Verlag, 2012).

25. See, for example, Roger Stahl, *Militainment, Inc.: War, Media, and Popular Culture* (New York and London: Routledge, 2010).

26. For an overview of these developments, see James Der Derian, *Virtuous War: Mapping the Military-Industrial-Media-Entertainment Complex*, 2nd ed. (New York: Routledge, 2009); Timothy Lenoir and Henry Lowood, "Theaters of War: The Military-Entertainment Complex," in *Collection, Laboratory, Theater: Scenes of Knowledge in the 17th Century*, ed. Helmar Schramm, Ludger Schwarte, and Jan Lazardzig, 427–56 (Berlin and New York: de Gruyter, 2005); Timothy Lenoir and Luke Caldwell, *The Military-Entertainment Complex* (Cambridge, MA: Harvard University Press, 2018); and Stahl, *Militainment, Inc.*

27. Detailed accounts of the opening can be found in Der Derian, *Virtuous War*, 160–76, as well as in Lenoir and Lowood "Theaters of War."

28. Institute for Creative Technologies, "Who We Are," n.d. https://vhtoolkit.ict.usc.edu/vhtk-who-we-are.html.

29. *20 Years in Excellence in Supporting the DoD and Society*. Los Angeles: USC Institute for Creative Technologies, 2019. https://ict.usc.edu/wp-content/uploads/2021/05/Historical-Achievements.pdf, 2.

30. *20 Years in Excellence*, 3. See also Lucy Suchman's analysis of one of these projects, *FlatWorld* (2001–2007), in "Configuring the Other: Sensing War through Immersive Simulation," *Catalyst: Feminism, Theory, Technoscience* 2, no. 1: 1–36.

31. *STRIVE* was subsequently awarded the 2014 Army Modeling and Simulation Award. See http://ict.usc.edu/news/strive-project-receives-2014-army-modeling-and-simulation-award/. In 2019, the ICT launched a new research program called EMPOWER—Enhancing Mental Performance and Optimizing

Warfighter Effectiveness and Resilience—that seeks to improve resilience through the integration of virtual human technology with AI and big-data analytics. *20 Years in Excellence*, 35.

32. *STRIVE*, Institute for Creative Technologies. 2015. http://ict.usc.edu/prototypes/strive/.

33. The system is currently distributed to over eighty sites, such as VA hospitals, military bases, and universities. See http://ict.usc.edu/prototypes/pts/ and *20 Years in Excellence*, 28. For a detailed analysis of the ICT and its virtual scenarios, see Anders Engberg-Pedersen, "Technologies of Experience: Harun Farocki's *Serious Games* and Military Aesthetics," *Boundary 2* 44, no. 4 (Fall 2017): 155–78.

34. For a perceptive critique of the virtual reality exposure therapy developed at the ICT, see Marisa R. Brandt, "Simulated War: Remediating Trauma Narratives in Military Psychotherapy," *Catalyst: Feminism, Theory, Technoscience* 2, no. 1: 1–42.

35. This project later received the 2010 American Psychological Association Award for Outstanding Contributions to the Practice of Trauma Psychology.

36. It has since been reorganized under the name PEO STRI (the US Army Program Executive Office for Simulation, Training, and Instrumentation).

37. Der Derian, *Virtuous War*, 87–89. Such adoptions are openly acknowledged. As Chris Morris, the technical manager for warfighting experimentation at Qinetiq, Britain's Ministry of Defence testing establishment, stated back in 2002: "We've been using flight and vehicle simulations for a long time now. . . . However, it is far more difficult to create a realistic synthetic environment for foot soldiers. . . . We decided to concentrate on the mental and procedural issues, so we started to look for a computer game we could modify." See John Crace, "War Game," *Guardian*, July 9, 2002. https://www.theguardian.com/education/2002/jul/09/furthereducation.uk1.

38. *Bravemind: Virtual Reality Exposure Theory*, Institute for Creative Technologies, 2015. http://ict.usc.edu/prototypes/pts/.

39. *Stress Resilience in Virtual Environments (STRIVE)*, Institute for Creative Technologies, 2015. http://ict.usc.edu/prototypes/strive/. There is also a clear connection to the emotional poetics of Hollywood war films. They have long made use of a varied series of pathos scenes or pathos formulas in order to manage the affective response of viewers. See Hermann Kappelhoff, "Der Kriege im Spiegel des Genrekinos: John Ford's *They Were Expendable*," in *Mobilisierung der Sinne: Der Hollywood-Kriegsfilm zwischen Genrekino und Historie*, ed. Hermann Kappelhoff, David Gaertner, and Cilli Pogodda, 184–227 (Berlin: Vorwerk 8, 2013). The affective modulation of Hollywood war films, however, targets the collective sense of an emotional community rather than

the individual trauma in the wargames, where the pathos scenes are also scripted live by the soldiers themselves. Moreover, to increase the experiential illusion further, recent VR trauma therapy includes features that enable the customization of sounds and smells. See "Virtual Reality Therapy Plunges Patients Back into Trauma. Here Is Why Some Swear by It," *New York Times*, June 3, 2021. https://www.nytimes.com/2021/06/03/well/mind/vr-therapy.html.

40. Alexander Gottlieb Baumgarten, *Aesthetica/Ästhetik* (Hamburg: Felix Meiner Verlag, 2007), 1:11.

41. See Jacques Rancière, *Malaise dans l'esthétique* (Paris: Editions Galilée, 2004); *Le Partage du sensible: Esthétique et politique* (Paris: La Fabrique Éditions, 2000); and *The Politics of Aesthetics: The Distribution of the Sensible*, trans. Gabriel Rockhill (London: Continuum, 2004); Jacques Rancière, Gavin Arnall, Laura Gandolfi, and Enea Zaramella, "Aesthetics and Politics Revisited: An Interview with Jacques Rancière," *Critical Inquiry* 38 (Winter 2012): 289–97; Jacques Rancière and Davide Panagia, "Dissenting Words: A Conversation with Jacques Rancière," *Diacritics* 30, no. 2 (Summer 2000): 113–26; and Jacques Rancière, Marie-Aude Baronian, and Mireille Rosello, "Jacques Rancière and Indisciplinarity," *Art & Research* 2, no. 1 (Summer 2008): 1–10.

42. Jacques Rancière, *Aesthetics and Its Discontents*, trans. Steven Corcoran (Cambridge: Polity Press, 2009), 25. See also *Politics of Aesthetics*, 13.

43. See Bernhard Stiegler, *Symbolic Misery*, vol. 1, *The Hyperindustrial Epoch* (Cambridge: Polity Press, 2014).

44. See especially chap. 4 in Pasi Väliaho, *Biopolitical Screens: Image, Power, and the Neoliberal Brain* (Cambridge, MA: MIT Press, 2014).

45. The game *America's Army*, developed by the US Army in 2002, clearly works as a recruitment instrument. Only six years after it came on the market, it had nine million registered users across the world, and an estimated 19 percent of all US recruits have played the game. At the same time, it is a very subtle form of military propaganda more akin to advertising. As Farocki notes: "In this sense, you introduce the war into the imaginary." As with war films, he continues, games expose the public to "danger, [to] the fact that you don't know who is firing on you, and that you are surprised, and all these things have become part of the common imaginary." See Stahl, *Militainment*, 106; Günzel, *Egoshooter*, 123; and ter Brink and Oppenheimer, *Killer Images: Documentary Film, Memory and the Performance of Violence* (New York: Wallflower Press, 2012), 70.

46. See Suchman, "Configuring the Other."

47. Claus Pias, "The Game Player's Duty: The User as the Gestalt of the Ports," in *Media Archeology: Approaches, Applications, and Implications*, ed.

Erkki Huhtamo and Jussi Parikka, 164–84 (Berkeley: University of California Press, 2011), 179.

48. Bohemia Interactive Simulations, product brochure, "VBS 3. Virtual Desktop Training and Simulation," 2020. https://bisimulations.com/products/vbs3. Moreover, in late 2021, Bohemia Interactive Simulations, the maker of the VBS platform, partnered with the Norwegian firm Kongsberg to develop the "Core™ Training Simulator" for in-vehicle virtual training. As Pia Andersen, a program director at Kongsberg, put it: "Because you are using real equipment, training with control grips and interacting with buttons, this approach to training improves and strengthens muscle memory. Combined with the stunningly realistic virtual world provided by VBS4, it's also more engaging, which improves knowledge retention and drives behavioral change." Bohemia Interactive Simulations, press release, "Kongsberg Defence & Aerospace Debut New Core™ Training Simulator Using BISIM's VBS4 at I/ITSEC 2021," November 29, 2021. https://www.bisimulations.com/company/news/press-releases/kongsberg-defence-aerospace-debut-new-core-training-simulator-using-bisim..

49. Baumgarten, *Ästhetik*, 1:38–39.

50. Baumgarten, 1:40–41.

51. Baumgarten, 1:40–41.

52. Baumgarten, 1:92–93.

53. Similar disjunctions structure the postbellum therapeutic scenarios. *Bravemind*, for example, prohibits the user from killing anyone in the virtual world, just as only male civilians can be injured. See Brandt, "Simulated War," 31–32.

54. John Dewey, *Art as Experience* (New York: Berkley Publishing Group, 2005), 54.

55. Douglas Maxwell, *Application of Virtual Environments for Infantry Soldier Skills Training: We Are Doing It Wrong* (Orlando, FL: US Army Research Laboratory, Advanced Training and Simulation Division, 2016).

56. Susan G. Straus, Matthew W. Lewis, Kathryn Connor, Rick Eden, Matthew E. Boyer, Timothy Marler, Christopher M. Carson, Geoffrey E. Grimm, and Heather Smigowski, "Collective Simulation-Based Training in the US Army: User Interface Fidelity, Costs, and Training Effectiveness" (Santa Monica, CA: Rand Corporation, 2019), 31.

57. Straus et al., "Collective Simulation-Based Training," 33.

58. Indeed, one review paper concluded, "Furthermore, we did not identify any empirical evidence that virtual exposure is particularly helpful for patients with imagination difficulties. This is surprising because it is a frequently cited argument for VRET." Thiemo Knaust, Anna Felnhofer, Oswald D. Kothgassner, Helge Höllmer, Robert-Jacek Gorzka, and Holger Schulz, "Virtual Trauma

Interventions for the Treatment of Post-Traumatic Stress Disorders: A Scoping Review," *Frontiers in Psychology* 11, art. 562506 (November 2020). https://www.frontiersin.org/articles/10.3389/fpsyg.2020.562506/full. See also L. V. Eshuis, M. J. van Gelderen, M. van Zuiden, M. J. Nijdam, E. Vermetten, M. Olff, and A. Bakker, "Efficacy of Immersive PTSD Treatments: A Systematic Review of Virtual and Augmented Reality Exposure Therapy and a Meta-Analysis of Virtual Reality Exposure Therapy," *Journal of Psychiatric Research* 143 (2021): 516–27; Ana Vianez, António Marques, and Raquel Simões de Almeida, "Virtual Reality Exposure Therapy for Armed Forces Veterans with Post-Traumatic Stress Disorder: A Systematic Review and Focus Group," *International Journal of Environmental Research and Public Health* 19, no. 1 (January 2022): 464; and David J. Morris, *The Evil Hours: A Biography of Post-Traumatic Stress Disorder* (Boston: Mariner Books, 2016).

59. Nelson Goodman, *Ways of Worldmaking* (Indianapolis, IN: Hackett, 1978), 22.

60. Goodman, *Worldmaking*, 7.

61. Goodman, 102.

62. Goodman, 104.

63. Elaine Scarry, *The Body in Pain: The Making and Unmaking of the World* (Oxford: Oxford University Press, 1985), 150.

64. Scarry, *Body in Pain*, 21.

65. Scarry, 145.

66. Scarry, 172.

67. I make use of Scarry's terms here, but in a slightly different manner. For Scarry, *making-up* denotes the process of mental invention, while *making-real* denotes the externalization and materialization that comes with the creation of an artifact. The operational purpose of military aesthetics, however, adds a dimension insofar as the made-up scenarios developed in and through the artifact might subsequently be realized in concrete military operations on the ground. Making-real, then, involves not only the externalization of mental processes in an object but the coordination of mental processes and the artifact to realize a given tactic or strategy. See Scarry, 146.

68. Johannes Kepler, *Die Astrologie des Johannes Kepler: Eine Auswahl aus seinen Schriften*, ed. H. A. Strauss and S. Strauss-Kloebe (Fellbach, Germany: Verlag Adolf Bonz, 1981), 239.

69. Väliaho, *Biopolitical Screens*, 24.

70. Rozman, "Synthetic Training Environment."

71. Stephany Nuneley, "US Army Spending $57 Million on Military Simulator Using CryEngine 3," *VG247*, May 27, 2011. http://www.vg247.com/2011/05/27/us-army-spending-57-million-on-military-simulator-using-cryengine-3/.

72. ter Brink and Oppenheimer, *Killer Images*, 76.

73. Entrust Solutions, "Military Training Simulation Software: Artificial Intelligence for Armed Servicemembers," November 13, 2020. https://www.entrustsolutions.com/2020/11/13/military-training-simulation-software-ai/.

74. "Dominate the Fight: The Army's Synthetic Training Environment," *YouTube*, https://www.youtube.com/watch?v=dWrquTLhMDU&list=PLv1hRo99y64zHduzCeK-v_PTXopZYHmpa&index=1. Quotation at 2:21.

75. Louise Amoore, *The Politics of Possibility: Risk and Security beyond Probability* (Durham, NC, and London: Duke University Press, 2013), 1.

76. Brian Massumi, *Ontopower: War, Powers, and the State of Perception* (Durham, NC, and London: Duke University Press, 2015), 3–19. For an insightful account of the military driver of future studies and a critique of the anticipatory paradigm that governed much Cold War military thought, see van Munster and Sylvest, *Nuclear Realism*.

77. Nick Montfort, *The Future* (Cambridge, MA: MIT Press, 2017), xi.

78. Montfort, *The Future*, 4.

79. Montfort, xi.

80. Montfort, xii.

CHAPTER 4

1. James Norman Mattis, *Memorandum for U.S. Joint Forces Command: Assessment of Effects Based Operations*. August 14, 2008. https://smallwarsjournal.com/documents/usjfcomebomemo.pdf.

2. Mattis, *Assessment*, 6.

3. Mattis, 6.

4. Mattis, 7.

5. James Norman Mattis, *Memorandum for U.S. Joint Forces Command: Vision for a Joint Approach to Operational Design*. October 6, 2009. http://www.jfcom.mil/newslink/storyarchive/2009/aod_2009.pdf , 2.

6. Beatrice Heuser, "Theory and Practice, Art and Science in Warfare," in *War, Strategy & History: Essays in Honor of Professor Robert O'Neill* (Acton: Australian National University Press, 2016), 179–96, 193. See also Heuser, *The Evolution of Strategy: Thinking War from Antiquity to the Present* (Cambridge: Cambridge University Press, 2010); and Milan Vego, "Science vs. the Art of War," *Joint Force Quarterly* 66 (2012): 62–70.

7. See Alice König, "Conflicting Models of Authority and Expertise in Frontinus' *Strategemata*," in *Authority and Expertise in Ancient Scientific Culture*, ed. Jason König and Greg Woolf, 153–81 (Cambridge: Cambridge University Press, 2017). See also Heuser, "Theory and Practice," 183.

8. For the science of war in the eighteenth century, see Azar Gat, *The Origins*

of Military Thought from the Enlightenment to Clausewitz (Oxford: Clarendon Press, 1991); Antoine Bousquet, *The Scientific Way of Warfare: Order and Chaos on the Battlefields of Modernity* (New York: Columbia University Press, 2009); and Anders Engberg-Pedersen, "The Refraction of Geometry: *Tristram Shandy* and the Poetics of War 1700/1800," *Representations* 123, no. 1 (Summer 2013): 23–52.

9. Heinrich Dietrich Freiherr von Bülow, *Geist des Neuern Kriegssystems, hergeleitet aus dem Grundsatze eines Basis der Operationen* (Hamburg: Benjamin Gottlieb Hofmann, 1799), 214.

10. Heuser, "Theory and Practice," 180–82.

11. Carl von Clausewitz, *Geist und Tat: Das Vermächtnis des Soldaten und Denkers*, ed. Walther Malmsten Schering (Stuttgart: Alfred Kröner Verlag, 1942), 53.

12. Otto August Rühle von Lilienstern, *Aufsätze über Gegenstände und Ereignisse aus dem Gebiete des Kriegswesens* (Berlin: Ernst Siegfried Mittler, 1818), 76–77.

13. Rühle von Lilienstern, *Aufsätze*, 77.

14. Rühle von Lilienstern, 46.

15. Rühle von Lilienstern, 45.

16. Rühle von Lilienstern, 72, 47.

17. Rühle von Lilienstern, 47

18. Rühle von Lilienstern, 46.

19. Rühle von Lilienstern, 42.

20. Rühle von Lilienstern, 41.

21. Rühle von Lilienstern, 249.

22. Immanuel Kant, *Kritik der Urteilskraft* (Hamburg: Felix Meiner Verlag, 2001), 193.

23. Otto August Rühle von Lilienstern, *Bericht eines Augenzeugen, von dem Feldzuge der während den Monaten September und October 1806 unter dem Kommando des Fürsten zu Hohenlohe-Ingelfingen gestandenen Königl: preußischen und Kurfürstl. sächsischen Truppen* (Tübingen, Germany: Cotta, 1809), 198–99. Georg Heinrich von Berenhorst, Rühle's friend and fellow reader of Kant, similarly linked military command with the aesthetics of genius. In his influential three-volume book *Observations on the Art of War, on Its Progress, Its Contradictions and Its Reliability*, he wrote that "the genius of the true commander is just as different from the mere art of maneuvering, as the Muse, who inspires odes and heroic poems, is different from the science that teaches how to count syllables and metrical feet." Georg Heinrich von Berenhorst, *Betrachtungen über die Kriegskunst, über ihre Fortschritte, ihre Widersprüche und ihre Zuverlässigkeit* (Osnabrück, Germany: Biblio Verlag, 1978), 341. For the wider

influence of Romantic thought on the military theories of the time, see also Wolf Kittler, "War and Romantic Thought," in *War and Literary Studies*, ed. Anders Engberg-Pedersen and Neil Ramsey (Cambridge: Cambridge University Press, 2023).

24. See, for example, Rühle von Lilienstern, *Aufsätze*, 249, and *Handbuch für den Officier zur Belehrung im Frieden und zum Gebrauch im Felde* (Berlin: Reimer, 1817), 68–70.

25. Rühle von Lilienstern, "Über Theorie und Praxis: über den Unterschied von Wissenschaft und Kunst," in *Aufsätze*, 72.

26. Rühle von Lilienstern, *Aufsätze*, 72.

27. Rühle von Lilienstern, 74.

28. Rühle von Lilienstern, 74–75.

29. Beatrice Heuser also notes the irony that Clausewitz gets credit for establishing the link between war and politics. See Heuser, *Evolution of Strategy*, 13. The overlaps with the ideas formulated by Rühle von Lilienstern, however, go well beyond this one argument.

30. Carl von Clausewitz, *Vom Kriege* (Bonn: Dümmler, 1980), 231–32.

31. Clausewitz, 232, 236.

32. As his letters to his wife, Marie von Clausewitz, reveal, Clausewitz was highly cultured and well read. He was equally comfortable commenting on Schiller's *Wallenstein* and Sterne's *Tristram Shandy* as he was writing sonnets. See *Karl und Maria von Clausewitz: Ein Lebensbild in Briefen und Tagebuchblättern*, ed. Karl Linnebach (Berlin: Verlag von Martin Warneck, 1925).

33. Clausewitz, "Über den Begriff des körperlich Schönen," in *Geist und Tat*, 166–70, 167.

34. Clausewitz, "Über den Begriff," 168.

35. Clausewitz, 169.

36. Clausewitz, 170.

37. Clausewitz, "Architektonische Rhapsodien," in *Geist und Tat*, 170–72.

38. Clausewitz, "Charakter der Privathäuser," in *Geist und Tat*, 172–78, 174.

39. For the reference to Mozart, see "Strategie aus dem Jahr 1804," in *Verstreute kleine Schriften*, ed. Werner Hahlweg (Osnabrück: Biblio Verlag, 1979), 6.

40. Clausewitz, "Über Kunst und Kunsttheorie," in *Geist und Tat*, 153–66, 158.

41. Clausewitz, "Über Kunst und Kunsttheorie," 159.

42. Clausewitz, 165.

43. Clausewitz, *Vom Kriege*, 302.

44. Clausewitz, *Vom Kriege*, 345.

45. Already in the opening chapter of *Vom Kriege*, Clausewitz defines the

relation between means and ends: "Violence then . . . is *the means*; to impose our will on the enemy is *the purpose*." *Vom Kriege*, 192. See his further reflections on the dual purpose of military victory and the achievement of the ultimate political goals in chap. 2, "Purpose and Means in War," 214.

46. Clausewitz, 345.

47. Clausewitz, 345 and 422–23. See further "Über den Zustand der Theorie der Kriegskunst," in *Geist und Tat*, 52–60; and *Schriften, Aufsätze, Studien, Briefe*, ed. Werner Hahlweg (Göttingen, Germany: Vandenhoeck & Ruprecht, 1966/1990), part 1, 2:77.

48. Clausewitz, *Vom Kriege*, 346.

49. Clausewitz, "Über Kunst und Kunsttheorie," 161.

50. Clausewitz, "Über Kunst und Kunsttheorie," 158.

51. Clausewitz, *Vom Kriege*, 303.

52. Clausewitz, 303.

53. Clausewitz, 302. In similar fashion, Ernst von Pfuel, who would later become minister of war and prime minister of Prussia, at once couches warfare in the language of aesthetics and notes the shortcomings of the analogy. See "Ueber das Studium der Kriegsgeschichte," *Deutsches Museum* 1 (1812): 221–37, 225–26.

54. Clausewitz, *Schriften, Aufsätze*, part 1, 2:74.

55. Clausewitz, *Vom Kriege*, 283.

56. Rühle von Lilienstern, "Apologie des Krieges," in *Aufsätze*, 101–79, 104.

57. Rühle von Lilienstern, "Apologie des Krieges," 101.

58. Rühle von Lilienstern, 146.

59. Karma Nabulsi, *Traditions of War: Occupation, Resistance and the Law* (Oxford: Oxford University Press, 2000), 81.

60. See in particular chap. 4, "High Priests of the Temple of Janus: The Martial Tradition of War." Nabulsi's discussion is insightful, but while Clausewitz, in particular the early Clausewitz, certainly expressed views that would seem to place him squarely within the martialist tradition, his historical writings, his letters, and *On War* itself frequently problematize a straightforward martialist reading. For one, we should take care not to mistake his philosophical concept of "absolute war" with his own promotion of it—regardless of the fate of this concept in the twentieth century.

61. The enduring power of this idea is evident in contemporary research on creativity. See, for example, R. Keith-Sawyer, *Explaining Creativity: The Science of Human Innovation* (Oxford: Oxford University Press, 2011).

62. See James Engell, *The Creative Imagination: Enlightenment to Romanticism* (Cambridge, MA: Harvard University Press, 1981). See also Andreas Reckwitz, *Die Erfindung der Kreativität: Zum Prozess gesellschaftlicher Ästhetisierung*

(Berlin: Suhrkamp Verlag, 2012), 63; and Larry Shiner, *The Invention of Art: A Cultural History* (Chicago and London: University of Chicago Press, 2001), 113–14.

63. Alexander Gerard, *An Essay on Genius* (London: W. Strahan, 1774), 8.

64. Reckwitz, *Erfindung*, 64.

65. Clausewitz, *Vom Kriege*, 213.

66. Helmuth von Moltke, *Moltke on the Art of War: Selected Writings* (New York: Presidion Press, 1993), 43, 93.

67. von Moltke, *Moltke on the Art of War*, 124.

68. The German army's official manual for World War II opens with the statement, "The conduct of war is an art, a free creative activity based on a disciplined [*wissenschaftliche*] foundation." See Deutsches Reich Heer Oberkommando, *Truppenführung* (Berlin: Mittler, 1933), 1:1.

69. See Ursula von Gersdorff, "Jähns, Maximilian," in *Neue Deutsche Biographie* 10 (1974): 284. https://www.deutsche-biographie.de/pnd117058750.html#ndbcontent.

70. Maximilian Jähns, *Die Kriegskunst als Kunst* (Leipzig: F. W. Grunow, 1874), 4.

71. Jähns, *Kriegskunst*, 5.

72. Jähns, 6.

73. Jähns, 6–7.

74. Jähns, 8.

75. Jähns, 9.

76. Jähns, 25.

77. Jähns, 39.

78. Jähns, 38.

79. A.T. Mahan, *Naval Strategy* (Boston: Little, Brown, 1911), 299–300.

80. James Mrazek, *The Art of Winning Wars* (London: Leo Cooper, 1968), 1–2.

81. See Luc Boltanski and Ève Chiapello, *The New Spirit of Capitalism* (London and New York: Verso, 2018). See also John Beck and Ryan Bishop, *Technocrats of the Imagination: Art, Technology, and the Military-Industrial Avant-Garde* (Durham, NC, and London: Duke University Press, 2020).

82. See Reckwitz, *Erfindung*, 15.

83. Reckwitz, *Erfindung*, 15, 17, 52–53.

84. Mrazek, *Art of Winning Wars*, 4.

85. As Mrazek puts it: "Regardless of the wide disparity between the two activities, they both originate from powerful creative insights and drives" (136).

86. Mrazek, 138.

87. Mrazek, 40–42, 160.

88. Mrazek, 103.
89. Mrazek, 121.
90. Mrazek, 123.
91. Mrazek, 103.
92. Mrazek, 123.
93. Mrazek, 167.
94. Mrazek, 160, 99, 134.

CHAPTER 5

1. In 2018, Dan Öberg published an important critique of military design in which he wrote that "it may be argued that military design has not had a comprehensive impact on war. Taken as a whole, it constitutes a microcosm with a somewhat limited scope." Dan Öberg, "Warfare as Design: Transgressive Creativity and Reductive Operational Planning," *Security Dialogue* 49, no. 6 (December 2018): 493–509, 10. The present chapter builds on Öberg's critique, but by situating military design within aesthetics, it also shows that military design is merely the most recent instantiation of a theoretical conception of war that has a deeper history. Moreover, the "microcosm" of design has expanded significantly in scope during the past couple of years. While its advocates have a tendency to overstate its importance, military design has by now become a significant movement across several Western militaries.

2. Chris Paparone, "Critical Military Epistemology: Designing Reflexivity into Military Curricula," *Journal of Military and Strategic Studies* 17, no. 4 (2017): 123–38, 123.

3. Stefan J. Banach and Alex Ryan, "The Art of Design: A Design Methodology," *Military Review* (March-April 2009): 105–15, 110, 112.

4. The origins of military design have been traced all the way back to nineteenth-century Prussia, with further developments in the Soviet Union in the 1920s and 1930s, and the wider adoption of its early forms by Western militaries in the 1980s. See Aaron Jackson, "A Brief History of Military Design Thinking," *Medium*, February 6, 2019. https://medium.com/@aaronpjackson/a-brief-history-of-military-design-thinking-b27ba9571b89#_ednref4. The main originator of military design in its current form, however, is the retired Israeli brigadier general Shimon Naveh.

5. William T. Sorrels, Glen R. Downing, Paul J. Blakesley, David W. Pendall, Jason K. Wlak, and Richard D. Wallwork, *Systemic Operational Design: An Introduction* (Fort Leavenworth, KS: School of Advanced Military Studies, 2005). For the early history of design discourse, see also Stephan De Spiegeleire, Tim Sweijs, Peter Wijninga, and Joris Van Esch, *Designing Future Stabilisation Efforts* (The Hague: The Hague Center for Strategic Studies, 2014).

6. Sorrells et al., *Systemic Operational Design*, 15.

7. Eyal Weizman, *Hollow Land* (London, Verso: 2012), 199–200.

8. Weizman, *Hollow Land*, 200–201.

9. See Weizman, *Hollow Land*, 214.

10. US Army, School of Advanced Military Studies (SAMS), *Art of Design: Student Text, Version 2.0* (Fort Leavenworth, KS: School of Advanced Military Studies, 2010), ii.

11. The statement belongs to Jeffrey M. Reilly. See Richard R. Dickens, *Operational Design: The Art of Framing the Solution* (Montgomery, AL: Air Command and Staff College, 2010), 1.

12. For the history of design theory, see Jackson, "Brief History of Military Design Thinking"; De Spiegeleire et al., *Designing Future Stabilisation Efforts*; Banach and Ryan, "Art of Design"; William F. Dufresne, *Design Doctrine in Military Planning* (Newport, RI: Naval War College, 2018); Jeffrey van der Veer, "The Rise of Design: Why an Innovative Concept Is Emulated around the Globe" (master's thesis, Royal Netherlands Defence Academy, 2015); Öberg, "Warfare as Design"; and Ben Zweibelson, Lars Hedström, Magnus Lindström, and Ulrica Pettersson, "The Emergent Art of Military Design: Swedish Armed Forces and the Contemporary Security Environment," *Analys & Perspektiv* 3 (July/September 2017): 83–97.

13. Zweibelson et al., "Emergent Art of Military Design," 94; Ben Zweibelson, "Fostering Deep Insight through Substantive Play," in *Design Thinking: Applications for the Australian Defence Force*, ed. Aaron P. Jackson, Joint Studies Paper Series, no. 3 (Canberra: Australian Defence Publishing Service, 2019), 110. See also Alex Ryan, "A Personal Reflection on Introducing Design to the U.S. Army," *Medium*, November 4, 2016. https://medium.com/the-overlap/a-personal-reflection-on-introducing-design-to-the-u-s-army-3f8bd76adcb2.

14. See, for example, Lawrence Freedman, *The Future of War—A History* (London: Allen Lane, 2017), 187–93, and Theo Farrell, Sten Rynning, and Terry Terriff, *Transforming Military Power Since the Cold War: Britain, France, and the United States, 1991–2012* (Cambridge: Cambridge University Press, 2013), 286–87.

15. Antoine Bousquet, *The Scientific Way of Warfare: Order and Chaos on the Battlefields of Modernity* (New York: Columbia University Press, 2009), 34, 185–234.

16. David Barno, "Military Adaptation in Complex Operations," *Prism* 1, no. 1 (December 2009): 27–36, 30.

17. See Philippe Beaulieu-Brossard, "Encountering Nomads in Israel Defense Forces and Beyond," in *Concepts at Work: On the Linguistic Infrastructure of World Politics*, ed. Piki Ish-Shalom (Ann Arbor: University of Michigan Press, 2021), 91–117.

18. See the *Commander's Appreciation and Campaign Design* (CACD), TRADOC Pamphlet 525-5-500, US Army, 2008, 9–10, 13.

19. CACD, 39.

20. Ben Zweibelson has recently argued that play should be adopted for the purposes of war as a central mode of learning. As he writes, "Play is not only useful *but essential in design praxis for the most challenging of society's military applications*." Zweibelson, "Fostering Deep Insight," 106.

21. James Norman Mattis, *Memorandum for U.S. Joint Forces Command: Assessment of Effects Based Operations*, August 14, 2008. https://smallwarsjournal.com/documents/usjfcomebomemo.pdf, 7; *Memorandum for U.S. Joint Forces Command: Vision for a Joint Approach to Operational Design*, October 6, 2009. http://www.jfcom.mil/newslink/storyarchive/2009/aod_2009.pdf, 6.

22. Carl von Clausewitz, *Vom Kriege* (Bonn: Dümmler, 1980), 208. See also Anders Engberg-Pedersen, *Empire of Chance: The Napoleonic Wars and the Disorder of Things* (Cambridge, MA: Harvard University Press, 2015).

23. CACD, 8–9.

24. Joint Chiefs of Staff, *Planner's Handbook for Operational Design* (Suffolk, VA: Joint and Coalition Warfighting, 2011), introduction, no page number.

25. *Planner's Handbook*, IV-3.

26. *Planner's Handbook*, I-4.

27. *Planner's Handbook*, III-8.

28. Andreas Reckwitz, *Die Erfindung der Kreativität: Zum Prozess gesellschaftlicher Ästhetisierung* (Berlin: Suhrkamp Verlag, 2012), 104. See also John Beck and Ryan Bishop, *Technocrats of the Imagination: Art, Technology, and the Military-Industrial Avant-Garde* (Durham, NC, and London: Duke University Press, 2020), 22.

29. In the 1950s, civilian design thinkers such as Buckminster Fuller and Herbert Simon came to regard design as a form of science. This was in part due to the strong influence of operations research and systems analysis following World War II. The association of design with art and creativity that dominates today, however, owes much to later civilian design theorists such as Melvin Webber, Horst Ritter, and Victor Papanek, who in the 1960s and 1970s explored how complex problems required innovative solutions that had more to do with the practical intuitions of the artist than the rational mind of the scientist. For an overview of this development, see Aaron P. Jackson, *Design Thinking in Commerce and War: Contrasting Civilian and Military Innovation Methodologies* (Maxwell Air Force Base, AL: Air University Press, 2020), 13–15.

30. Quoting design theorist Klaus Krippendorff, Paparone states that "'design is a sense creating activity' that can claim perception, experience, and, perhaps, esthetics as its fundamental concern." Chris Paparone, "A Primer for Key

Terms and Concepts Associated with *Design Thinking*," *Archipelago of Design*, August 2019, 7. https://aodnetwork.ca/wp-content/uploads/2019/08/Primer_Associated_Terms_and_Concepts_V_08_22_19-post.docx.pdf.

31. Tom Kelley, *The Art of Innovation: Lessons in Creativity from IDEO, America's Leading Design Firm* (New York: Doubleday, 2001), 69.

32. Julian Bleecker, *Design Fiction: A Short Essay on Design, Science, Fact, and Fiction*, Near Future Laboratory, March 2009, 6. http://drbfw5wfjlxon.cloudfront.net/writing/DesignFiction_WebEdition.pdf.

33. De Spiegeleire et al., *Designing Future Stabilization Efforts*, 14.

34. De Spiegeleire et al., 20.

35. See Chris Paparone, *The Sociology of Military Science: Prospects for Postinstitutional Military Design* (New York and London: Bloomsbury, 2013). Paparone was an early proponent of military design and articulated his views in three articles in the online *Small Wars Journal*: "Design and the Prospects of a Military Renaissance," *Small Wars Journal*, May 2010. https://smallwarsjournal.com/blog/journal/docs-temp/429-paparone.pdf; "Design and the Prospects for Deviant Leadership," *Small Wars Journal*, September 2010. https://smallwarsjournal.com/blog/journal/docs-temp/530-paparone.pdf; and "Design and the Prospects for Mission Analysis," *Small Wars Journal*, October 2010. https://smallwarsjournal.com/blog/journal/docs-temp/569-paparone.pdf.

36. Paparone, *Sociology of Military Science*, 4, 94.

37. Christopher R. Paparone and George L. Topic, "Design and the Prospect for Artistry," *Small Wars Journal*, December 2010. https://smallwarsjournal.com/blog/journal/docs-temp/618-paparonetucker.pdf , 9.

38. Paparone, *Sociology of Military Science*, 49.

39. Paparone, *Sociology of Military Science*, 55–56. See also Paparone, "Primer," 7.

40. Paparone, *Sociology of Military Science*, 135.

41. Paparone, 58.

42. Paparone, 65. See also 29.

43. Paparone, 134.

44. Paparone, 134.

45. Paparone, 102.

46. Hannah Arendt, *On Violence* (San Diego, CA: Harcourt Brace Jovanovich, 1970), 7.

47. Richard Swain, *Fundamentals of Operational Design* (Washington, DC: Booz Allen Hamilton, 2009), 7.

48. Anna Grome, Beth Crandall, Louise Rasmussen, and Heather Wolters, *Army Design Methodology: Commander's Resource* (Arlington, VA: Army Research Institute for Behavioral and Social Sciences, 2012), 42, 25.

49. Grome et al., *Army Design Methodology*, 18.

50. Grome et al., 22.

51. Öberg, "Warfare as Design," 6.

52. Banach and Ryan, "Art of Design," 106.

53. SAMS, *Art of Design*, 9.

54. Paparone, *Sociology of Military Science*, 67.

55. Zweibelson et al., "Emergent Art of Military Design," 94.

56. See the online military design hub *Archipelago of Design*, https://aodnetwork.ca/about-archipelago/.

57. John Stanczak, Peyton Talbott, and Ben Zweibelson, "Designing at the Cutting Edge of Battle: The 75th Ranger Regiment's Project Galahad," *Special Operations Journal* 7, no. 1 (2021): 1–16, 7.

58. Stanczak et al., "Designing at the Cutting Edge of Battle," 7.

59. Paparone, *Sociology of Military Science*, 59.

60. Paparone, 59.

61. Paparone, 60.

62. Paparone, 61–62.

63. Paparone, 62–63.

64. Paparone, 63.

65. Beaulieu-Brossard, "Encountering Nomads," 99, 95, 107. See also Zweibelson, "Fostering Deep Insight."

66. *Planner's Handbook for Operational Design*, II-1; Paparone, *Sociology of Military Science*, 10. See also Zweibelson, "Emergent Art of Military Design, 88.

67. CACD, 15; Banach and Ryan, "Art of Design," 110; Grome et al., *Army Design Methodology*, 22.

68. Banach and Ryan, "Art of Design," 112

69. Swain, *Fundamentals of Operational Design*, 8, 13.

70. van der Veer, "Rise of Design," 7.

71. With inspiration from Nietzsche, Dan Öberg writes: "The ideal military designer does not simply wage war at the edge of chaos but heeds Nietzsche's insight that to create one should aspire to become chaos: making the uncertainty of war into an artistic medium to redesign future worlds." Öberg, "Warfare as Design," 9–10.

72. Banach and Ryan, "Art of Design," 107

73. Recently, the link between military design and VR games has been tightened even further as a group of military designers have sought to create their own immersive virtual artifacts by designing not just abstract concepts and problem solutions but actual games in order "to enhance critical and creative thinking required for mastering advanced design leadership." See Project Albatross, led by Philippe Beaulieu-Brossard, *Archipelago of Design*. https://aodnetwork.ca/project-albatross/.

74. Mattis, *Assessment of Effects Based Operations*, 6.

75. Banach and Ryan, "Art of Design," 109.

76. Banach and Ryan, 105.

77. In the words of Charles Eames, "One could describe design as a plan for arranging elements to accomplish a particular purpose." Quoted in Nick Montfort, *The Future* (Cambridge, MA: MIT Press, 2017), 134.

78. See Montfort, *The Future*, 133–134; Bruce Sterling, *Shaping Things* (Cambridge, MA: MIT Press, 2005); and Julian Bleecker, *Design Fiction*.

79. Bleecker, *Design Fiction*, 15.

80. Bleecker, 8.

81. Bleecker, 84.

82. Bleecker, 84.

83. Bleecker, 86.

84. Jens Bartelson, *War in International Thought* (Cambridge: Cambridge University Press, 2018), 15.

85. Bartelson, *War in International Thought*, 16.

86. For critiques of the discourse on humanitarian war, see Eyal Weizman, *The Least of All Possible Evils* (London: Verso, 2011); and Sam Moyn, *Humane: How the United States Abandoned Peace and Reinvented War* (New York: Farrar, Straus and Giroux, 2021).

87. Bartelson, *War in International Thought*, 190.

88. Öberg, "Warfare as Design," 3.

89. Kofi Annan, "Report of Secretary-General on Recent Events in Jenin, Other Palestinian Cities," August 2002, UN press release (doc. nr. SG2077), 1.

90. Clausewitz, *Vom Kriege*, 192.

EPILOGUE

1. Army Futures Command, "Year in Review 2021," n.d. https://armyfuturescommand.com/year-in-review/.

2. US Army Combined Arms Center, "Synthetic Training Environment (STE). Statement of Need," April 2018, 11. https://usacac.army.mil/sites/default/files/documents/cact/STE_Industry_Day_Statement_of_Need.pdf.

3. Theresa Hitchens, "Army Envisions Global 3D Terrain Map as Future PNT Aid for Operations," *Breaking Defense*, October 18, 2021. https://breakingdefense.com/2021/10/army-envisions-global-3d-terrain-map-as-future-pnt-aid-for-operations/.

4. See US Army Combined Arms Center, "Synthetic Training Environment (STE)"; Department of Defense, "Soldier Virtual Trainer (SVT). Statement of Need," August 2021. https://govtribe.com/file/government-file/svt-statement-of-need-son-final-dot-pdf , 5; Jeremiah Rozman, "The Synthetic

Training Environment," the Association of the United States Army, December 2020. https://www.ausa.org/publications/synthetic-training-environment; Ivan Martinez, "SFC Paul Ray Smith Simulation and Training Technology Center Overview," DEVCOM, 2021. https://www.trainingsystems.org/-/media/sites/ntsa/events/2021/11to/presentations/thu-17-june/17-june_1125-1_martinez_st-tc-overview.ashx; Mandy Mayfield, "Army Has High Hopes for One World Terrain Training Tool," *National Defense*, November 25, 2019. https://www.nationaldefensemagazine.org/articles/2019/11/25/army-has-high-hopes-for-one-world-terrain-training-tool; Maxar Technologies, "Maxar's Vricon Awarded Phase 2 of U.S. Army's One World Terrain Contract," press release, February 24, 2021. https://www.maxar.com/press-releases/maxar-s-vricon-awarded-phase-2-of-u-s-army-s-one-world-terrain-contract; and US Department of Defense, "Contracts for Dec. 1. 2021," https://www.defense.gov/News/Contracts/Contract/Article/2858648/.

5. Clausewitz, *Vom Kriege* (Bonn: Dümmler, 1980), 192.

6. *The 9/11 Commission Report: Final Report of the National Commission on Terrorist Attacks upon the United States. Executive Summary*, 9–10. https://govinfo.library.unt.edu/911/report/911Report_Exec.pdf.

7. Phil Klay, *Missionaries* (Edinburgh: Canongate, 2021), 401.

8. August Cole and P. W. Singer, "Thinking the Unthinkable with Useful Fiction," *Journal of Future Conflict*, no. 2 (Fall 2020): 5.

9. Cole and Singer, "Thinking the Unthinkable," 5.

10. See Lawrence Freedman, *The Future of War—A History* (London: Allen Lane, 2017), 4, 97.

11. As Freedman also notes, there are forerunners. But Singer and Cole have sharpened the criteria of the genre and developed a whole realist poetics of the martial novel. Their close ties to the military establishment also enable them to push the concept with great impact. See Freedman, *Future of War*, 4, and Singer and Cole's website, www.useful-fiction.com.

12. P. W. Singer and August Cole, "How to Write about World War III: Can Fiction Help Prevent Another Conflict between Great Powers?" *The Atlantic*, June 30, 2015. https://www.theatlantic.com/international/archive/2015/06/ghost-fleet-world-war-III/397301/?utm_source=copy-link&utm_medium=social&utm_campaign=share.

13. Cole and Singer, "Thinking the Unthinkable," 2.

14. Peter Singer, "The True Story of Using Fiction to Enhance Risk Intelligence." *YouTube*. October 28, 2021. https://www.youtube.com/watch?v=qP_i94eP2Ho.

15. Cole and Singer, "Thinking the Unthinkable," 3–4.

16. Cole and Singer, 6.

17. Marine Corps Warfighting Lab, *Science Fiction Futures; Marine Corps Security Environment Forecast: Futures 2030–2045* (Quantico, VA: US Marine Corps, 2016).

18. Trina Marie Phillips and August Cole, *Visions of Warfare: 2036* (Norfolk, VA: Allied Command Transformation, 2016).

19. Army Cyber Institute, *Dark Hammer: A Retrospective of Science Fiction Prototyping* (West Point, NY: 2018), 9. See also Brian David Johnson and Natalie Vanatta, "What the Heck Is Threatcasting?" Future Tense, *Slate*, September 15, 2017. https://slate.com/technology/2017/09/threatcasting-in-futurism-attempts-to-imagine-the-risks-we-might-face.html.

20. James A. Winnefeld and Michael J. Morrell, "The War That Never Was?" US Naval Institute, *Proceedings* 146/8, August 2020. https://www.usni.org/magazines/proceedings/2020/august/war-never-was.

21. Brian David Johnson, Sandy Winkelman, Don Hudson, and Kinsun Loh, *Quantum Winter* (West Point, NY: Army Cyber Institute, 2018).

INDEX